CRYPTOGRAPHY IN THE DATABASE

CRYPTOGRAPHY IN THE DATABASE

THE LAST LINE OF DEFENSE

KEVIN KENAN

Upper Saddle River, NJ • Boston • Indianapolis • San Francisco
New York • Toronto • Montreal • London • Munich • Paris • Madrid
Capetown • Sydney • Tokyo • Singapore • Mexocio City

Publisher Symantec Press: Linda McCarthy
Editor in Chief: Karen Gettman
Acquisitions Editor: Jessica Goldstein
Cover Designer: Alan Clements
Managing Editor: Gina Kanouse
Project Editor: Christy Hackerd
Copy Editor: Gayle Johnson
Indexer: ICC
Proofreader: Christal Andry
Compositor: ICC
Manufacturing Buyer: Dan Uhrig

The publisher offers excellent discounts on this book when ordered in quantity for bulk purchases or special sales, which may include electronic versions and/or custom covers and content particular to your business, training goals, marketing focus, and branding interests. For more information, please contact:

U. S. Corporate and Government Sales
(800) 382-3419
corpsales@pearsontechgroup.com

For sales outside the U. S., please contact:

International Sales
international@pearsoned.com

Visit us on the Web: www.awprofessional.com

ISBN 0-321-32073-5 05-29-07

Text printed in the United States on recycled paper at R.R. Donnelley & Sons in Crawfordsville, Indiana.
First printing, October 2005

Library of Congress Cataloging-in-Publication Data
Kenan, Kevin.
  Cryptography in the database : the last line of defense / Kevin Kenan.
    p. cm.
  ISBN 0-321-32073-5
  1. Database security. 2. Cryptography. I. Title.

QA76.9.D314K45 2005
005.8'2—dc22

2005018455

For mom and dad.
Thank you.

Contents

Contents

Contents

Acknowledgments

First, thank you to my family who made the real sacrifices that made this book a reality: Ella, who shared her birth and first months with a manuscript; Skyler, who for far too many weekends waved goodbye as I drove off to the "Daddy work" of writing; and Stephanie, whose abundant love covered for her often delinquent husband. This book would simply not exist if weren't for your generous support.

Thanks also to Linda McCarthy from Symantec Press and Jessica Goldstein from Addison-Wesley who enthusiastically endorsed this project and, with the assistance of Frank Vella, carried it forward. Christy Hackerd took my "completed" manuscript and, with the help of the talented Addison-Wesley team, transformed it into an actual book.

Many insightful reviewers examined this text and code. Particular thanks go to Bob Bruen, Alan Krassowski, Don MacVittie, Ulf T. Mattsson, Drew Simonis, Anton Stiglic, and Mark R. Trinidad whose comments on various drafts made this a much stronger book. I appreciated and gave serious consideration on how to best implement all of the comments. I'm sure that readers of the published book will not be short of comments, as well. Please refer to `http://www.kevinkenan.com` for the latest news and errata relating to this book.

Also, a thanks to the staff members of the Delta and Green Acres Starbucks who cheerfully supplied me with espresso and electrical power during many months of long, weekend afternoons. There is something so *right* about sipping an espresso and writing code.

Finally, a deep thank you to Professor Emeritus Richard Koch at the University of Oregon. His patient encouragement and explanations helped myself and a legion of other undergraduates decipher the elegance of mathematics. My pursuit of cryptography began in his office.

About the Author

Kevin Kenan leads Symantec's IT application and database security program. In this position, he works with application development teams to ensure that the applications and databases Symantec deploys internally are secure. This work includes specifying cryptographic solutions to protect sensitive information wherever it is stored.

Prior to his work in Symantec's information security department, Kevin designed and developed applications for Symantec's information technology and product development teams often with an emphasis on security and cryptography. He previously provided enterprise support for Symantec's development tools, and he holds a Bachelor of Science in Mathematics from the University of Oregon.

Preface

About This Book

This book is about using established cryptographic techniques and algorithms to protect information while it is at rest in a database. The emphasis is on designing and building (or selecting and integrating) a cryptosystem to protect against clearly identified threats against the database. Security is assumed to be a top priority. As such, the discussions in this book cover not only encrypting the data, but also attacks against the encrypted data.

If the cryptography is not implemented carefully, attackers can recover data even if it is protected by strong encryption. Many examples of this have been seen in the field of secure communications. For instance, the widely publicized weaknesses in the encrypted wireless protocol WEP have prompted many to move to WPA even at the cost of buying new equipment. Database encryption can suffer from the same sort of weaknesses. Simple, naïve encryption of the data is not enough. My goal is to provide a solid blueprint and execution plan so that a team charged with the task of encrypting sensitive information in a database will be successful.

The cryptosystem presented in this book should be seen as a template that outlines threats against data at rest and provides safeguards against those threats. Problems and pitfalls common to implementing cryptography, such as mode selection and key management, are identified and addressed. The architecture is flexible and should be adaptable to many environments.

For situations where some element of the presented solution simply does not fit, you should find enough information and guidance to pursue variations in the design. Similarly, when you're evaluating database cryptosystems from vendors, you can use the design in this book and the reasons behind the decisions that shaped that design as a sort of baseline.

Even if the proposed system differs markedly from the design in this book, it will still have to map keys to columns and rows and provide a key life cycle. It will still have to store and protect keys, select an appropriate encryption mode, and handle initialization vectors. Most importantly, any solution must adequately reduce the risks outlined in an organization's threat model. You must consider all these details. By working through these issues and presenting a working cryptosystem, my hope is that this book will enable a team to successfully build or buy a database cryptosystem.

Who Should Read This Book

The core audience for this book is the technical lead responsible for protecting sensitive information in a database. This person might be an architect, a senior system or security analyst, a database administrator, or a technical project manager. Because success requires that the team implement the cryptographic architecture correctly and securely, the lead must provide guidance throughout the project on secure development practices as well as technology.

This book assumes that the technical lead is a senior application security analyst. Our analyst is part of a team responsible for an application that handles and stores sensitive information in a database. The analyst's job begins with convincing the team, its management, and the customer that encryption is necessary. From there, the analyst contributes to each stage of the project to ensure that the team specifies, designs, and implements the cryptographic solution correctly and securely.

For projects that don't have a dedicated security analyst, one of the other roles, such as architect or system analyst, may serve just as well so long as security is explicitly called out as a core responsibility. In some projects, the security analyst role described here might be best split across multiple people. A logical split would be between a security-focused technical lead, such as the architect, and the project manager.

Prerequisites

This book assumes that you are familiar with databases and have a passing knowledge of cryptography. A brief refresher is offered on databases, and cryptography is introduced and treated in more depth. Experience with Java or some other programming language is necessary to get the most out of the code examples included at the end of the book. Knowledge of application development methodologies will also help provide context for the discussion of secure development practices.

Structure

This book is divided into four major parts. The opening covers database security at a high level, and the second part details a database cryptosystem design. The third part discusses development practices necessary to implement a cryptosystem securely, and the final part provides working code examples of the design.

Part I, "Database Security," opens, unsurprisingly, with Chapter 1, "The Case for Database Security," which looks at why database security is important and what sort of attacks databases face. This discussion culminates in a generalized threat model for database security. The chapter concludes with a brief survey of regulatory requirements to secure data. Then, Chapter 2, "Securing Databases with Cryptography," discusses the kinds of protection that cryptography can provide to a database. This chapter also introduces the idea that the cryptography itself can introduce new risks and sets the groundwork for examining the cryptosystem itself for weaknesses. We can't just assume that encrypted data, even when encrypted with strong algorithms, is secure.

Part II, "A Cryptographic Infrastructure," details the design of a cryptographic infrastructure. Chapter 3, "An Overview of Cryptographic Infrastructure," provides an overview of the cryptosystem and presents the fundamentals of key management and how keys are assigned to data for encryption. Chapter 4, "Cryptographic Engines and Algorithms," covers algorithms and engines. An engine is the component that actually carries out the cryptographic operations. Different types of engines are discussed. There are several ways to apply the cryptographic algorithm used in this book (which is AES), and the discussion of modes at the conclusion of this chapter explores these as well as considers the vulnerabilities that improper use of a mode can introduce. Chapter 5, "Keys: Vaults, Manifests, and Managers," covers the components that store and manage keys, and Chapter 6, "Cryptographic Providers and Consumers," describes how an application interacts with the cryptosystem.

At first, Part III, "The Cryptographic Project," may seem somewhat out of place because it focuses on secure development practices. If you're an expert on developing secure applications, these six chapters may be review. However, experience has shown (not to mention the plethora of successfully attacked applications gracing the weekly news) that secure application development expertise is far from common. A database cryptosystem is a primary element of an organization's security infrastructure. Other applications will depend on the cryptosystem's security, so every effort must be made to ensure that the implementation is as secure as possible. Vulnerabilities in the database cryptosystem put data throughout the organization at risk. The seriousness of this situation earned the topic this prominent placement.

The discussion of secure development practices begins with an overview of managing a cryptographic project in Chapter 7, "Managing the Cryptographic Project." Chapter 8, "Requirements Hardening," covers specifying security and cryptographic requirements and includes a discussion of data classification. Securing the design itself is the subject of Chapter 9, "Design Hardening," which consists of guidelines, threat modeling, and the application of security patterns. General guidelines for secure programming (what most people think of as development) are covered in Chapter 10, "Secure Development." The last two chapters of this part, Chapters 11, "Testing," and 12, "Deployment, Defense, and Decommissioning," cover testing and the three Ds—deployment, defense, and decommissioning.

Part IV, "Example Code," consists of code examples and explanations. Each component discussed in Part II is represented, along with nearly all the core functionality. This code lets you explore and experiment with the functioning of a live database cryptosystem. Hopefully these concrete examples will help remove any ambiguities introduced by the more theoretical exposition in the earlier parts of the book and will prepare you to implement or evaluate a production cryptosystem. The final chapter, Chapter 21, "The System at Work," shows the example system at work. It illustrates everything from setting up key-encrypting keys to searching for encrypted data.

PART I

DATABASE SECURITY

Chapter 1

The Case for
Database Security

A typical database in a large company might contain financial forecasts, acquisition targets, customer information, and product plans. For legitimate users, this central database is a convenient repository for critical information. From an attacker's point of view, cracking that database is far more lucrative than the alternative: eavesdropping on network connections. Electronic eavesdropping, or, as it is more commonly known, packet sniffing, is difficult[1] and generates a flood of information, of which only a tiny fraction is actually valuable to an attacker.

Cracking a database, on the other hand, yields refined information in one accessible location. An attacker with database access might be able to simply query the database and retrieve *every* item of interest: every credit card number, every customer, every employee, every company under acquisition review. Like thieves who rob banks because "that's where the money is," computer attackers target databases because that's where the data is.

Ironically, most organizations spend more resources protecting data in its ephemeral form as it transits the network. Technologies such as HTTPS, SSH, and VPNs all use encryption to keep data safe from packet sniffing. However, once the data arrives at its destination—say, an e-commerce site—the packets are decrypted, processed, and then stored in a convenient, readable format in a database.

---

1. *While readily available tools ease the technical challenges of sniffing, an attacker must still locate and compromise a machine through which a significant portion of your traffic passes.*

If such an online storefront were a brick-and-mortar shop, an analogous security policy would have the highways and loading docks tightly secured with cameras, RFID tags, and guards but would neglect to place anything but the most rudimentary shoplifting countermeasures in the store itself.

This chapter looks at why database security is or should be an important concern for any organization. First we look at the kinds of attacks against which a database is typically vulnerable. In this section we don't describe the technical details of specific attacks, but rather approach vulnerabilities from a high level and look at common features. The second section considers the legislative, compliance, and other external pressures for database security.

1.1 Attacks Against Databases

Experts explain that computer security consists of three basic principles: confidentiality, integrity, and availability. Confidentiality pertains to allowing only authorized individuals access to information. Integrity provides assurance that information is authentic and has not been subject to tampering. Availability means that users can access information and computing resources as needed. In this book, we are concerned primarily with confidentiality. Integrity will be touched on briefly, but availability is beyond our scope.

A complete database security strategy consists of much more than just cryptography. Many other books and Web sites go into detail about standard database security techniques. Access controls to both the database and the objects in the database are essential. Other important practices include backup and recovery plans, regular audits, and secure network connections. While these practices are necessary for a secure database, defending against today's sophisticated attackers requires additional protection. This last line of defense is provided by cryptography.

1.1.1 Types of Attacks

We generally deal with two classes of attackers: external and internal. External attackers, in most cases, face a more difficult task because they must navigate firewalls, intrusion detection systems, and an unknown network without any authorization. An internal attacker has the primary advantages of being within the perimeter firewall and having access to information about the network's topology. Most organizations seem to worry more about the external attacker because there are so many more of them. However, given their insider knowledge and access, the threat from internal attackers is often much more serious.

In particular, the threat from administrators is often underestimated. A database administrator has access to everything in the database. Administrators also can cover up most, if not all, traces of their attack. They can read everything and write to anything. Cryptography, if implemented correctly, can significantly reduce and, in many cases, eliminate the threat posed by database administrators.

We also have two basic categories of attacks: one-offs and persistent. A one-off is an attack in which the attacker accomplishes his goal and then vanishes. A persistent attack is one in which the attacker returns to the compromised database many times to carry out additional attacks.

At first glance, the persistent attack may seem more dangerous, but consider for a moment if the one-off attacker's goal is to download your entire database. Once the attacker has the database on his own machine, he can work on it in leisure without fear of his work raising alarms. The persistent attacker, on the other hand, risks discovery with every attack.

1.1.2 Confidentiality Attacks

Most databases supporting large organizations contain sensitive information, or, at least, information that should not be disclosed to some of the database's users. An attack against the confidentiality of this information is one of the most fundamental threats to an organization's databases. In such an attack, an unauthorized person accesses the sensitive information.

Imagine an attacker who gains full access to a database server. With the entire machine at his mercy, one of the first things he might do is download the entire database file. Once the database file is on his own machine, the attacker can take his time and scan it for interesting text or other data. Or perhaps the attacker loads the stolen database file into a database engine and then uses the database like any other user. In either case, all unencrypted information in the database is compromised.

Many organizations rely on access controls to protect their databases. As mentioned earlier, access controls are an essential component of security, but in many cases they are not enough. One of their obvious weaknesses in terms of confidentiality is that they allow administrators to view data. In addition, access controls are often misconfigured or subverted (through techniques as technical as cracking the access control software to those as simple as social engineering a password), and most organizations also have authorized backdoors into the database that are not subject to the otherwise strict access controls. These backdoors include read-only accounts, nonproduction environments, and backups.

When a problem occurs in a database, IT troubleshooters typically need a way to look at the database to see what went wrong. To prevent them from doing harm, accidentally or intentionally, a read-only account is often provided. This, of course, doesn't prevent a confidentiality attack. The staff members with access to the read-only account usually include application developers, QA staff, and the configuration management team, any of which might also be contract staff. Should any of these individuals become malicious insiders, or should they simply lose control of the read-only password (after all, it's an account not tied to any individual and is good *only* for reading data), a confidentiality compromise is but a few keystrokes away.

Another common backdoor situation that is a prime candidate for a confidentiality compromise involves nonproduction databases. Most organizations have separate databases for development, testing, staging, and production. Typically, nonproduction databases have far fewer access controls than production databases, and the nonproduction databases are generally created by cloning the production database. This, of course, places sensitive information in a database without the necessary controls.

Similar to the backdoor-like problem of nonproduction instances is the problem of securing database backups. In many organizations, backup tapes are stored off-site and often by a third party. Firewalls, intrusion detection, and access controls provide very little protection should an adversary gain access to the backups.

A final example of a confidentiality attack requires neither the compromise of a server nor insider access to a backdoor. Instead, the attacker finds a poorly coded Web application that queries the target database and then executes an SQL injection attack. This attack leverages the Web application's own access privileges and allows the attacker to issue database queries against any table that the application can access.

Because a Web application generally must read and write information pertaining to many customers, an SQL injection attack has access to all of that information. In general, encryption protects against SQL injection attacks, but it is possible to implement cryptography in such a way that SQL injection is not prevented. Many transparent encryption schemes, as discussed in the next chapter, fail to protect against such application-level attacks.

1.1.3 Integrity Attacks

An integrity attack alters information in the database. Given that information is stored to be used at a later date, integrity attacks are as serious as confidentiality attacks. The attack could be blatant and easily discovered, such as altering the content of Web pages stored in a database, or very subtle and hard to discover, such as a tiny change to the base tax rate in a table used to generate aggregate financial reports. When attempting to protect against integrity attacks, we are not concerned with keeping an attacker from reading information. We only want to keep him from writing changes to the database, or, failing that, we want to at least know that the change occurred.

Unlike confidentiality threats, which have a rich array of targets ranging from the production system to offsite backup tapes, an integrity attack requires the ability to write to the live production database. This requirement alone somewhat limits the threat posed by integrity attacks, but it certainly does not remove it. In addition to the ever-present threat posed by malicious administrators, common integrity attacks include subverting faulty applications, using stolen accounts with write privileges, and escalating the privileges of otherwise limited accounts.

The fundamental threat to the integrity of a database is the introduction of an *inappropriate* change. An inappropriate change is any change that is counter to the organization's policy, such as might be made in the case of fraud. Unfortunately, identifying inappropriate changes is beyond the capability of most computer systems. When the value of a sale is entered, the system has no way of determining if that is the actual, correct value. Boundary conditions might be checked, but some variance is expected. Otherwise, the field should be fixed and uneditable.

Given that protecting against inappropriate changes is generally not realistic, a computer system instead relies on the separation of duties and allows only authorized users to use approved applications when making the change. If the appropriate, authorized individuals all complete their steps using the approved application, the system considers the change *authentic*, which is a surrogate for appropriate because we can't verify appropriateness.

Of these three elements—separation of duties, authorizing users, and application approval—only the latter is a good candidate for database cryptography. Separation of duties means that more than one person is required to finalize the change. This is a policy issue the system must enforce. It is not a problem that requires database cryptography. Authorizing users is a task of the access control system. While cryptography will no doubt be involved, it is not cryptography in the database.[2]

Limiting which applications can be used to make changes is also an issue of access control, but it is possible to use database cryptography to check that

---

2. *Cryptography in the database could be used to tie changes to particular individuals, but this is a question of nonrepudiation. Robust and pervasive logging is likely a better solution.*

information in the database was written by an official mechanism. In this case, the system cryptographically stamps the row in the table in such a way that should any change be made to that row, it will be detected. This technique does not prevent the change from occurring but does generate an alert that a security breach occurred sometime in the past.

This protection is nice to have but probably is not worth too much effort because it is effective only against threats that target the database directly. Because databases are generally easier to secure than custom applications, security failures are more likely to occur in the application. If an attacker can exploit one of these failures to convince the application that he is an authorized user, the application will stamp the attacker's change as authentic, and the cryptographic protection will not detect any corruption. Hence, the cryptographic integrity protection protects only against attackers who compromise the database. Because the application is the weakest link in this chain, this book recommends that limited security resources be spent on bolstering the application's security rather than using cryptography to further protect against direct database threats.

Finally, while integrity threats may be viable only against the production system, the threat to the production system is much more diffuse than the threat of a confidentiality breach. Confidentiality threat targets are generally well defined in that we know specifically which information is confidential, and that information is grouped in the database. Integrity threat targets, on the other hand, are scattered throughout the database, and to be effective, integrity protection needs to be as ubiquitous. In the end, nearly every transaction would involve at least one integrity check. While cryptographic confidentiality protection impacts performance when the system is processing confidential information, which in most cases does not occur frequently, integrity checks introduce a constant drain on performance.

Given this discussion, this book does not spend too much time developing integrity protection. Obviously, if encrypted data doesn't decrypt, there is an integrity problem, but this side effect of encryption will not thwart many attackers. As discussed in later chapters, the use of wide key scopes can make integrity attacks more difficult, and it is possible to embed integrity checks into decryption requests. Overall, though, we focus much more on confidentiality than integrity.

1.1.4 Availability Attacks

While cryptography generally doesn't apply to availability, two points are worth considering. While neither point directly counters availability threats such as denial of service attacks, the first shows how cryptography can increase availability while keeping security constant, and the second emphasizes the importance of protecting the cryptographic system itself.

By providing strong protection, cryptography can increase the availability of information because that information can now be more easily placed where authorized users can access it. If given proper security, unencrypted sensitive information should by kept deep inside an organization's firewalls and surrounded with strict access controls. Unfortunately, such precautions frequently limit the availability of that information or other information within the same database. However, with proper encryption of the sensitive information, it might not be unreasonable to provide more liberal access to that database. In this sense, availability is increased.

By integrating cryptography into applications, the system becomes dependent on having access to the cryptographic keys.[3] Should an attacker delete or corrupt those keys, the system breaks. Another possibility that must be guarded against is the case where the attacker loads his own key into the system. The system won't break, but data will be encrypted with this key. Eventually, the attacker removes the key, and at that point the system breaks. The attacker now holds the data hostage and might offer to sell the key for a high price.

Cryptography must be used carefully lest it become a new avenue for attack. Care must be taken that the cryptographic system does not become the weakest link in a database's security. As mentioned, in the interest of availability, a database protected with encryption, even a poorly implemented system, may be placed in a less secure location. There, the cryptosystem can be more easily attacked, and should it fail, the information's availability, not to mention its confidentiality and integrity, are at serious risk.

1.1.5 Threat Models

A threat model describes the threats against a system. The attacks just discussed can form the basis of the threat model for our database. In this book we are particularly concerned about confidentiality threats. Our threat agents include system and database administrators, development staff, network intruders, application crackers,[4] legitimate users, and traditional thieves.

Constructing a threat model (see section 9.3, "Threat Modeling," for more information) involves considering how each of these agents might compromise the system's security. In our particular case, we consider how each of the listed agents

---

3. *Cryptographic keys, as used here, are secret data that enables encryption and decryption.*
4. *Application crackers are individuals who exploit vulnerabilities in applications.*

might gain unauthorized access to confidential information. Our threat model consists of the following:

Administrators   Administrators are privileged users who generally have full access to everything in their administrative domain. In most cases, it is best to assume that a dedicated administrator will eventually be able to access anything that the administered machine can access. Given this, the goal is to make it difficult and time-consuming for administrators to casually read confidential information and to layer other controls, such as employment screening and separation of duties, to compensate.

Development Staff   Development staff is responsible for designing, building, and testing applications that use the database. Their intimate knowledge of the system coupled with the fact that their code is ultimately what handles the confidential information makes them a significant threat. Especially because development staff often obtain troubleshooting, read-only rights to the database to deal with emergency production problems (best practices keep development out of production by default). The goal is to prevent compromise of the information even when development staff have access to the database.

Network Intruders   A network intruder is an unauthorized individual who has gained access to the network. The intruder might attempt to eavesdrop on communications to gather confidential information or authentication credentials (transport level cryptography provides solutions for these problems), or might attempt to crack an application. This book assumes transport level encryption is in place and places controls to limit application cracking, as discussed next.

Application Crackers   Like safecrackers, application crackers attempt to circumvent application security to gain unauthorized access. Generally, an application cracker is considered to be an unauthorized user, but he may gain the appearance of a legitimate user via a successful attack. The most dire scenario is a cracker who gains administrative privileges. In such a case, the goal mirrors the goal described for administrative malfeasance. Access should be difficult and time-consuming. This gives monitoring software the time and opportunity to note that something is not right. Less severe scenarios, such as access via SQL injection, should be prevented.

Legitimate Users   A legitimate user could attempt to leverage the limited user privileges to gain additional unauthorized access. In such a case, the user is essentially an application cracker and the comments just made apply. Impersonating a legitimate user is another related threat, and while

authentication controls should make impersonation very difficult, our goal is still to prevent a confidentiality breach even if the authentication controls fail.

Thieves Traditional thieves might steal the database or the backup media. Databases and other sensitive equipment is typically kept in locked, limited-access data centers to help reduce this risk. Backup media, unfortunately, must leave the premises and therefore are more exposed to theft. The goal is to prevent the information on backup media from being read by unauthorized individuals.

This basic threat model is referred to throughout this book. Each organization must decide which threats are relevant and how severe each is. Deeper analysis is often done where each basic threat is refined with a set of specific attacks. For instance, attacks such as SQL injection and statistical analysis of the encrypted data within the database file could be considered for each of the threat agents mentioned here.

A threat model is one of the most important tools to have when considering a database cryptosystem. The threat model shapes the design of the cryptosystem to ensure that it protects against the threats the organization ranks highly. Without a carefully crafted threat model, a cryptosystem can easily be built or purchased that protects against only a single class of low-priority threats.

For instance, a cryptosystem that encrypts backup tapes will not protect against the other threats. A system that automatically encrypts and decrypts data for a particular user role might protect against backup tape theft and access from users assigned to other roles, but it still leaves a wide set of threats unmitigated.

Before any decision to buy or build a cryptosystem can be made, the threat model must be evaluated in light of the proposed solution. Only systems that mitigate the organization's most highly ranked threats should be considered. Any threat unmitigated by the cryptosystem should have other controls applied to ensure that it doesn't become the weak link that attackers use to bypass the protection provided by the cryptosystem.

1.2 External Requirements to Secure Databases

While some organizations encrypt their databases to protect proprietary information, many more face external policies that require encryption. These policies originate in privacy and security legislation, corporate compliance agreements, and trade regulations. Other organizations may not worry much about the value of the information in their databases, but instead fear the damage to their reputation should a successful attack become public knowledge.

1.2.1 Legislation

Governments throughout the world have enacted laws covering data security and privacy. Often, these laws apply to any company doing business in the region, even if the company itself is based in a different jurisdiction. We briefly discuss a sampling of these laws, but each organization should work with a legal advisor to determine which laws are applicable and what precisely the law requires for the organization.

Health Insurance Portability and Accountability Act

Introduced in 1996, this U.S. law, commonly referred to as HIPAA, impacts the privacy and security of health care data. Of the standards developed in accordance with the law, two are relevant to database security. The privacy standard requires data safeguards that protect against

> [I]ntentional or unintentional use or disclosure of protected health information in violation of the Privacy Rule and to limit its incidental use and disclosure pursuant to otherwise permitted or required use or disclosure. [16]

Clearly this rule is designed to protect confidentiality of patient information, but it does not explicitly require encryption. Given that databases are notoriously insecure, and access to protected health information by system and database administrators and development and QA staff are not in agreement with the "minimum necessary use and disclosure" principle of HIPAA, it would not be surprising to find that, in practice, encryption becomes a *de facto* standard for meeting the privacy requirements.

The second standard, the security rule, does explicitly mention encryption in the context of stored protected health information. In general, the rule requires that an organization (referred to as a "covered entity" in HIPAA-speak)

> Ensure the confidentiality, integrity, and availability of all electronic protected health information the covered entity creates, receives, maintains, or transmits.[5]

More specifically, as part of the technical safeguards, the rule requires an organization to

> Implement a mechanism to encrypt and decrypt electronic protected health information.[6]

---

5. *45 CFR §164.306(a)(1).*
6. *45 CFR §164.312(a)(2)(iv).*

This requirement is considered "addressable," which means that the requirement applies only when an organization determines that it is a "reasonable and appropriate" safeguard in its environment. If the requirement is not implemented, the rule requires documentation explaining the reasons behind the decision.

Following the guidance provided by the general requirement to secure the confidentiality, integrity, and availability of data, encryption would seem reasonable and appropriate in many cases. The existence of other access controls might be deemed sufficient in small organizations, but, as we discussed earlier, depending only on access controls is risky. For a large healthcare provider with a diverse user base and a complex environment, relying only on access controls may very well be seen as inadequate.

Sarbanes-Oxley Act

In the aftermath of various accounting scandals in the early 2000s, the U.S. Congress passed the Sarbanes-Oxley Act in 2002. The law, frequently referred to as SOX, aims to improve the accuracy of financial reports as well as increase accountability among those responsible for producing the reports. The law requires auditors to assess and report on the effectiveness of the company's internal controls on information pertaining to financial reporting.

While SOX focuses on internal accounting controls, its requirements do extend into the realm of IT and software security controls insofar as those controls pertain to information used in financial reporting or as those controls protect information assets whose value is reflected in financial reporting. Because the prevention or detection of fraud is a key concern, integrity controls top the list of relevant solutions. Repudiation and confidentiality controls follow closely behind.

Gramm-Leach-Bliley Act

Formally known as the Financial Modernization Act of 1999, or, more compactly, GLBA, this law requires financial institutions to comply with standards that provide

[A]dministrative, technical, and physical safeguards—

(1) to insure the security and confidentiality of customer records and information;
(2) to protect against any anticipated threats or hazards to the security or integrity of such records; and
(3) to protect against unauthorized access to or use of such records or information which could result in substantial harm or inconvenience to any customer.

Neither the law nor the accompanying Safeguards Rule explicitly calls for encryption, but as discussed earlier, existing controls for securing confidentiality and integrity generally are insufficient. A robust and comprehensive response to GLBA includes encryption among its roster of safeguards.

California Information Practices Act

This California law was amended by AB 1950 in January 2005. It now requires businesses to implement and maintain reasonable security procedures and practices to protect personal information[7] about California residents. In addition, businesses must contractually require third parties who handle such information to also protect that information. Section 1798.81.5 defines personal information as "an individual's first name or first initial and his or her last name in combination with any one or more of the following data elements, when either the name or the data elements are not encrypted or redacted" and lists elements such as social security number, driver's license number, financial account information, and medical information.

Should a business fail to provide reasonable safeguards, section 1798.82, introduced by SB 1386, requires any company that conducts business in California to notify its California customers of any breach of their unencrypted personal information. The law defines breach as "unauthorized acquisition of computerized data that compromises the security, confidentiality, or integrity of personal information maintained by the person or business."

California law clearly favors cryptographic protection of its residents' information. In a sense, adequately encrypting personal information creates a safe harbor that shields a business from the other requirements of the law. Businesses with poor security practices and that store unencrypted personal information risk legal penalties, civil suits, and a tainted reputation.

Children's Online Privacy Protection Act

Passed in 1998, this law is not well known outside of industries that deal with children. However, section 312.8 requires a company to "establish and maintain reasonable procedures to protect the confidentiality, security, and integrity of personal information collected from children." In many cases, particularly cases in which a database supports a Web site designed for children, encryption is not only reasonable, it is the only robust solution.

---

7. *Such information is generically referred to as personally identifiable information (PII) and broadly includes any information that is likely to uniquely identify a person. Many laws and regulations are much more specific about what constitutes PII.*

1.2.2 Business Compliance

The government isn't alone in requiring security controls around data. Companies that accept credit cards are expected to be in compliance with security programs specified by the major credit card companies, including Visa, MasterCard, and American Express.

In late 2004, many of these separate programs were fused into the Payment Card Industry (PCI) Data Security Standard, which is aimed at ensuring that credit card information remains secure from the moment a customer makes a purchase until the merchant disposes of it. The requirements cover a wide range of security techniques, including network security, anti-virus, patch management, access controls, and encryption.

In particular, requirement 3.4 specifies that stored cardholder data must be rendered unreadable, and it includes cryptographic methods in the recommended controls. American Express, MasterCard, and Visa, along with several other payment card companies, have all adopted the PCI data security standard.

1.2.3 Trade Regulations

The Federal Trade Commission has also launched a campaign to secure stored data. Its approach, though, is unique. Instead of just pursuing outright encryption legislation (the FTC is involved with laws such as the Gramm-Leech-Bliley Act and the Children's Online Privacy Protection Act), the Commission works to make sure that companies comply with their own privacy policies.

Most companies doing business online post a privacy policy that describes the steps taken to protect customer information. Empowered by Section 5 of the FTC Act, which prohibits unfair or deceptive practices, the Commission pursues cases against companies that do not protect customer information to the extent specified in their privacy policy.

1.2.4 Reputation Damage

A publicized security breach, or even a hint of insecurity, can damage any organization's reputation. While many companies strive to keep news of intrusions or security weaknesses quiet, this is becoming increasingly difficult due to forces such as Sarbanes-Oxley, which requires an assessment of internal controls to be included as part of financial reporting, the California Information Practices Act, and the FTC's enforcement efforts.

The online world is especially sensitive to reputation, and customers are rightfully wary of a business that has suffered because of insecure practices.

A company with a reputation for insecurity may also find few willing business partners. As our economy becomes more dependent on information and information sharing, keeping the information to which we've been entrusted becomes a crucial skill.

1.3 Summary

The two sections of this chapter examined, first from a technical perspective and then from a business and legislative perspective, why securing a database is a key concern in any organization. We looked at the fundamental principles of computer security and how they apply to databases and in the process discussed how databases are vulnerable to attacks against confidentiality, integrity, and availability.

From a legislative perspective, we covered HIPAA, Sarbanes-Oxley, GLBA, the new provisions in the California Information Practices Act introduced by AB 1950 and SB 1386, and the Children's Online Privacy Protection Act. We also looked at the requirements for database security imposed by the major credit card companies and the role of the FTC in enforcing privacy and security policies. Finally, we considered the impact of insecurity on an organization's reputation. Throughout this section, embedded in legislation and policy, we heard echoes of the previous section's emphasis on the security theme of confidentiality, integrity, and availability.

Now that you understand why database security is important and the types of threats on which you need to focus, we'll examine how cryptography can help mitigate the risk posed by those threats.

Chapter 2

Securing Databases with Cryptography

This chapter discusses how cryptography can address the concerns raised in the previous chapter. After explaining what cryptography is and providing a general idea of how it works, we dig into the various types of cryptographic algorithms and see where the strengths and weaknesses of each lie.

Finally, we look at where database cryptography sits in an organization's security portfolio. With respect to threats against confidentiality and integrity, we examine how cryptography can help with security. We also look at the common pitfalls and difficulties encountered in implementing a cryptographic system. Not only does a poorly implemented system not provide the needed protection, it can actually weaken overall security. We spend time looking at what kinds of risks a poor cryptographic system introduces.

2.1 A Brief Database Refresher

For the most part, this book assumes knowledge of databases, but we'll quickly go over the fundamentals in case you've been away from the topic for some time. A relational database stores information in tables consisting of rows and columns. A field or cell is the intersection of a row and column.

Tables are related to each other through primary and foreign keys (these keys are quite different from cryptographic keys, which are discussed later). A primary key is a subset of the information in a row that uniquely identifies that row from all the other rows in the table. A foreign key links a row in one table to a row in another table by referencing the latter table's primary key.

Indexes allow for quick searching through a table. By specifying an index on a column, the database creates a special data structure that allows it to rapidly find any information stored in that column. Primary key columns are typically indexed.

A standard language, structured query language (SQL), is used to manage data. Database objects, such as tables and indexes, are created, modified, and destroyed using a subset of SQL known as data definition language (DDL). Information is entered, viewed, altered, and deleted from a database using another subset of SQL called data manipulation language (DML).

The most common interaction with a database is the `select` statement, which is an element of DML. The `select` statement allows an operator to dig though one or more database tables and display just the data that meets specific criteria. A basic `select` statement contains three clauses. The *select* clause specifies which columns should be displayed. The *from* clause specifies which tables should be included in the search. The *where* clause details the criteria a row must meet to be selected.

The where clause frequently contains *join* statements, which tell the database how to include multiple tables in the query. Typically, a join follows the link established by a foreign key.

Other frequently used statements include `insert`, for inserting new data into a table; `update`, for modifying existing data in a table; and `delete` for removing rows. All of these statements also include from and where clauses.

Programs typically interact with databases by building and passing these statements to the database. For instance, when a customer wishes to see the items she added to her shopping cart last week, the application passes a `select` statement to the database to select all of the items in that customer's cart. Then, when the customer adds an item, the application might pass an `insert` to the database.

Stored procedures offer another avenue for an application to interact with a database. A stored procedure is a program that is loaded into the database itself. Then, instead of the application building an `insert` statement to add a new item to the customer's cart, the application would call the `add_item_to_cart` stored procedure and pass the item and quantity as arguments.

Databases are much more complex and feature-rich than what we've described here, but this overview should provide enough context to help you make sense of the database terminology used in this book. The code examples at the end of the book contain many examples of SQL statements. See Chapter 21, "The System at Work," for example.

2.2 What Is Cryptography?

Cryptography is the art of "extreme information security." It is extreme in the sense that once treated with a cryptographic algorithm, a message (or a database field) is expected to remain secure even if the adversary has full access to the treated message. The adversary may even know which algorithm was used. If the cryptography is good, the message will remain secure.

This is in contrast to most information security techniques, which are designed to keep adversaries away from the information. Most security mechanisms prevent access and often have complicated procedures to allow access to only authorized users. Cryptography assumes that the adversary has full access to the message and still provides unbroken security. That is extreme security.

A more popular conception of cryptography characterizes it as the science of "scrambling" data. Cryptographers invent algorithms that take input data, called *plaintext,* and produce scrambled output. Scrambling, used in this sense, is much more than just moving letters around or exchanging some letters for others. After a proper cryptographic scrambling, the output is typically indistinguishable from a random string of data. For instance, a cryptographic function might turn "Hello, whirled!" into `0x397B3AF517B6892C`.

While simply turning a message into a random sequence of bits may not seem useful, you'll soon see that cryptographic hashes, as such functions are known, are very important to modern computer security. Cryptography, though, offers much more.

Many cryptographic algorithms, but not all, are easily reversible if you know a particular secret. Armed with that secret, a recipient could turn `0x397B3AF517B6892C` back into "Hello, whirled!" Anyone who did not know the secret would not be able to recover the original data. Such reversible algorithms are known as *ciphers*, and the scrambled output of a cipher is *ciphertext*. The secret used to unscramble ciphertext is called a *key*. Generally, the key is used for both scrambling, called *encryption*, and unscrambling, called *decryption*.

A fundamental principle in cryptography, Kerckhoffs' Principle, states that the security of a cipher should depend only on keeping the key secret. Even if everything else about the cipher is known, so long as the key remains secret, the plaintext should not be recoverable from the ciphertext.

The opposite of Kerckhoffs' Principle is security through obscurity. Any cryptographic system where the cipher is kept secret depends on security through obscurity.[1] Given the difficulty that even professional cryptographers have in designing robust and efficient encryption systems, the likelihood of a secret cipher providing better security than any of the well-known and tested ciphers is vanishingly small. Plus, modern decompilers, disassemblers, debuggers, and other reverse-engineering tools ensure that any secret cipher likely won't remain secret for long.

Cryptographic algorithms can be broadly grouped into three categories: symmetric cryptography, asymmetric (or public-key) cryptography, and cryptographic hashing. Each of these types has a part to play in most cryptographic systems, and we next consider each of them in turn.

2.2.1 Symmetric Cryptography

Symmetric key cryptography is so named because the cipher uses the same key for both encryption and decryption. Two famous ciphers, Data Encryption Standard (DES) and Advanced Encryption Standard (AES), both use symmetric keys. Because symmetric key ciphers are generally much faster than public-key ciphers, they are suitable for encrypting small and large data items.

Modern symmetric ciphers come in two flavors. *Block ciphers* encrypt a chunk of several bits all at once, while *stream ciphers* generally encrypt one bit at a time as the data stream flows past. When a block cipher must encrypt data longer than the block size, the data is first broken into blocks of the appropriate size, and then the encryption algorithm is applied to each. Several *modes* exist that specify how each block is handled. The modes enable an algorithm to be used securely in a variety of situations. By selecting an appropriate mode, for instance, a block cipher can even be used as stream cipher.

The chief advantage of a stream cipher for database cryptography is that the need for padding is avoided. Given that block ciphers operate on a fixed block size, any blocks of data smaller than that size must be padded. Stream ciphers avoid this, and when the data stream ends, the encryption ends. We'll return to block and stream ciphers in the algorithm discussion in Chapter 4 "Cryptographic Engines and Algorithms."

The primary drawback of symmetric key ciphers is key management. Because the same key is used for both encryption and decryption, the key must be distributed to every entity that needs to work with the data. Should an adversary

---

1. *A military cipher would seem an exception, except that most likely the cipher is designed in accordance with Kerckhoffs' Principle in the not-too-unlikely case that an enemy discovers the cipher.*

obtain the key, not only is the confidentiality of the data compromised, but integrity is also threatened given that the key can be used to encrypt as well as decrypt.

The risks posed by losing control of the key make distributing and storing the key difficult. How can the key be moved securely to all the entities that need to decrypt the data? Encrypting the key for transmission would make sense, but what key would be used to encrypt the key, and how would you get the key-encrypting key to the destination?

Once the key is at the decryption location, how should it be secured so that an attacker can't steal it? Again, encryption offers a tempting solution, but then you face the problem of securing the key used to encrypt the original key.

We'll look at these problems in more detail in Chapter 5 "Keys: Vaults, Manifests, and Managers." In terms of the key distribution problem, cryptographers have devised an elegant solution using public-key cryptography, which we examine next.

2.2.2 Public–Key Cryptography

Public-key cryptography, also known as asymmetric cryptography, is a relatively recent invention. As you might guess from the name, the decryption key is different from the encryption key. Together, the two keys are called a key pair and consist of a public key, which can be distributed to the public, and a private key, which must remain a secret. Typically the public key is the encryption key and the private key is the decryption key, but this is not always the case. Well-known asymmetric algorithms include RSA, ElGamal, and Diffie-Hellman. Elliptic curve cryptography provides a different mathematical basis for implementing existing public-key algorithms.

Public-key ciphers are much slower than symmetric-key ciphers and so are typically used to encrypt smaller data items. One common use is to securely distribute a symmetric key. A sender first encrypts a message with a symmetric key and then encrypts that symmetric key with the intended receiver's public key. He then sends both to the receiver. The receiver uses her private key to decrypt the symmetric key and then uses the recovered symmetric key to decrypt the message. In this manner the speed of the symmetric cipher is still a benefit, and the problem of distributing the symmetric key is removed. Such systems are known as hybrid cryptosystems.

Another important use for public-key cryptography is to create digital signatures. Digital signatures are used much like real signatures to verify who sent a message. The private key is used to sign the message, and the public key is used to verify the signature.

A common, easily understood digital signature scheme is as follows. To sign a message, the sender encrypts the message with the private key. Anyone with the corresponding public key can decrypt the message and know that it could only have been encrypted with the private key, which presumably only the sender possesses. Note that this does not protect the confidentiality of the message, considering anyone could have the sender's public key. The goal of a digital signature is simply to verify the sender.

Because the public key can be distributed to anyone, we don't have the same problem as we do with symmetric cryptography. However, we do have a problem of unambiguously matching the public key with the right person. How do we know that a particular public key truly belongs to the person or entity we think it does? This is the problem that public key infrastructure (PKI) has tried to solve. Unfortunately, PKI hasn't lived up to its promise, and the jury is still out on what the long-term accepted solution will be.

Public-key cryptography is mentioned here to help readers new to cryptography understand how it is different from symmetric algorithms. We do not use public-key cryptography in this book, and we do not cover particular algorithms or implementation details. As is discussed in section 2.3, "Applying Cryptography," public-key schemes aren't necessary for solving the problems in which we're interested.

2.2.3 Cryptographic Hashing

The last type of cryptographic algorithm we'll look at is cryptographic hashing. A cryptographic hash, also known as a *message digest,* is like the fingerprint of some data. A cryptographic hash algorithm reduces even very large data to a small unique value. The interesting thing that separates cryptographic hashes from other hashes is that it is virtually impossible to either compute the original data from the hash value or to find other data that hashes to the same value.

A common role played by hashing in modern cryptosystems is improving the efficiency of digital signatures. Because public-key ciphers are much slower than symmetric ciphers, signing large blocks of data is very time-consuming. Instead, most digital signature protocols specify that the digital signature is instead applied to a hash of the data. Given that computing a hash is generally fast and the resulting value is typically much smaller than the data, the signing time is drastically reduced.

Other common uses of cryptographic hashes include protecting passwords, time-stamping data to securely track creation and modification dates and times, and assuring data integrity. The well-known Secure Hash Algorithm family includes SHA-224, SHA-256, SHA-384, and SHA-512. The older SHA-1 and MD5 algorithms are currently in wider use, but flaws in both have been identified, and both should be retired in favor of a more secure hash.

2.3 Applying Cryptography

Now that you've freshened your recollection of database terminology and surveyed the basics of modern cryptography, we examine how cryptography can help secure your databases against the classes of threats covered in Chapter 1.

As we discuss the types of solutions offered by cryptography, we'll also consider the threats that cryptography is expected to mitigate. This threat analysis, as discussed previously, is an essential component of any cryptographic project, and the answers significantly shape the cryptographic solution. Unfortunately, in practice, a requirement to encrypt data is rarely supported with a description of the relevant threats. Encrypting to protect confidentiality from external attackers launching SQL injection attacks is different from protecting against internal developers with read-only access to the production database. The precise nature of the threat determines the protection.

2.3.1 Protecting Confidentiality

A breach of confidentiality occurs when sensitive data is accessed by an unauthorized individual. Encrypting that sensitive data, then, seems to make excellent sense: if the data is encrypted, you've secured it against unauthorized access. Unfortunately, the solution is not this simple. Cryptography only changes the security problem; it doesn't remove it.

The initial problem was to protect the confidentiality of the business data. Encrypting that data changes the problem to one of protecting the confidentiality of the key used for the encryption. The key must be protected with very strong access controls, and those controls must cover both direct and indirect access.

Direct access is access to the key itself. An attacker with direct access may copy the key and use it without fear of detection. Indirect access is access to an application or service that has access to the key. With indirect access, an attacker can feed encrypted data to the application or service and view the decrypted information. An attacker exploiting indirect access faces additional risk, because the application or service, due to its sensitivity, is generally well monitored. From an attacker's point of view, the advantage that might make the indirect access worth the additional risk is that the application or service will continue to provide decryption even after the key is changed. An attacker who has a copy of the key will find the key useless as soon as the data is encrypted with a different key.

The problem of securing access to the key lies behind much of the complexity of key management systems. Cryptography is often said to transform the problem of protecting many secrets into the problem of protecting one secret. Protecting this one secret, despite the complexity, is generally easier than protecting the many secrets. Because of this, encryption is a strong and preferred method of protecting confidentiality in a database.

Consider the confidentiality threats identified in the previous chapter. The potential attackers included individuals with a copy of the database, privileged administrators, IT troubleshooters, development staff using nonproduction environments, individuals with access to backup media (often stored off-site), and attackers exploiting application weaknesses. In each of these cases, encryption protects the data so long as access to the keys is tightly controlled.

While tightly controlling direct access to keys is a relatively solvable problem (this book recommends dedicated key storage hardware but offers suggestions if such protection is unavailable), controlling indirect access is more difficult. Information is stored because the business is likely to need it at a later date, and to use it at that later date, encrypted information will need to be decrypted. The application that provides the decryption service is a weak link in the security chain. Rather than attack the encryption or the controls protecting direct access to the key, a smart attacker targets the decrypting application. We'll consider this issue in more detail in section 2.5.1, "Indirect Access of Keys."

Protecting against attackers with access to a copy of the database, whether stolen from a production machine or a backup tape, requires that the key not be stored within or, ideally, on the same machine as the database. In the case of attacks exploiting backup media, backups of keys must be stored separately from the backups of encrypted data. Access to those backups must also be restricted to different individuals. How deep that separation goes depends on the threat model. If the relevant threat is the off-site backup staff, two different staffs (perhaps two different backup companies) are all that is necessary. If the relevant threats extend all the way to internal system administrators, separate administrators should manage the backups of each system.

Protecting against administrators with full access to database or application servers is primarily a matter of strong indirect access controls to the keys. However, even with just moderate access controls protecting the keys, encryption prevents casual attacks from administrators. In particular, encryption significantly increases the amount of effort required for an administrator to compromise confidentiality and keep the risk of detection low. Such protection is often described as "keeping the honest, honest." If the threat model rates the risk of administrator compromise sufficiently low, keys may need only a moderate level of protection from indirect access.

Most threat models should identify the presence of sensitive production data in nonproduction environments as a significant threat. Because encryption does such a fine job of preserving confidentiality, encrypted production data can't be decrypted in a nonproduction environment.[2] While this is good from a security perspective, the failure in decryption typically results in a malfunctioning environment.

The best solution is to replace all the encrypted data with mock data. Ideally, the mock data reflects the entire data model specified by the application's design, including common, general-use scenarios as well as edge cases. Depending on resource availability, the mock data might be encrypted after it is written to the database. In some cases, it might be possible to encrypt the mock data first and then update the table with the encrypted mock data wherever it is needed. This latter strategy avoids the row-by-row encryption of the mock data.

2.3.2 Assuring Integrity

Cryptography can help detect and prevent integrity attacks, which are unauthorized modifications of data. In some cases, both integrity and confidentiality protection are desired, while in other cases just integrity protection may be needed. When integrity protection alone is called for, the data itself remains unencrypted, and some other operation protects integrity.

The naive solution for both confidentiality and integrity is to simply encrypt the information with a symmetric cipher. Later, if it doesn't decrypt properly, someone has tampered with the information.

Unfortunately, the naive solution is not very robust. A clever attacker will attack integrity in a less obvious fashion. For instance, an attacker might move encrypted fields around so that the rows containing my information now have someone else's encrypted credit card number. Or the attacker might swap blocks within the ciphertext or between ciphertexts. In such an attack, much of the field could decrypt to the correct value, but selected portions of it would decrypt to something else. This attack might result in some garbled data, but the rest of the field would look fine.

---

2. *This assumes that the keys for decrypting the data are not available in nonproduction environments; if they are, the key management procedures are seriously flawed. This is discussed further in Part II, "A Cryptographic Infrastructure."*

A better solution, and one that works even if confidentiality protection is not needed, is to use a message authentication code (MAC). A MAC is generated from the plaintext and a unique ID for that row (the ID thwarts attacks that move entire fields around). To confirm the integrity of the data, we check to make sure that the MAC still corresponds to the data.

While this will detect a past integrity attack, a MAC can also prevent integrity attacks. When data and its MAC are inserted into a table, the database can first check to ensure that the MAC is the correct MAC for that data. If it is the wrong MAC (or the MAC is not included), the database can reject the change.

Every database threat model should consider integrity threats, but as described in the previous chapter, cryptographic integrity protection is typically not a good fit for databases. The threat model will help make this clear. Integrity threats against the database may be carried out by attackers directly targeting the database or by attackers targeting the application providing access to the database, which also stamps changes with the MAC. In general, attacks against the application are more likely to be successful than attacks directly against the database, so, in this context, the risk posed by the application is greater than the risk posed by the database itself. To be effective, security should be applied to the higher-risk items. Because the protection offered by a MAC further increases the difficulty of directly attacking the database successfully (which is already a lower risk), those resources should be applied to securing the application instead, thus reducing the overall risk. Refer to section 1.1.3, "Integrity Attacks," for a more detailed discussion.

2.4 Cryptographic Risks

Cryptography should not be undertaken lightly. While it can significantly help secure information in a database, cryptography carries risk as well.

Perhaps the most obvious risk is the danger of lost keys. Should a key become lost, either corrupted or deleted or even accidentally thrown away, any data encrypted with that key is also lost. There is no "undelete" or "data recovery" program that can undo the encryption. All it takes is the loss of just 128 bits (the recommended size of a key in this book), and megabytes of data become meaningless. This threat is one of the reasons that key management is such an important topic in cryptography.

As mentioned earlier, weaknesses in key management tools and procedures can put overall security at risk. If an attacker can access the key, directly or indirectly, or insert a known key into the system, the cryptography is broken.[3] If the key generation routines aren't based on sufficiently random numbers, the attacker may be able to guess the key.

Implementation bugs also introduce risks. If other data used in the encryption process, such as initialization vectors, which are covered later, does not possess the appropriate properties, attackers will likely be able to discern patterns in the encrypted data and possibly deduce the real data. If the data is written to logs or even not wiped from memory, it is vulnerable to attackers. Even if the key management is perfect and the implementation bug-free, indirect access to the keys is still a significant issue.

Because poor encryption looks so similar to good encryption, it generates misplaced confidence, which can amplify the risks posed by the data. An encrypted system may not have as many other controls placed around it, so any vulnerabilities are even more exposed. In this way, a bad cryptographic system can decrease the data's security.

It is vitally important that the cryptographic infrastructure be designed and implemented correctly. Later chapters go into detail on the design of a cryptographic infrastructure.

2.5 Cryptographic Attacks

Cryptographers classify attacks against cryptosystems into several categories. These attacks attempt to either retrieve the key or expose the plaintext. The algorithms discussed in this book are strong and resist all the attacks discussed here. However, the demands of a practical cryptosystem can easily introduce vulnerabilities even though the algorithm itself is strong. Much of the design presented in this book is aimed at mitigating these weaknesses.

A *known-ciphertext* attack is what most people think of as a cryptographic attack. The attacker has access only to the ciphertexts produced with a given key. These attacks can target either the key or the plaintext. Generally, we'll assume that the attacker has all the ciphertexts.

In the case of a database, this is tantamount to the attacker's having access to the database. Perhaps the attacker has found a weakness in the operating system that allows the database file itself to be downloaded, or perhaps a SQL injection

---

3. *Adding to the risk is the fact that such situations can be very difficult to detect.*

attack is exposing the encrypted data. A properly placed insider often has easy access to all the data.

When the attacker has access to both the plaintext and the ciphertext, the attacker can mount a *known-plaintext* attack. People new to cryptography often dismiss known-plaintext attacks as a sort of "cheating." After all, if the attacker already has all the plaintexts, all the secrets have been exposed. We generally assume, though, that only some of the plaintext-ciphertext pairs are known. Perhaps all the past plaintexts prior to a certain date were compromised. The goal of a known-plaintext can be to recover the key or to uncover plaintext.

In a database context, it is often not too hard to find known plaintexts. The system might temporarily cache the plaintext prior to encryption, or the system might store the data unencrypted elsewhere in the system. This last case is far more common than you might think. For instance, say customer data is stored encrypted, but the data is decrypted in order to e-mail the invoice. The invoice might very well be stored in the database as well. If the invoice isn't also encrypted, the attacker has a source of plaintexts to match with ciphertexts.

An even more subtle example is when data taken together must be encrypted but when the data is separate, it can be unencrypted. For instance, a customer's name and credit card number might be encrypted when they are together in the order table. But another table, in the call tracking system, perhaps, might have the customer's name unencrypted. If these two tables can be linked in a series of joins, the attacker has access to the plaintext. Database normalization can help security in this case, but in practice many databases are not highly normalized, so leaks like this are common.

As its name implies, a *chosen-plaintext* attacker can construct plaintext for the system to encrypt. This is a much more powerful version of a known-plaintext attack. An even more powerful variation is when the attacker can experiment by constructing new plaintexts based on the results of previously constructed plaintexts.

This attack is generally quite easy to mount against a database. In the case of an online ordering system, the attacker simply places additional orders with whatever data he would like to see encrypted. If he would like to see the ciphertext for "Kenan," placing a false order with that information would be suffucient. Unless the cryptosystem is designed carefully, the attacker would then be able to identify all the rows in the table with an order for "Kenan" (and encrypted with a particular key) by searching for the ciphertext produced by the chosen-plaintext attack.

2.5.1 Indirect Access of Keys

The general strategy to protect against direct access of keys is to design the cryptosystem to ensure that the keys are never available outside the code that uses them. Ideally, the keys are locked in dedicated tamper-proof hardware that also contains the cryptographic code. Indirect access, though, as discussed earlier, is a much thornier problem since programs must be able to decrypt the data in order to process it.[4] If automatically launched programs can decrypt the data, a sufficiently motivated and skilled attacker will eventually be able to do the same.

In practice, an indirect access of keys is typically made through a function that passes data to the cryptosystem for decryption. This decryption function is often the weakest link in the security chain protecting encrypted data. If compromised, it will enable an attacker to decrypt arbitrary ciphertexts.[5]

Ideally, the cryptosystem is guarded by strong access controls that require authentication and authorization for each decryption call. To make this effective, though, the authorization check needs to occur as close to the actual decryption as possible. If a dedicated cryptographic device (discussed in Chapter 4, "Cryptographic Engines and Algorithms") is in use, the device should make the check itself. Unfortunately, that capability is very rare. The goal of these measures is to prevent the attacker from following the chain of function calls until a decryption call is found *after* the authorization check. If such a call is found, the attacker uses it for the decryption compromise attack.

Automated processes throw a wrinkle into this strategy. Automation, such as a batch credit card payment process, often needs access to decrypted data, and while it is certainly possible to require the automation to provide credentials prior to decrypting data, those credentials must also be stored and protected. The following discussion of data obfuscation covers this situation in more detail, but it is best to assume that if the attacker is sophisticated enough to break the application sufficiently to access the decryption function, he also will be capable of retrieving any credentials used by the automation.

Our approach is one of containment and observation. First, we ensure that the decryption function decrypts only the fewest necessary columns. This contains the damage in the case of a decryption compromise; the attacker won't be able to

---

4. *Do not store unneeded data, especially unneeded sensitive information such as customer data. Storing and protecting unneeded data increases your risk and costs and provides no business value.*

5. *A decryption compromise exploiting indirect key access is related to the* chosen-ciphertext *class of attacks. The primary difference is that the general goal of a chosen-ciphertext attack is to recover the key, whereas a decryption compromise generally ignores attempts to recover the key (our algorithms are not susceptible to chosen-ciphertext attacks) and is content with decrypting all encrypted information in the system.*

decrypt all protected data in the system. Our next layer of defense, observation, is the critical control.

Extensive logging of decryption requests will expose sudden spikes caused by an attacker. Correlation of the logs with server processing and customer request logs helps reveal skimming.[6] Honeycombing is also a valuable technique against an attempted decryption compromise.

Honeycombs are to applications and databases what honeypots are to networks. A honeycombed application has several APIs that are named and look like they should do what the attacker wants, but in reality they simply trigger alerts. A honeycombed database contains tables and views that look promising to potential attackers, but any `select` against them triggers an alert. In some cases, honeycombs can take the form of special rows in a table that look legitimate, but the data is fake and any query against them results in an alert. Any alert fired by a honeycomb is by definition suspicious since the honeycomb serves no actual business purpose and there is no reason in the normal course of business that the honeycomb would be accessed.

2.6 Obfuscation

Cryptography can be applied so as to provide strong security or weak security. Generally, since cryptography is expensive and introduces risk, you want only as much security as is necessary. This book uses the term *obfuscation* to describe situations where encryption is used to provide a minimal amount of security. Obfuscation is used simply to make reading data more difficult and thereby prevent casual attacks.

Obfuscation should be used rarely. Strong encryption, not obfuscation, is necessary for nearly every threat requiring a cryptographic solution. Obfuscation is generally appropriate only as a solution of last resort and relies on other controls for adequate protection. For instance, consider the situation described in the previous section, where a program must, in order to decrypt data, log into a dedicated decryption machine over the internal network. The dedicated machine requires a password, so the program must have access to that password. The problem of how to protect that password is an issue.

Encrypting the password makes sense, but how would it be decrypted? The strong cryptographic solution would be to use the dedicated decryption machine,

---

6. *Skimming is where the attacker grabs only a few items at a time as opposed to going for bulk. It is a tactic more appropriate for an insider, who typically has a longer attack window.*

but that won't work because the decrypted password is necessary to access the machine. Another option would be to encrypt the password with a key stored elsewhere and not use the dedicated machine. Then the problem becomes a matter of protecting that key while also making it available to the program when it needs to use the password.

Complicated schemes where the credentials are entered manually by a security administrator when the program first starts and are then stored only in primary memory, perhaps split into several pieces, further shift the problem to one of protecting the key when it is in the administrator's possession. Such measures also increase the program's fragility and introduce dependencies for restarting the program. Additionally, the security of such techniques is, ultimately, questionable. A skilled and patient attacker with the right tools and access can simply wait until the program decrypts the password, at which point the attacker picks it out of memory. While this isn't trivial, it certainly isn't impossible. The threat model helps you determine if such a complex scheme is appropriate in a given situation.

Alternatively, the password could simply be obfuscated. An obfuscated password might be encrypted and stored in one file while the key used for the encryption is stored in another file. Anybody simply browsing through files won't accidentally compromise the password, but, obviously, if that individual were dedicated to retrieving the password, it would not be difficult to get both the encrypted password and the key. Various schemes could be employed to increase the difficulty, but by calling the protection obfuscation, we recognize that the security is rather easily broken, so we are reminded to maintain other controls appropriately. In this case, we want to ensure that only administrators and the necessary programs have access to both files.

2.7 Transparent Encryption

Several products on the market advertise transparent encryption. The name itself should raise a few questions: what kind of security does *transparent* encryption provide? The assumption is, of course, that the cryptography is transparent to the legitimate, authorized user but not to attackers. The security in such a system depends not only on the cryptosystem and key storage, but also on how well legitimate users can be distinguished from attackers.

Attackers are notoriously good at looking like legitimate users. Internal attackers typically *are* legitimate users. Many of the attacks discussed in the previous chapter are not stopped by transparent encryption, including SQL injection and "sanctioned" backdoors. The threat model must be considered carefully to see if transparent encryption offers the necessary protection.

For instance, triggers and views (features of some databases) can offer automatic encryption and decryption for authorized users. The trigger in this case is a program embedded in the database that runs every time a row is inserted and encrypts the necessary data. The view is a "virtual" table that decrypts the data before returning it to the requester. A `select` against the view (by an authorized user) returns decrypted data.

Which threats does this system protect against? Assuming that the keys are secured on another machine,[7] the risk posed by thievery of the database or backups is mitigated. Of course, if an attacker can steal the database file, it is not too much of a stretch to assume that he can attack the transparent encryption system itself or the database's authorization mechanism.

Also, threats from legitimate users with direct access to the database via an account that allows them to `select` against the encrypted table but not against the auto-decrypting view are reduced. However, such users are rare. Development staff engaged in troubleshooting is perhaps the most likely scenario, but, depending on the problem, they may need access to the auto-decrypting view. Most other users will access the data through an application that typically uses its own account, so they will not directly access the database. This is a rather minimal gain.

Most of our other threats still pose a risk for the database. Administrators can easily don the "authorized" user role and have the cryptosystem happily decrypt the data. Application crackers have the option of attacking the application or the database. If either succeeds, the attacker will be well on the way to accessing the encrypted data.[8] Application subversion attacks, such as SQL injection, will also likely remain viable since such attacks generally leverage the application's access privileges, and the application will likely access the database through an account that is authorized to view the decrypted data.

In a nutshell, the trigger and view solution described here reduces the data's online security to the security level of the passwords to the accounts that are authorized to select against the auto-decrypting view. Should any of those accounts be compromised, the cryptography is circumvented. In terms of online threats, if this level of security were acceptable, cryptography in the database wouldn't be necessary in the first place.

---

7. *If the keys are actually stored in the same database as the encrypted data or even on the same machine as the database, the solution provides very little protection against all but the most simple threats.*

8. *One of the design goals of a secure system is to minimize the number of attack points, and this book attempts to remove the database as an attack point.*

If the local threat model consists of only offline attacks, transparent encryption, such as the scheme just discussed, might be sufficient.[9] The threat model considered in this book, though, is more extensive. To mitigate online threats, we can, at the very least, require that an attacker gain access to both the database for the encrypted data *and* a cryptography service to decrypt it. The cryptography service can then be protected with much better security controls. We can better limit which machines may communicate with it, monitor it more closely, significantly strengthen its access credentials, increase the frequency with which the credentials are changed, and better protect the handling of those credentials.

When considering a transparent encryption solution, an organization's security analysts must carefully compare the threat model the solution targets with the organization's threat model. In addition, key storage must be considered. Ideally, the solution will support the use of a dedicated cryptographic hardware module for protecting the key and performing cryptographic operations. At the very least, the keys should be kept and used on a different machine.

A final word of caution. As you'll see later, using a good algorithm is not enough. How it is used is of equal importance. This *how* is captured in the *mode*, and selecting the right mode depends on many conditions. While no single mode is correct in every situation, some modes are very rarely the right choice. Always ask which mode is used, and be very suspicious if a vendor indicates that no mode was used or if electronic code book (ECB) mode was used. In either case, the system is likely to be vulnerable to chosen-plaintext attacks, as described earlier in this chapter. This is covered in more detail in Chapter 4.

2.8 Summary

This chapter looked at database cryptography as a hardening solution to what is often referred to as the "soft, chewy center" of most organizations. This hardening is the last line of defense between data and attackers.

The chapter opened with introductory coverage of databases and cryptography. The cryptographic overage included symmetric cryptography, asymmetric (or public-key) cryptography, and cryptographic hashing. While the material certainly won't turn you into a database expert or cryptographer, it should provide enough background for you to follow the rest of the book.

---

9. *If the threat model is concerned only about access of backup media, a dedicated backup-only encryption solution might be most appropriate. Such a scheme is generally much easier to implement than cryptography in the database.*

With the introductory material out of the way, the discussion turned to examining, at a high level, how cryptography can be applied to protect the confidentiality and integrity threats identified in the previous chapter. Confirming the principle that security is always a balance of trade-offs, the risks of attacks against a database cryptosystem were considered. In particular, we explored the idea that encryption turns the problem of protecting the confidentiality of a large quantity of business data into the problem of protecting a small set of keys.

This chapter also discussed obfuscation, the purposeful use of poor key protection to obtain a minimal amount of data security, and transparent encryption, the problematic technique of automatically decrypting information for any "legitimate" user.

This chapter hopefully provided a taste of what cryptography can and cannot do. With the promise and limits of cryptography covered, we now move on to exploring the details of a functioning cryptosystem.

PART II

A CRYPTOGRAPHIC INFRASTRUCTURE

Chapter 3

An Overview of Cryptographic Infrastructure

Protecting databases with cryptography requires careful thought and design. When confronted with a requirement to encrypt a field in a database, it is quite easy for a developer to simply use an existing encryption library and begin encrypting data using a key embedded in the code. This, of course, provides very little security. To make this point as clear as possible, let's briefly consider such a poorly conceived system.

Over time, as more applications and programs need access to the encrypted data, the developer duplicates the key. Soon, the key is embedded in dozens of programs and resides on a handful of servers and perhaps even on end-user machines. The old developer leaves the company, and new developers take up the code. Contractors come and go. Staff from the QA team reviews the code with the embedded key. In very little time, the number of people who have looked at the key is quite large, and that number includes individuals who are no longer employees.

The chances that an attacker can find the key are quite high. If the attacker is one of the many who have already had access to the key, or perhaps is associated with one of that multitude, the cryptography is easily circumvented. Alternatively, the attacker can easily extract the key from the code. Using modern tools, this is barely an inconvenience.

Once the company realizes that the key is compromised and decides to install a new key, a new wrinkle develops. The key is embedded in dozens of programs, and each needs to be tracked down, changed, and tested. Imagine the confusion that would result if one program were missed and still used the old key. Plus, all the existing data encrypted with the current key will need to be decrypted and then re-encrypted with the new key. This convoluted procedure will need to happen fairly frequently because good security requires that old keys are retired and new keys are brought into service.

Given that there will likely be many different embedded keys, each of which will need periodic changing, it is clear that the quick encryption solution is a long-term maintenance disaster. The amount of work required to support this "system" is certainly not worth the minuscule amount of security gained.

Proper design and careful implementation will yield a cryptographic system that provides the needed security (for both the data and the keys), scales well, and supports management of keys throughout their life cycle.

3.1 Application Architecture

To provide a context for the rest of the discussion, we'll consider a database in a typical application environment consisting of three tiers: a presentation tier, an application tier, and a database tier. This is a fairly standard arrangement where, in most cases, the presentation tier is composed of Web servers that present the Web pages forming the user interface. Occasionally the Web pages may contain embedded applets or other code that executes locally on the client machine.

The application tier is typically where the business logic resides. Composed of application servers, this tier processes requests from the presentation tier according to business rules and interacts with the database. The results are passed back to the presentation tier, which responds to the user.

The database tier, of course, contains database servers. While the primary purpose of the database tier is to provide storage and easy retrieval, often business logic is also found in the database tier. Either embedded in the database itself or located on a back-office server, business logic in this tier is typically automated data processing that occurs on a scheduled basis.

These three tiers might support an organization's external Web site, so the presentation tier would be exposed to the Internet. In such a situation, the three tiers together form an *extranet*. Alternatively, the architecture could be deployed for an organization's internal business applications, in which case the presentation tier would likely be exposed only to the intranet. Figure 3.1 illustrates an application architecture for an extranet.

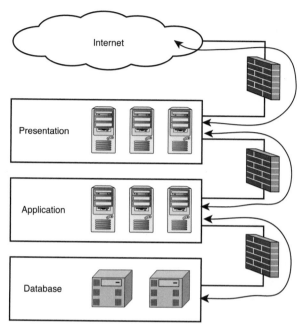

Figure 3.1: Application architecture

The figure shows a firewall protecting the gateway into each of the tiers (or zones in network parlance). Network traffic is only allowed to flow with the arrows. Accordingly, servers in the presentation tier are allowed to connect to the servers in the application tier but not to servers in the database tier.[1] Traffic coming from the Internet would only be permitted to target the presentation tier and is explicitly blocked from entering any of the other tiers.

In cases where additional business logic resides on back-office servers, particularly in architectures for Web sites, an intranet (not shown) might connect to the same firewall that filters Internet access. Unlike Internet traffic, appropriate traffic originating from the intranet would be permitted into each of the three tiers. However, typically the connection can be initiated only from the intranet. None of the servers in the extranet is permitted to initiate a connection to an intranet server; they may only respond to requests from the intranet.

The point of this brief firewall discussion is to introduce the question of where to place database cryptography. It probably never belongs in the presentation tier.

---

1. *In many networks, the application and database tiers are joined, and only a single firewall controls access to the combined zone. We'll assume that the zones are separate; in cases where they're joined, the implementation of cryptography may be easier, but of course the network is somewhat less secure.*

Not only is the presentation tier the most exposed and where a compromise is most likely to occur, but firewall rules would prevent the cryptostystem from directly accessing the database. Not a useful situation for a database encryption solution.[2]

Other than ruling out the presentation tier, no other obvious configurations, right or wrong, are immediately apparent. The decision depends on such factors as the desired level of security, the location of the consumer or consumers, and the budget (for software, hardware, and administrative staff). We'll work through these considerations as we continue through the book.

3.2 Cryptographic Architecture

The cryptographic architecture developed in this book is a flexible, modular system that can be adapted to many situations. Unfortunately, as a system's flexibility and modularity increase, so does the difficulty of keeping the system secure. As presented, the system strikes a balance between security and functionality.

The design contains seven logical components consisting of three data stores and four processes. These components are illustrated in Figure 3.2, which shows interactions involving an encryption operation.

The entities that interact with the system include end users such as data input staff or Web site customers and the security officers in charge of key administration. In addition, there are typically automated jobs that need to enter, process, and extract encrypted data. The seven components are as follows:

Cryptographic Engine   Performs the actual cryptographic operations.

Key Vault   Securely stores keys for the engine.

Key Manifest   Tracks details of keys, including aliases, family, state, and engine.

Key Manager   Manages keys in the key vault and the key manifest.

Cryptographic Provider   Provides a bridge between the cryptographic engine and the consumer.

Cryptographic Consumer   Maintains or processes data that needs encryption or decryption.

Protected Data   The data that needs to be secured with cryptography.

The interaction between the components begins with an administrator using the key manager to create a new key in the key vault and then adding it to the key

---

2. *Some types of encryption belong in the presentation tier, such as the encryption needed to support HTTPS or encryption to protect data in primary memory.*

manifest. As part of adding the new key to the manifest, the administrator assigns the key to a key family (described in section 3.3, "Cryptographic Keys") and sets an activation date.

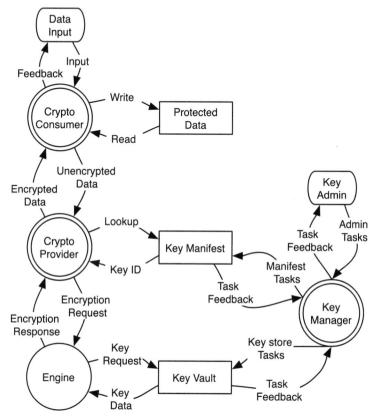

Figure 3.2: Cryptographic infrastructure

The interesting work occurs when a cryptographic consumer has data it needs encrypted. The consumer hands the data to the provider for encrypting and identifies which family of keys should be used for the job. The provider uses the manifest to look up which key in that family is currently in use and which key vault and engine are assigned to that key. It also gathers or generates any ancillary data that might be needed, such as an initialization vector.

All of this information is handed off to the cryptographic engine, which retrieves the actual key from the key vault and performs the encryption. The encrypted data is then handed back to the provider, which prepares a receipt consisting of information such as the ID of the key used and any other necessary information. The receipt is returned with the encrypted data to the consumer.

The consumer writes the encrypted data and the receipt to the database. Later, when the consumer needs the data decrypted, it passes the receipt and encrypted data back to the provider. The provider extracts what information it needs from the receipt and checks to make sure the key is in a valid state in the manifest. If everything checks out, the provider passes the request on to the engine. The engine decrypts the data and passes it back to the consumer through the provider.

3.3 Cryptographic Keys

As mentioned in previous chapters, cryptography reduces the problem of protecting many secrets into a problem of protecting just a few secrets. Those few secrets are the cryptographic keys, and because those keys are of primary importance, the rest of this chapter is devoted to examining their properties. These properties include the state of the key, its family and scope, and when it should be replaced. Many of these properties will be dealt with in more depth in later chapters.

The key length is a special property that significantly affects the security provided by the algorithm using the key. While, for a given algorithm, longer keys provide greater security than shorter keys, we cannot make general statements about the security provided by key lengths when used by different algorithms. For instance, we can't always say that a 128-bit key in algorithm A is always more or less secure than a 128-bit key used in algorithm B. For this reason, discussion of key length is deferred to the sections covering the algorithms themselves in Chapter 4, "Cryptographic Engines and Algorithms."

3.3.1 Key Separation

Key separation is a security concept that requires that a cryptographic key be used for only a single purpose. The primary goals and benefits of key separation are

- Minimize the number of entities that need access to the key.
- Keep the amount of data handled during a key replacement manageable.
- Reduce the amount of data encrypted with a given key so that attackers have less information to use in breaking the encryption.
- Limit the damage if a particular key is compromised.
- Allow different levels of security to be applied to different types of data.

Given that the security of a cryptographic system depends on the security of the keys, it is best if the number of entities that need access to the key is kept to the absolute minimum. By limiting the use of a key to a single purpose, fewer entities need access to the key. In the context of database cryptography, this mandate keeps keys limited to just a single database.

As we'll discuss later, keys must be periodically replaced to maintain security. During a key replacement, all the data encrypted with an old key is decrypted and then re-encrypted with a new key. Key separation can help keep this task manageable by allowing a variety of replacement schedules and, in some cases, enabling parallel replacements.

One class of attacks against cryptographically protected data, *known-ciphertext attacks*, relies on having a large collection of data encrypted with the same key. Using several different keys limits the effectiveness of this class of attacks because a smaller amount of data is encrypted with each key.

Should a key be compromised, perhaps due to a malicious insider, everything encrypted with that key is vulnerable. Key separation limits the extent of the loss because any given key protects only some of the data, and the rest of it is protected by other keys. The attacker might get customer names, but not their credit card numbers.

Finally, rather than protecting all data at the highest level of protection, key separation lets the strength of the protection be tailored for the data. For instance, if most of a database requires 128-bit keys replaced quarterly, but a few columns require 256-bit keys replaced weekly, then without the use of key separation, everything in the database would have to be re-encrypted every week with a 256-bit key.

Exactly what constitutes a "single purpose" is somewhat vague. We can say that keys should not be used in more than a single database, but beyond that rule, we must refer to the points mentioned here in deciding what is appropriate. In our design, key separation is achieved through key families and key scopes.

3.3.2 Key Families

A *key family* is a group of keys that are used to operate on the same set of data. For instance, one family might be used for credit card numbers and another for medical records. Keys are labeled with their family names.

The keys in a family have specific roles that determine how they can be used. For instance, at any given moment, only one key in a family can be used for encryption, and while multiple keys can be used for decryption, a family often contains old keys that cannot be used for encryption or decryption. These roles change over time and are determined by the key life cycle, as discussed in the next section.

The best practice is to assign a single, unique family to each column that needs encryption. If a table has five protected columns, ideally five families would cover the table. Figure 3.3 illustrates two protected columns covered by two families.

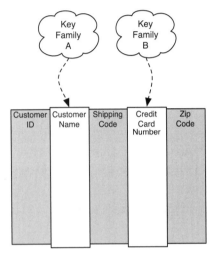

Figure 3.3: Two families

However, a one-to-one relationship between families and protected columns requires each key to be marshalled and applied in order to read the entire row. This might present noticeable performance penalties. Letting the family span all the columns can reduce the performance overhead somewhat, but the degree of the savings depends on how the engine processes requests.[3] Testing is required to determine the effect of a column-spanning family on performance. Often, the gains, if any, are so slight that they aren't worth sacrificing the advantages and additional security. A stronger case for column-spanning families takes into consideration the storage requirements for tracking each of the keys for each row. We look more deeply into this situation in section 3.3.4, "Key Scope." Figure 3.4 illustrates a single family covering two columns.

---

3. *Typically, even with a spanning family, each column requires a separate encryption or decryption request.*

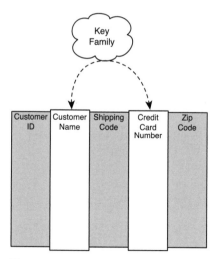

Figure 3.4: A column-spanning family

Striping

Another family assignment strategy maps multiple families to a column and uses more sophisticated criteria to select which family is applicable for a given row. This creates tables that are *striped* with different families: one set of rows would be encrypted with one family, and another set of rows would be encrypted with a different family. The stripes might be interleaved or contiguous, depending on the family selection criteria. Figure 3.5 shows an example of striping.

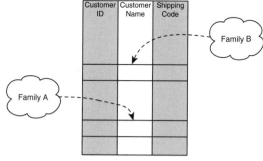

Figure 3.5: Striping

As an example, if each row of a table were tagged with a unique "row ID" (perhaps an incrementing primary key), that number could be used to determine the family. If ten families were desired, the family could be based on the row ID modulo 10. In such a scenario, families zero through nine would cover the column, and subsequent updates would still fall into the same family because the row ID wouldn't change. Conceptually, this creates interleaved encryption stripes (assuming that new rows are always appended to the table). A scheme using the month of row creation as the determining factor for the family would create contiguous zones of stripes sharing the same family.

This strategy can be further extended so that multiple families also cover multiple columns. Our ten families could span several columns. The simple case would require that all the columns in a given row be covered by the same family (the discussion of key scopes later in this chapter removes this constraint). For this to work, the family selection criteria must operate independently of the columns: No matter which column is to be encrypted, the criteria must evaluate to the same family. Our row ID and creation date schemes meet this property.

Family and striping affect only the encryption of new or updated data. Decryption is always determined by the information in the receipt. So if the family assignment changes while data is encrypted, nothing happens until that data is updated and needs to be re-encrypted. At that point the new receipt references a key in the new family.

If an architecture allows changes to which families are assigned to which tables, there could be disagreement between the family currently assigned to a table and the family of the key referenced in the receipt. This could pose a risk if the encrypted data is backed up and the family assignment is used to determine which keys should be matched with that backup.[4] For this reason, always use the receipts to determine which keys are needed for decryption.

3.3.3 Key Life Cycle

Keys, unlike diamonds, are not forever. The more data a key encrypts, the weaker it becomes. Not only does a long service life mean that the key has faced more opportunities for compromise, it also means that an attacker has more data to use in breaking the encryption. To counter this inherent weakness, cryptographic keys must be periodically replaced.

When replacing a key, all the data encrypted with the old key must be decrypted and then re-encrypted with the new key. Then the old key should be

---

4. *Of course, the key backups must be stored separately from the data backups.*

deleted so it can't be used again. The key life cycle provides a model that captures and organizes these various states. The states in the life cycle, described next, are illustrated in Figure 3.6.

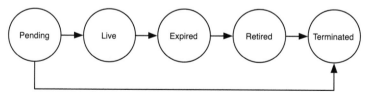

Figure 3.6: Cryptographic key life cycle

Pending   A key that becomes Live when its activation date is reached. There may be several Pending keys in a family.

Live   A key that is currently used for encryption and decryption. There may be only a single Live key in a family.

Expired   A key that was once Live but has been supplanted by a newer Live key. Expired keys are used to decrypt data encrypted with old keys. There may be several Expired keys in a family.

Retired   A key that is no longer in use. There may be several Retired keys in a family.

Terminated   A key that has been deleted from the key vault. There may be several Terminated keys in a family.

Table 3.1 indicates which cryptographic operations are permitted in each state and summarizes the criteria that cause a key to transition from one state to another. Note that the transition criteria apply to the keys within a given key family, so life cycle events in one family do not affect keys in another family. For instance, each family may have at most one Live key, and when a Pending key becomes Live in one family, key states in the other families are not changed.

Table 3.1

Key States		
State	**Encryption**	**Decryption**
Pending	No	No
Live	Yes	Yes
Expired	No	Yes
Retired	No	No
Terminated	No	No

As mentioned earlier, when a key is created, it is assigned a family and an activation date. The activation date indicates the date (and time) when the key becomes Live. Until that date passes, the key is in the Pending state and can't be used for any cryptographic operations.

Once the current date passes a key's activation date, that key becomes Live, and any previously Live key is thereby pushed into the Expired state. The Live state is the only state that permits encryption, and all encryption requests for that key's family use whichever key is currently Live.

Keys in the Expired state are never used for encryption. An Expired key can only be used to decrypt data that was encrypted when the key was Live. The Expired state is essentially a holding state until the key can be replaced. It is best to replace keys as soon as possible once they've been Expired.

Once all the data that was encrypted with an Expired key has been re-encrypted with a new key, the Expired key should be set to a Retired state. Retired indicates that the key is no longer in use but is still resident in the key vault.

The difference between Retired and Terminated is simply that a Terminated key has been deleted from the key vault. In both cases, though, the key cannot be used. It is best to delete a Retired key from the key vault as soon as possible. Even keys no longer in use present a risk because an attacker might have access to old data that was encrypted with that key. Careless handling of Retired or Terminated keys can easily lead to data compromise.

A common theme throughout the key life cycle is that keys should not linger in any particular state longer than necessary. As soon as a key has reached the end of its term in a given state, it should move to the next state. Similarly, for Pending keys, it's best not to create keys too far in advance—say, more than a quarter out. The goal of this prompt advancement is to ensure that keys are stored and used for the shortest period possible. The longer a key is in existence, the greater the opportunity for compromise.

3.3.4 Key Scope

While families map keys to columns, key scopes indicate how keys are used to encrypt across rows. When a row is inserted into a table with protected columns, we must track which key or keys were used. Recall from section 3.2, "Cryptographic Architecture," that the receipt returned by the cryptographic provider contains this information. In a sense the key scope determines how many receipts the consumer needs to manage.

For the narrowest scope, each protected column needs its own receipt. This is the default case when the best practice of using a separate, unique family for each column is followed, but even if a single family is used for the entire table, the keys can still be scoped narrowly. In such a case, each protected column is associated with its own receipt. On the initial insert, all the receipts reference the same key. Over time, though, the keys in the receipts will likely drift apart as individual items of data are updated and others are left unchanged.

Narrowly scoped keys create complex key management schemes and require more space to hold all the receipts. They are also much more flexible and provide better security. The best practice is to use the narrowest scope possible.

At the widest scope, only a single receipt is needed because all the protected columns are encrypted with a single key. This makes for the simplest key management scheme but creates more complex key migration scenarios because all the protected columns need to be re-encrypted even when just one of them is updated (key migration is discussed in more depth in section 3.3.6, "Key Migration"). Wide scopes[5] are useful for grouping columns containing data that generally changes as a group. For instance, the credit card number and expiration date could be scoped together because when one changes, the other is likely to change as well. Figure 3.7 illustrates how scopes and receipt storage are related.

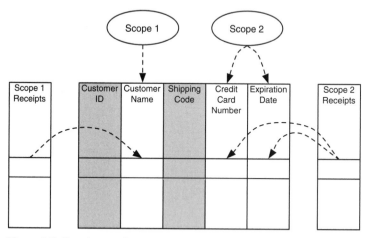

Figure 3.7: Receipts and scopes

5. We'll say that a key has a wide scope when a receipt covers more than one column. A narrow scope indicates that the receipt is for a single column. We'll say that a key's scope is narrower or wider than another key's when we mean that its receipt covers fewer or more columns, respectively.

The actual storage of receipts could be in the same table as the data or in a separate table. While Figure 3.7 implies that a single column holds the receipt, this is generally not the case, unless perhaps an object-oriented database is being used. In practice, most receipts are decomposed into multiple types of data, including the encrypted data, a reference to the key used, and additional cryptographic material (such as the initialization vectors described in Chapter 4). Each of these is then stored in its own column.

The number of families covering a table cannot be greater than the number of scopes.[6] A table that has six protected columns might be structured such that three columns are under one scope, two other columns are under a different scope, and the remaining column is in its own scope. We would then say that the table is covered by three scopes.

To support our three-scope table, we need to allocate storage space for three receipts. We can then assign one, two, or three families to cover the table. If we tried to assign four families to cover the table, we would run into problems because we haven't allocated a place to store the necessary receipts for that fourth family.

Scoping and Striping

When family striping is used, the family selection criteria must evaluate to the same family for all the columns in a scope. For instance, if the family selection were based on the first letter of the column's value,[7] the columns for the first name and last name could not be in the same scope because it is very likely that each of these would have different first letters. If the criteria were instead the first letter of just the first name, both columns could be included in the same scope. Figure 3.8 shows how receipts are linked to striped scopes.

Of course, the best strategy for striping is to base the selection on a value that isn't likely to change and is independent of the encrypted data. A column or columns dedicated just to storing the family selection data is advantageous as it is simple, enables precise control over the family, and is less likely to change.

---

6. This conclusion depends on the receipt's storage of only a single set of parameters for the cryptographic operation. The structure of the receipt is detailed later.

7. Using the first letter as the selection criteria for striping is not recommended; it's used here only as an easy example. A more realistic (and more complicated) criteria might be based on the value of a foreign key.

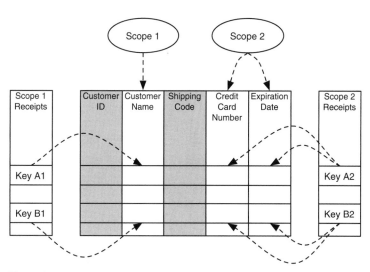

Figure 3.8: Receipts and striped scopes

3.3.5 Key Fatigue

When assigning families and scopes, the amount of data to be protected by a key must be considered in order to counter a possible threat of information leakage. Information leakage describes the faint traces of the plaintext that linger in the ciphertext. While the system in this book strives to use cryptography in a secure manner, some information leakage is simply unavoidable with the tools we have to work with. Here we look at the impact of information leakage on family and scope specifications.

As more data is encrypted with a key, the more likely it becomes that the encryption leaks information, so the system must limit the amount of data encrypted with that key. The analysis of information leakage described in [8] in the Bibliography provides excellent guidance on how to determine this limit and is highly recommended. Once the limit is reached, the likelihood of leaking information becomes a near certainty. The key is essentially "fatigued," and continued use weakens security.

Let's assume that an encryption scheme supports the encryption of up to 2^{36} bytes with a given key before leakage becomes a concern.[8] Such a limit would support storing and maintaining a kilobyte of encrypted data, 2^{10} bytes, for up to

---

8. *As described in [8], this limit is appropriate for AES in cipher block chaining mode (see Chapter 4) with 128-bit keys.*

2^{24} customers (over 15 million). Once all that data is encrypted, though, the key protects only 2^{34} bytes. This allows each customer to completely change the stored data once a quarter, so that after a year the total amount of data that has been encrypted with that key is 2^{36} bytes.

Any key used in this scheme would be fatigued by the end of the year. Encrypting additional information increases the likelihood of information leakage (the local threat model should be consulted to determine how much risk from leakage is appropriate). Expiring the key and replacing it with the current Live key is not a solution because as soon as all the information has been re-encrypted with the current Live key, that key too will be fatigued.

In practice, this particular problem is not too likely. Because we require keys to be specific to a table, the problem would appear only if 2^{36} bytes (64 gigabytes) of encrypted information were stored in a *single* table. Most designs would split that much data across multiple tables and possibly across multiple database servers to keep performance high. Given that each table has its own key, the problem would be minimized.

Another scenario involving key fatigue has to do with determining how long a key should remain Live. Consider if we have a half million (2^{19}) customers who are changing their kilobyte of data once a week. After 128 weeks, about two and a half years, the limit of 2^{36} bytes would have been encrypted with the key. At any given time, though, only 512 megabytes would be encrypted and stored in a table.[9] In this case, 128 weeks is the maximum amount of time the key should remain Live.

These scenarios illustrate two ways of dealing with data sets so large that they threaten to fatigue the key. In the first case, the problem was side-stepped by using multiple families. Even if we hadn't been able to side-step the problem by specifying multiple tables, assigning multiple families to cover the single table would still have provided an effective solution. By determining the maximum amount of information to be stored in the table, a set of families can be devised, using striping, to ensure that the keys never become fatigued.

In the second case, the key was fatigued even though the overall amount of encrypted data was never at any given time very close to the key's limit. The solution here doesn't depend on multiple families so much as ensuring that the key doesn't remain Live after the encryption limit is reached. Generally, limiting a key

---

9. We'll assume that the database can support this table just fine. For the example, we could always reduce the number of customers and increase the frequency of their changes or the length of time over which the changes occur.

to a year in the Live state is reasonable. Should data flow rapidly through the system, the period should be shortened appropriately. Leaving the key in the Live state for more than a year opens the door to key theft, because the longer the key remains available, the more opportunity there is for compromise. We'll return to this subject in the discussion of key replacement in a moment.

3.3.6 Key Migration

When protected data is altered, it is subject to a key migration if the key that was used to originally encrypt the data has become Expired. In such a situation, the data is decrypted with the Expired key, but the changes are encrypted with the current Live key.

For instance, when the data was originally inserted into the table, say key K_1 was used for encryption. A year later K_1 has become Expired, and key K_2 is the new Live key. If the data is then changed, the changed data is encrypted with K_2. In this way, data naturally migrates away from Expired keys.

Key migration is similar to what happens when the family assigned to a column changes, perhaps due to striping criteria. The primary difference is that all the keys used in a key migration are members of the same family. In a family reassignment, obviously the new encryption key is in a different family from the decryption key. Family reassignment should also be a rare and somewhat exceptional occurrence; key migration, on the other hand, is a typical occurrence in the use of a key.

Key migration does introduce an interesting situation when dealing with wide scopes. Even if only a subset of the columns covered by the scope are updated, all the scope's columns must undergo the migration.

As an example, consider what would happen if the keys for unchanged columns in a scope were not migrated when others were. Say we have two columns in scope of K_1. When data is initially inserted, it is encrypted and the receipt R_{K_1} contains the cryptographic information necessary for the engine to decrypt the data.[10]

A year later K_1 is Expired and K_2 is the Live key. If one of the columns changes, the changed data is encrypted with K_2 and noted in receipt R_{K_2}. When this receipt is saved, it overwrites the previous receipt, R_{K_1}. Later, if data from the other, unchanged column is needed, the system attempts to decrypt it with data contained in the scope's receipt: R_{K_2}. Because this receipt contains the wrong information for that column, the decryption fails.

---

10. *The receipt doesn't contain the key itself, but instead a reference to the key.*

To correctly handle this, both columns must be migrated to the new key even if only one is changed. The new receipt then contains accurate information for both columns, and future decryptions won't fail.

Narrow scopes prevent this situation altogether because each column has its own receipt. Also promptly replacing Expired keys minimizes the frequency of key migrations, and because Expired keys are Expired because they have reached the end of their useful life, they should be replaced as soon as possible. The next section covers key replacement.

3.3.7 Key Replacements and Schedules

Key replacement, also known as rekeying, describes the procedure to replace an Expired key with the current Live key. The replacement process requires any data encrypted with the Expired key to be decrypted and then re-encrypted with the new Live key. Once all data has been re-encrypted, the Expired key should be marked as Retired to indicate that it is no longer needed.

The best practice of limiting one family to one column simplifies key replacement. In such a case, only a single column needs to be examined for the existence of the Expired key, so the risk of accidentally missing a use of the key is minimized. The more columns covered by a family, especially if those columns are in other tables, the greater the risk that one is missed, perhaps due to an undocumented update to the cryptographic scheme.

The risk of missing data in an update carries serious consequences because once the expired key is retired, it is soon deleted from the key vault. While keys deleted from the key vault might be retained in a secure, offline key archive, a kind of graveyard of cryptographic keys, recovery using such archived keys is difficult. Should the key be removed from even the archive, any data that remains encrypted with that key is essentially lost. A cryptographic system that prevents even authorized users from accessing needed data is useless.

As mentioned earlier, an Expired key should be replaced as soon as possible. The longer the key remains in the system, the greater its risk of compromise. However, key replacement is often a significant consumer of processing given that a large quantity of data is decrypted and then re-encrypted in a relatively short period of time. The computational expense of frequent key replacement can be prohibitive. Key replacement also introduces additional administrative interaction, including configuring and backing up keys. The risk of error or compromise in the manual steps of the replacement procedure must also be considered when determining when to replace keys.

Replacing a key within a year of its expiration is reasonable. If the key is Live for a year and then Expired for another, the key's complete operational period is two years. Two years is a long time for an attacker to craft attacks against the key vault, key backups, or key administration procedures. If the key is protected in a tamper-proof hardware device, it might be reasonable to extend the Expired state to two years.

3.3.8 Key Aliases and the Key Manifest

The key vault, as shown in Figure 3.2, stores and protects the actual key. The only other entity that should ever have direct access to the key is the cryptographic engine. All other entities in the infrastructure reference the key through the key alias.

The key alias is an identifier that is unique to each key throughout the entire cryptosystem. Because most key vaults support multiple keys, vaults typically assign an ID to each key. This ID is unique only within that particular vault. If an organization has multiple vaults, it is possible that two different keys have the same ID in different vaults. Along with providing a way to reference keys securely, the key alias resolves this ambiguity.

Responsibility for tracking the mapping between key IDs and key aliases falls to the key manifest. The key manifest maintains a list of all the key IDs available in a vault and their associated key aliases. In addition, the Key Manifest tracks the family to which a key is assigned, the key's activation date, and whether the key has been retired or terminated.

Given the amount of information the key manifest must maintain, it is apparent that creating a new key also entails a fair amount of configuration before the new key can be used. Typically, key creation begins when the key manager instructs the vault to create a new key. The vault creates the key and returns the key's ID to the manager. The manager then creates a new, unique key alias and places it in the appropriate key manifest along with the key ID, the key's engine, the activation date, and the family assignment.

Because only engines can retrieve the key from the vault, and not all engines have access to all key vaults, the manifest tracks which engine is assigned to the key. Engines always work with a single key vault. When the cryptographic provider accesses the manifest to determine the key ID, it also notes the engine so that it can correctly pass on the request.

3.4 Summary

This chapter began with a discussion of the high-level architecture of a typical Web application that might need to store encrypted information in a database. The architecture theme continued with an outline of the infrastructure that this book describes. Figure 3.2 shows this architecture in a data flow diagram.

The bulk of the chapter addressed the properties of keys. The security of the cryptosystem depends on the security and careful handling of these keys, so a proportionate amount of time was spent on them. Coverage included emphasis that while any given key should be used for a single purpose, families of keys share that purpose. Within a family, keys shift through a variety of states as they move through their life cycle. Key scope describes how keys are applied across a row and determines how the cryptographic receipts must be handled.

Key fatigue looked at the limits of a key's use and considered how much data a key should encrypt and for how long before becoming Expired. The transformation of Expired keys into Retired keys was covered in sections on migration and replacement. Finally, the purpose behind key aliases and the manifest was examined.

Much of the terminology used later in the book was introduced in this chapter. The key life cycle and concepts such as the key family, key scope, migration, and replacement are fundamental to understanding how a database cryptosystem functions. The next chapter covers engines and the algorithms that power them.

Chapter 4

Cryptographic Engines and Algorithms

The cryptographic engine lies at the core of the infrastructure. It implements algorithms, such as AES, upon which the rest of the system depends. Any request to encrypt, decrypt, or hash data ultimately passes through the engine.

Building and maintaining a secure and efficient cryptographic engine is not the easiest task. The best practice, in nearly all cases, is to use an engine that's already available and tested.

Engines come in two flavors: local and dedicated. A local engine is one in which the cryptography occurs on the same CPU as the rest of the application's processing. Typically for a local engine, the algorithms are included as part of the application or as a library to which the application is linked. Examples of local engines include RSA's Crypto-J, Cryptix, the default providers in Sun's Java Cryptography Extension, and Mcrypt for PHP.

Dedicated engines contain a separate CPU dedicated to cryptography. A typical example of a dedicated engine is a Hardware Security Module[1] (HSM) in which the cryptographic CPU is mounted within a standalone, typically tamper-resistant, enclosure. An HSM might communicate with the application through a PCI connection, SCSI, or over the network using SSL.

---

1. The goal of an HSM is to provide a secure environment for keys. Thus, most HSMs combine the functionality of a key vault and engine. This chapter covers the engine aspects of an HSM; the key vault capabilities are covered in Chapter 5, "Keys: Vaults, Manifests, and Managers."

Another type of dedicated engine is an accelerator that simply handles the cryptographic processing and offers no key vault capabilities. Accelerators are most appropriate when a local engine is desired but the performance is too slow. An HSM can provide many of the benefits of an accelerator along with much better key security.

While most dedicated engines are devices specifically constructed for cryptography, some dedicated engines might be general-purpose computers running standard operating systems but stripped of all but the most essential services. Among those services would be a cryptographic server and perhaps a key storage module. At the heart of the server would most likely be a library such as the ones used for a local engine. For that reason, these types of dedicated engines could be thought of more as hybrid engines.

Local and dedicated engines (and hybrids) have their place in a cryptographic infrastructure, and often both are used. A dedicated engine generally provides better security for the keys and off-loads the cryptographic processing so that the main application CPU isn't burdened with the intensive demands of cryptography. On the downside, dedicated engines are expensive, and the cost quickly adds up when building a highly available system. Key management can also be troublesome with dedicated engines because a security officer frequently needs to be physically present at the device for many key management tasks.

A local engine is often easier to implement because there is no need to configure a separate hardware interface. Because there is no special hardware to purchase, the local engine can be significantly less expensive—even free. Of course, the keys used by the engine are also significantly less secure. The application's performance will also suffer to some extent by the inclusion of cryptographic processing on the application's CPU.

This chapter describes these different types of engines, how they are used, and which algorithms database cryptography requires them to support.

4.1 Local Engines

A local engine is essentially just another library that an application loads and uses. The benefit of a local engine is perceived simplicity and cost savings. However, as we'll discuss, these advantages apply only if a lower level of security is acceptable. Because of this, local engines are primarily recommended for obfuscation.

Compared to a dedicated engine, a local engine offers a reduction in complexity in some areas. A dedicated engine requires the installation and configuration of a separate layer of hardware. Local engines avoid this. Simply placing a library on the classpath might be all the installation needed for a Java engine.

However, dedicated engines typically store the key away from the data and application and then wrap the key in layers of encryption and tamper-resistent hardware. Approximating this level of security using a local engine is difficult, and any attempt to do so quickly reintroduces complexity.

In a straight comparison of costs, local engines are generally cheaper than dedicated hardware. However, once the cost savings are balanced against security and performance issues, the savings are less impressive.

As mentioned before, cryptography consumes a fair amount of CPU cycles; with a local engine, application performance could certainly suffer due to encryption. Dedicated engines off-load the encryption to a different CPU. To reduce the relative CPU load of a local engine, a more powerful, and costly, machine is required. Even then, some dedicated engines also use special processors designed for a particular algorithm. Coaxing similar performance out of general-purpose hardware could quickly become quite expensive.

The security concerns mentioned here also play into the cost equation. Attempting to attain the same degree of key security with a local engine will reduce if not eliminate any cost savings. Extra hardware to store the key and additional software to protect the key all add upfront and ongoing maintenance costs.

A final security consideration with local engines is due to the fact that the same physical memory is shared between the local engine and the application. Should an attacker compromise the application, memory-scanning techniques or judicious use of a good debugger could pick the key out of memory. If the attacker can crash the local engine, or in some cases the application, there's a good chance that a crash log such as a core dump contains the key. Swap files also expose the key to risk because it is quite likely that eventually the key will be written to a swap file, and once it is written, it is likely to stay there until that disk location is overwritten.

Memory attacks may seem theoretical, much like finding a needle in a haystack, but cryptographic keys, unlike most other data in computer memory, are random. Looking through memory structures for random data is very likely to reveal key material. Well-made libraries for use as local engines go to great efforts to protect keys even in memory. Key-encrypting keys are used to encrypt the key while it is in memory, and then the encrypted key is split into several parts and spread throughout the memory space. Decoy structures might be created that look like valid key material. Memory holding the key is quickly zeroed as soon as the cryptographic operation is finished.

These techniques reduce the risk of memory attacks, but at some point the key must exist in memory unencrypted in order for the algorithm to operate on the data. At that exact moment, the key is exposed. Should the operating system switch states at that moment (and there's nothing a developer can do to prevent this in most operating systems), the key will be written in plaintext to the disk.

To be fair, dedicated engines are also vulnerable to memory attacks. However, a well-made dedicated engine runs only the minimum number of services. Because Web servers, application servers, and databases have no place on a dedicated cryptographic engine, these common attack points aren't a threat. This severely constrained attack surface makes it much more difficult to gain the access needed to launch a memory attack.

Local engines can offer cost and complexity savings, but the cost is less security. This doesn't, however, rule out local engines. Their use, though, should be limited to obfuscation roles, and then only in environments where other controls make up for the lowered security. Even then, consider how backups are managed. Does the same set of tapes contain the encrypted data and the keys? If so, the data is at risk. Any extra security provided by the data center does nothing to protect against threats to backups.

4.2 Dedicated Engines

Dedicated engines, particularly those that offer strong key protection, should always be used unless the goal is simple obfuscation. A dedicated engine is typically a specially constructed device that is connected via a cable to the computer needing cryptographic services. Possible connection technologies include PCI or SCSI for directly connected engines or Ethernet for network-attached cryptography.

When selecting a dedicated engine, consider performance, scalability, and availability. Most dedicated engines perform cryptographic operations considerably faster than local engines, but the interface to the hardware can add overhead. This overhead may not be noticable on directly connected engines. Network-based engines, though, might carry a performance penalty from the need to negotiate a secure TCP connection. If the connection remains open between requests, the overhead may be negligible, but it certainly should be tested.

Many modern application architectures scale by adding servers. In the case of directly connected engines, each new server requires a new engine. Not only does this increase purchase costs, but the management of keys in a server farm can be difficult and time-consuming because each engine needs an identical set of keys.

Directly connected engines in a highly available cluster of servers provide built-in cryptographic availability. Should one engine fail, processing could shift to the other servers where the engines were still operational. A network-attached engine, on the other hand, does not provide high availability unless multiple engines are purchased and configured into a high-availability cluster.

Denial-of-service attacks are another related concern with network-attached engines. Because the engine is available over TCP/IP, an attacker could flood the engine with traffic and block legitimate cryptograhic requests. If required information can't be decrypted, a customer may not be able to place an order or access account information. If the database stored encrypted medical records, a successful denial-of-service attack could prove fatal.

None of these are reasons not to use dedicated engines, but rather factors to keep in mind when selecting a dedicated engine. Also look for industry-standard API support. Adopting a standard such as PKCS 11 [14] will help ease the transition from one vendor's engine to another and in some cases between different engines from the same vendor.

4.2.1 FIPS 140

Typically these standalone HSMs are compliant with the U.S. Government's Federal Information Processing Standard (FIPS) 140-2 [18]. This standard covers the security requirements a cryptographic module must meet if it is to protect sensitive but unclassified information. Four levels of security are identified, with Level 1 being the weakest and 4 the strongest:

Security Level 1   Applicable to local and hybrid engines. So long as the equipment is production-grade, no special requirements apply in terms of hardware.

Security Level 2   Hardware must feature tamper-evident casings and pick-resistent locks. Role-based authentication must be supported.

Security Level 3   Hardware must provide intrusion prevention as well as tamper evidence around the keys and other critical security information. Identity-based authentication must be supported with role-based authorization.

Security Level 4   Hardware must provide intrusion prevention across the entire module and must resist attacks using fluctuations in voltage and temperature.

For our purposes, hardware meeting level 2 or 3 is sufficient. If FIPS is required, and a local engine is desired, software implementations are available. For instance, IBM has released a Level 1-compliant module for Java [5].

4.3 Cryptographic Algorithms

This section is very conservative. Only well-known, public algorithms that have been widely tested are recommended. Even then, the use of the algorithms is conservative. Performance and storage are often sacrificed for better security.

Should the temptation to use a different algorithm prove irresistable, proceed with great caution. In accordance with Kerckhoffs's Principle, never use a secret algorithm. If the algorithm is public, ensure that it has been thoroughly vetted by the cryptographic community. Finally, if it's a known and tested algorithm, peruse the latest research to see if any recent discoveries have revealed weaknesses in the algorithm. Cryptography doesn't stand still. In the summer of 2004, the venerable MD5 finally succumbed to mathematical advances: a method for producing two messages that hashed to the same value was discovered [22]. New systems should not use MD5.

4.3.1 Symmetric Algorithms

Symmetric algorithms are the workhorses of database cryptography. The purpose of most cryptography found in databases is to protect the confidentiality of the data; this is the bread and butter of symmetric algorithms. The symmetric algorithm of choice in this book is Advanced Encryption Standard (AES). This algorithm is a block cipher that the U.S. Government has approved for encryption of nonclassified data. The specification for AES is found in FIPS 197 [17].

This algorithm certainly meets our criteria. It is public and was extensively studied prior to its acceptance. Cryptographers have been closely studying it since its introduction, and no weakness has yet been found. It is also widely available in a variety of engines, both local and dedicated.

Analysis of the algorithm and its underlying security properties is beyond the scope of this book. However, because AES was selected through public cryptanalysis of many candidate ciphers, information about its security (and, to some extent, its design) is easily found on the Internet. In particular, [17] and [8] are excellent places to start.

Figure 4.1 presents a rather simplistic illustration of our treatment of AES. *Plaintext* represents a 128-bit block of data, and *Key* is a 128-bit key. Both of these are inputs into AES, and a 128-bit *Ciphertext* is produced.

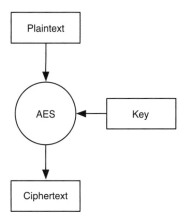

Figure 4.1: A simplistic diagram of AES

4.3.2 Modes of Operation

The AES algorithm works with blocks of 128 bits. For data that is not exactly 128 bits long, several *modes* have been specified [7] that allow AES to work with data of arbitrary lengths. The modes used in this book are *cipher block chaining* (CBC) and *counter* (CTR). Counter mode is preferred, but it is not as widely supported. Most engines support CBC mode, but, as discussed next, CBC requires padding and may not be as fast as optimized implementations of CTR.

Cipher Block Chaining Mode

In CBC mode, the plaintext is broken into multiple blocks, each of which is 128 bits long. The final block, if less than 128 bits, is padded to 128 bits. Encryption consists of first XORing each plaintext block with the previous ciphertext block and then encrypting that result with the key. The process is bootstrapped because there isn't a previous ciphertext for the first plaintext, by XORing the plaintext with an *initialization vector* (IV) that is also 128 bits long. Figure 4.2 illustrates CBC mode with a small diamond representing the XOR operation.

The IV must be unique and unpredictable, but it need not be secret. To understand why this is so, first note that protected data stored in many database is smaller than 128 bits. First names, last names, credit card numbers,[2] driver's

---

2. *Credit card numbers are often exactly 16 digits long (which is 128 bits with 1-byte characters), and under our padding scheme, plaintexts of exactly 128 bits are padded to 256 bits. However, most applications display the last four digits for confirmation of the number. In such a case, only the first 12 digits should be encrypted, which brings us to under 128 bits.*

license numbers, and social security numbers are all typically smaller than 128 bits. In CBC mode, each would be padded to be exactly 128 bits, so it would fill one block.

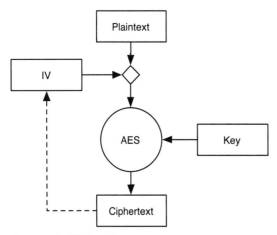

Figure 4.2: CBC mode

In addition, these values are typically predictable. Credit card numbers include information indicating card type, issuing bank, and a check digit. Social security numbers often include information about the issuing state. Names are perhaps the most predictable of all.

The following two chosen-plaintext attacks demonstrate how protected data could be compromised without breaking the encryption if the IV is either predictable or nonunique. Recall from section 2.5, "Cryptographic Attacks," that in a chosen-plaintext attack, the attacker can have the system encrypt any data he wants and can view the resulting ciphertext. These attacks don't necessarily lead to wholesale exposure of all data, but they certainly are useful for targeted attacks, which at the very least can violate privacy. We'll assume that the IV as well as the ciphertext is accessible to the attacker (both are typically stored in the cryptographic receipt).

Consider first, though, what happens in the extreme case when the IV is a constant value. When the attacker examines the database and finds the same ciphertext in several fields, he knows that those fields represent the same plaintext. For some databases, statistical methods can be used to determine the most likely values of those plaintexts. In such situations, the encrypted database leaks information even if it is copied to the attacker's machine.

Alternatively, the attacker can manipulate the cryptosystem to encrypt some plaintext P. Then he simply needs to search for the resulting ciphertext in the original encrypted data. Any ciphertext matches indicate fields that would decrypt to P. This is a fairly serious breach of a supposedly secure database.

So it is quite easy for an attacker to tease information from an encrypted database when strong algorithms are used in CBC mode with constant IVs. These same vulnerabilities are present when the algorithm is used without a mode or in electronic code book (ECB) mode, neither of which uses an IV. Often, a counter is suggested as the solution to the constant IV problem. As you'll see next, counters, which are predictable, have their own problems.

Say our attacker would like to confirm his speculation that an encrypted field in a database contains the value P when decrypted. Because this is a chosen-plaintext attack, we assume he has the ciphertext C and the IV I. The attacker, for the moment, assumes that P is the plaintext and computes the input block $P \oplus I$.

Given that the IVs are predictable, the attacker can predict a future IV, I', and then construct a value P' such that $P' \oplus I'$ is identical to the known input block $P \oplus I$:

$$P' = P \oplus I \oplus I'$$

The attacker then inserts P' into the encryption path so that P' is encrypted with I' to produce C'.

If C and C' are identical, the original plaintext P was indeed the encrypted value in the column. If they are different, the attacker knows that P was not the real plaintext, which can be just as compromising in some cases.

Imagine a database used by a physician's office, where a table stores the results of tests. This attack would allow an attacker to test various results until he found the actual result. It might be time-consuming, but it is not particularly difficult, and if the target is valuable enough, the attack is well within the reach of some crypto-paparazzi.

To counter that attack, we want unpredictable IVs. If the attacker cannot predict a future IV, this attack fails. Unpredictability, though necessary, is insufficient.

If IVs are duplicated, we have another problem because identical ciphertexts generated with the same IV imply identical plaintexts. Say the cryptosystem randomly selects an IV from a pool of previously generated random IVs.[3] If our attacker wants to find fields in the table that contain P, he manipulates the cryptosystem to repeatedly encrypt P.

Eventually the attacker will have a complete set of ciphertexts C_i, where each is P encrypted with one of the IVs from the pool. The attacker then looks for any

---

3. *The pool in this example is small, but the attack applies to any scheme where IVs repeat with a relatively short frequency.*

situation where one of his ciphertext-IV pairs is identical to an actual ciphertext-IV pair found in the database. Any such match indicates a field where P is encrypted.

The attacker doesn't have to cycle through the complete set of IVs. Even a partial set of pairs can reveal information about the contents of the database.

To avoid this attack we must add uniqueness to our conditions. We want IVs that are both unpredicatable and unique. Nonrepeating random numbers would work. The nonrepeating criteria is difficult to achieve efficiently. Generating a random number and then searching the table to see if that number has already been used isn't terribly fast. However, consider that for a 128-bit random number, the chances of getting a duplicate are fairly small at first. Only after about 2^{64} random numbers have been generated can we expect to have a duplicate.

Because a random number is generated for each new encryption, the system would have to perform 2^{64} encryptions with the *same* key before we would expect the first duplicate. As discussed in section 3.3.5, "Key Fatigue," this situation is not too likely because the key should be expired well before this limit is reached.[4]

The most significant drawback of using random numbers is that all 128 bits of the random number must be stored. Each encrypted column must be matched with another column containing these 16 bytes for each row. This can be a significant amount of extra data that the database must now store.

Another solution is to give each key its own counter. Each time the key is used for an encryption, the counter is incremented. The IV itself is generated by encrypting the counter value with AES using the counter's key. Because encryption produces what appears to be random data, we meet the unpredictable criteria. The uniqueness criteria is also met because we keep incrementing the counter.[5] The storage benefit is that we have to store only the counter value and not the full 128-bit IV. The downside, though, is that now we must make two encryption calls for each operation (one for the IV and one for the data).

Each project needs to look at the trade-offs involved with both strategies and decide which is most appropriate. Neither solution is always the right choice.

Finally, we consider padding. The need for padding is the primary drawback of CBC mode because it increases the amount of stored data. For data that is exactly a multiple of 16 characters long (assuming 1-byte characters), an additional 16 bytes of padding is needed. Data where the last block is less than 16 characters must be padded to a full 16 characters. The database could eventually end up with more

---

4. *This doesn't mean that a duplicate can't occur before 2^{64} generations, just that it's unlikely. If the threat model shows that the risk of "unlikely" isn't acceptable, do not use random numbers.*

5. *If two IVs were identical, they would have to decrypt to the same counter value, and that isn't possible because we increment the counter for each IV.*

encrypted padding than actual data. The padding scheme used here is specified in [13]. Many engines support this padding, so it is convenient.

Counter Mode

Because CTR mode allows AES to be used as a stream cipher, it does not require any padding. It encrypts exactly the number of bytes needed by XORing the plaintext with a *key stream* generated by encrypting the value of a unique *counter*. Figure 4.3 illustrates CTR mode's operation.

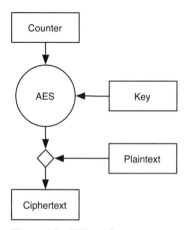

Figure 4.3: CTR mode

The encryption function produces 128 bits of key stream each time it encrypts a counter value (the counters are 128 bits long). When those 128 bits have been used, another counter value is encrypted to generate the next 128 bits of key stream. Any key stream bits remaining after the final bit of plaintext has been encrypted are discarded.

So unlike CBC mode, which requires an IV only for the first block, CTR requires a counter value for each block of key stream generated. Furthermore, each counter used for a given key must be unique. This uniqueness requirement applies to each block of key stream generated. If a particular counter value was used to encrypt a field, that value must not be used again with that key.

If the uniqueness property is not met, an attacker can recover information despite the encryption. Say the attacker notices that a particular counter value, T, was used repeatedly. If the attacker can identify the plaintext for any of those cases, or if he can launch a chosen-plaintext attack so that a plaintext of his design is encrypted when the counter is T, the attacker can recover all the plaintexts where T was used.

To demonstrate this, consider that a block of ciphertext C is known to the attacker and is computed as

$$C = E(T) \oplus P$$

where E is the encryption function and P is an unknown plaintext. If the attacker knows some plaintext P', by the assumptions of a chosen-plaintext attack, he can find the ciphertext C'. Given that

$$C' = E(T) \oplus P'$$

implies

$$E(T) = C' \oplus P'$$

the value of P can be derived as

$$P = C \oplus E(T) = C \oplus C' \oplus P'.$$

Once the attacker has the value of $C' \oplus P'$, any ciphertext generated with T as its counter value can be decrypted.

To ensure the uniqueness of the counter, we concatenate an invocation counter with a block counter. The invocation counter is incremented each time a key is invoked[6] to encrypt a field. The block counter is incremented for each block of key stream needed to encrypt the field. While the exact arrangement can be tuned for a given situation, we'll specify that the leftmost 64 bits of the counter are reserved for the invocation counter and the rightmost 64 bits are reserved for the block counter.

This scheme implies that no field can be longer than 2^{64} blocks. This size constraint can be altered by reserving a different number of bits for the block counter. In addition, a key in this scheme can be invoked only 2^{64} times. This constraint can be altered by reserving a different number of bits for the invocation counter.

In practice, these limitations rarely have any impact. Keys that are replaced annually will not often be invoked more than 2^{64} times. If a single invocation needs to encrypt more than 2^{71} bits, over a billion terabytes, storage space is more likely to be an issue than limitations of the block counter. Especially given that this is presumably just a single field of a multiple-field database.

To conserve space, the receipt will contain just the invocation counter. The block counter always starts with zero and is incremented by 1 for each block. To determine the number of counter values needed, compute the ceiling of the length

---

6. A key is invoked whenever it is used to encrypt a field. In a single invocation, the key could be used several times to generate multiple key stream blocks.

in bits of the plaintext divided by the block size of 128. If $\ell(P)$ is the length of the plaintext in bits, the number of counters needed is

$$\left\lceil \frac{\ell(P)}{128} \right\rceil$$

So for a plaintext of 80 bits, a single counter value would be needed. A plaintext of 270 bits would need three counter values.

Modes and Scopes

Now that we've seen how modes require initialization vectors or counters in order to protect data, we need to expand our concept of a receipt so that it can efficiently handle this extra data. A *compound receipt* combines several receipts. The compound receipt contains a single key alias and an IV or counter for each of its base receipts. So a compound receipt for a three-column scope encrypted with CBC mode would contain the key alias and three IVs.

The only component concerned much with compound receipts is the cryptographic consumer. We'll return to this subject, but in general, our discussion of a receipt is not impacted if the receipt happens to be compound.

4.4 Summary

This chapter explored the differences between local and dedicated engines. While the preference for dedicated engines, which generally provide much better protection for keys, is strong, it is clear that dedicated engines don't fit in every architecture or budget. Each organization must decide which approach best fits its specific needs.

The discussion of cryptographic algorithms focused on Advanced Encryption Standard (AES) in both cipher block chaining mode (CBC) and counter mode (CTR). In CBC mode, the necessity for uniqueness and unpredictability was shown, and techniques to achieve these criteria were given. A method for constructing a suitable unique counter for CTR mode was also described.

The preference is for counter mode, but unfortunately, counter mode is not as widely supported as CBC. Counter mode requires less storage space considering it encrypts only the data needed (no padding is necessary) and just needs to store a counter value. Its counterpart, CBC mode, requires padding so that even short fields contain 128 bits of encrypted data, and either needs to store 128 bits of an IV or must engage in an additional encryption call to compute the IV from a counter.

Next, we turn to the components that manage and store keys.

Chapter 5

Keys: Vaults, Manifests, and Managers

Given the importance of cryptographic keys, it should not be too surprising that a large portion of a cryptosystem is devoted to protecting and handling keys. The three components devoted to keys are the key vault, the key manifest, and the key manager.

The key vault stores the key in a highly protected environment. The vault allows only the engine and, in some cases, the key manager to access keys. The rest of the system works with key aliases. Mapping these aliases to actual keys is the responsibility of the key manifest. The manifest also tracks key attributes such as key state and key family. As its name implies, the key manager allows a key administrator to create, delete, and otherwise manipulate keys in both the manifest and the vault.

5.1 Key Vaults

If the data secured by cryptography is valuable, the keys securing the cryptography are at least as valuable. The problem of protecting these few small secrets is the job of the key vault.

Access to the key vault (at least the section of the vault that actually contains the keys) should be granted to only security officers and the cryptographic engine. Even in those cases, it is best to configure the vault so that keys are never removed from the vault unless they are first encrypted with a key-encrypting key.

As we discussed in Chapter 4 "Cryptographic Engines and Algorithms," many modern dedicated engines include key vaults. More accurately, because key protection is generally the primary purpose of dedicated hardware, the engine is included simply to further protect the key. The onboard engine means that the key never has to leave the hardware. In this book, we will assume that an HSM includes both the engine and the vault.

For local engines, the key vault generally needs to be implemented separately. The drawback with local engines, as mentioned earlier, is that the key is exposed outside the vault during the encryption. Generally this means that access to the engine implies access to the key vault. We'll discuss ways to limit this risk, but generally it is always a weakness with local engines and their key vaults.

Dedicated engines in the form of an HSM have a better opportunity to separate engine access from vault access. Unfortunately, not all of them provide this separation. Most HSMs typically provide an account or interface, protected by a password, that enables applications to access the cryptographic engine. Unfortunately, this same password frequently provides access to the key vault as well.

While most key vaults allow keys to be configured so that they are secure even in such cases, it is best if access to the engine does not automatically imply access to the vault.[1] Ideally, a separate account, or at least separate passwords, would be provided for the vault. This way an application could be set up so that it has access to only the engine. It could encrypt and decrypt data, but little else. Key management tools, on the other hand, would only have access to the vault. They could create, delete, and otherwise modify or copy keys, but they could not encrypt or decrypt data.

In either case, we can think of the vault as a module that contains the actual key, an ID specific to that vault, and attributes indicating such things as appropriate algorithms, allowed uses, and handling requirements. Services provided by the vault include transferring keys to the engine, loading new keys, extracting existing keys, deleting keys, and configuring key attributes. The vault does not manage key state. The key manifest handles that task as well as other attributes relating to a key's life cycle.

We only allow keys for a given engine to be stored in a single vault. That way an engine always accesses a single location for its keys. A vault may store keys for multiple engines, but keys are assigned to one engine only. In database terms, there is a many-to-one relation between engines and vaults but a one-to-one relation between engines and keys.

---

1. *Even if the vault protects existing keys from compromise, an attacker may still be able to delete keys, overload the vault with random keys, or, worse, load custom keys into the vault.*

5.1.1 Protecting Key Vaults

This section focuses on key vaults for local engines given that dedicated engines include their own vaults. Any dedicated hardware that meets FIPS 140-2 level 2 or higher provides sufficient key protection in most cases. The two types of key vaults considered here are key servers and key stores.

Key Servers

A key server is a key vault housed in its own hardware and attached to the network. When a local engine needs a key, it sends a query across the network to the key server for the appropriate key. The key server authenticates and authorizes the requestor and, assuming that the requestor passes those checks, delivers the key.

Needless to say, the protocol used must be secure. A good strategy would be to use Kerberos, which would provide both authentication and encryption of the key delivery. If Kerberos isn't available, SSL or TLS with mutual authentication could be used instead. Unless the design team has experience with designing secure protocols, stick with known and tested protocols.

The keys in the vault should be encrypted when in storage. A key used to encrypt another key is called a key-encrypting key. This raises a bit of a catch-22: what key will protect the key-encrypting key. Ideally, an HSM would be used for encrypting the keys in a key server. Even if only limited use of HSMs is possible, they should be used where they'll do the most good, and that would be to protect the key server.

If HSMs won't fit within a particular design, the key server needs its own local engine to protect the stored keys. This local engine will use a *master key* to encrypt the keys in the vault, and adequately protecting this master key is a problem. Ultimately, the solution relies on obfuscation or administrator trust at some point (refer to section 2.6, "Obfuscation").

The master key could be split into two parts, with one part placed in a file read when the server starts and the other supplied as a parameter during start-up. Each time the server starts, an administrator needs to enter the parameter. Variations are possible, but the goal is to place as much protection around the master key as the threat model requires. In some cases, mere obfuscation may be perfectly acceptable, and the master key could simply be stored in another database table.

In line with earlier recommendations, access to key management functionality should be kept separate from key transfer. Specifically, access to key transfer capability should not also grant access to key management. When a key server authenticates an engine, it should only allow the engine to request keys, not create or alter keys. Keys should be assigned to specific engines, and only that assigned engine should be permitted to download the key.

Similarly, when a key administrator logs in through the key management tool, although she may have full access to the key and the ability to create, delete, and manipulate keys, a cryptographic engine should not be available. The key adminsistrator does not need access to decrypt arbitrary data. If a testing facility is needed so that the administrator can verify that the key is working, the system can generate a random block of text and encrypt and then decrypt it.

Assuming that key administration is carried out across a network, that connection should also be secured via SSL or a similar protocol. If the administrator needs to copy the key from the server, ideally the copy would be encrypted with a key-encrypting key when saved to the destination machine. However, this presents a question as to how the administrator will know the key-encrypting key so that the copy can be decrypted later if needed.

Where possible, the destination system should provide a key-encrypting key automatically with the key server. For instance, if the administrator is copying the key to a key archive, the "backup key" function might automatically generate a key-encrypting key and use it to encrypt the copy. If automation isn't possible, public-key cryptography could be used. The destination system would have a key pair, and the administrator would enter the public key into the key server. The key server would encrypt the key with the public key. The destination could later decrypt the key using its private key.

Key Stores

If the vault must be on the same system as the engine, if at all possible, use an HSM to encrypt the keys. Of course, if an HSM is available, there's not much of a need to use a local engine. Assuming that an HSM is not available, encrypt the keys with a master key and separate the master key from the operational keys. This obfuscation of the keys will provide at least some protection.

Additional protection can be extended to the master key by spliting it into multiple parts[2] and then storing those parts separately. Splitting the key in this case means XORing the key with a randomly generated *obfuscation key*. The result (which we'll call the *key mask*) and the obfuscation key are stored. When the master key is needed, these two parts are XORed together to reproduce the real key.

---

2. *While this discussion covers splitting a key into two parts, the technique can easily be extended to include more than two parts.*

If K is the real key, and K_O is the obfuscation key, the key mask K_M is

$$K_M = K \oplus K_O$$

and we store K_M and K_O. Recovery of K is simply

$$K = K_O \oplus K_M$$

For best results, K_O should be generated with a cryptographically strong random-number generator. However, because this is simply an obfuscation technique (and a weak one at that), using a weaker random-number generator is acceptable. In general, an attacker will find it far easier to recover K_O and K_M than to break the random-number generator. That said, if a strong random-number generator is available, and one typically is when working with cryptographic libraries, by all means use it.

Ideally, the two parts would be stored on separate machines. One strategy is to place one part of the key in a file on the application server and place the other part in the database itself. When the key store needs to access operation keys, it reads in the two keys parts, recovers the master key, and applies it to decrypt the needed operational key.

As soon as the master key or key parts have been used, the key store should zero them in its memory. *Zeroing* is the technique of overwriting sensitive data in memory to prevent memory-scanning attacks. Typically, zero bytes, `0x00`, are written to the memory space, but in some cases random data might be used as well. Additionally, the key store should also zero the operational key as soon as it has passed it to the engine. In practice, though, this can introduce a considerable performance burden because each cryptographic operation must again marshall the necessary keys (the engine should not be caching keys).

To ease the burden, the key store can cache the split key parts (as separately as possible). All other keys should be zeroed as soon as they've been used. Additional gains can be made by also caching the encrypted operational keys in the store's memory. The primary drawback here is that it is more difficult to keep the key store apprised of changes to a key's state or the introduction of new keys.

Architecturally, the key store considered in this book consists of a module on the application server that handles the logic and a table in the database that actually stores the operational keys. The master key is split as just described, with one part residing on the application server and the other stored in its own table in the database.

The key store provides key access and management interfaces. The key access interface simply lets engines request keys. The management interface allows administrators to create, delete, and configure keys. We assume that the key store itself is located on the application server, so the key access interface does not need to be accessible via the network. The management interface, though, might be best used across the network—especially if there are several application servers and each needs to have the same set of keys. To provide for this case, and to provide an extra layer of security around the keys, we require a password to access the management interface.

5.1.2 Key Backups and Restores

Like any other valuable data, keys need to be safeguarded from accident and disaster. Typically this is done with backups, both local and off-site. Cryptographic keys, however, present a challenge with backups because unauthorized access to keys circumvents the entire cryptosystem and places all the data protected by that key at risk.

In addition, key backups need to be maintained and updated far more aggressively than other data. Indeed, the cryptographic protection provided by a key is what enables the less stringent protection of backups containing other sensitive information. Changes in key states should be reflected in backups as soon as possible. Terminated keys should be deleted from nearly all backups.[3]

Vaults included in HSMs typically have provisions (often proprietary) for backups, but backing up a custom key store is a more complicated endeavor. At its simplest, the backup is simply a text dump of the keys. Every time a key is created, it is added to the list. Ideally, the keys on the list are encrypted with the public key of an asymmetric key pair. The private key is stored in a physical vault—perhaps one vault on-site and a safe-deposit box off-site. The list of keys should be stored in separate vaults, both on-site and off.

For an added layer of protection, the private key could be protected by an m of n scheme, which allows n people to have fragments of the key in such a way that the key can be recovered if m people combine their fragments. While this is not a bad idea, consider that such schemes (and the additional overhead they require) imply very sensitive data that needs the strongest protection. In such cases, key stores and local engines should not be used. It is better to invest instead in well-tested and supported HSMs.

When selecting a format for the backup, reliability and convenience should be weighed. The most reliable storage is perhaps paper, but it is not too convenient.

---

3. *A tightly controlled repository for keys that includes terminated legacy keys is not a bad idea, so long as the risk it poses is recognized and appropriate safeguards are in place.*

Electronic media is more convenient when a restore is necessary but is subject to corruption. Consider storing both.

During a restore, the IDs in the restored vault must match the appropriate IDs in the key manifest. In some cases, this might mean that IDs in the manifest may need to change if the vault gave new and unchangeable IDs to the keys during the restore.

Every change to a key vault should be followed by a new backup. Failing that, every backup of encrypted data must be accompanied by a backup of the key vault (assuming a change in the keys). If the encrypted data is backed up without the key vault, in case of a disaster, data encrypted with keys created since the last vault backup will be unrecoverable even though the encrypted data itself was recovered.

5.2 Key Manifests

The key manifest is the component that tracks keys and engines for the cryptographic provider. The manifest supplies a layer of abstraction so that a provider can use multiple key vaults even if the IDs given to keys in different vaults are identical. If the engine-vault pair needs to be changed, only the manifest needs to be updated. The manifest also maintains a key's state. Specifically, the manifest maintains the following information:

- Alias ID
- Key alias
- Key family
- Key status
- Key activation date
- Engine
- Key ID

To uniquely identify a key throughout the cryptosystem, the manifest maintains an alias ID for each key. Whereas the key ID is used to uniquely identify a key within a particular key vault, the alias ID is unique across vaults, so even if two vaults have keys with the same key ID, the alias ID is still unique.

The key alias itself is just a name or label for an alias. It is a convenience for the system's human operators and doesn't serve any functional purpose.

We discussed key families in section 3.3.2, "Key Families." When an administrator assigns a key to a family, the key manifest stores that assignment. Key scope, though, is not represented in the manifest. Determining key scope and knowing how to handle the receipts is the consumer's responsibility.

Key state is a function of key status and activation date. Recall from section 3.3.3, "Key Life Cycle," that a key moves through five states during its life:

1. Pending

2. Live

3. Expired

4. Retired

5. Terminated

Each of these states is defined by key status and the activation date. Key status ranges through three values: Active, Retired, and Terminated. If the status is Retired or Terminated, the state matches the status. However, if the status is Active, the state depends on the activation date.

For keys with an Active status, if the activation date is in the future, the state is Pending. The key with the most recent activation date is the Live key. Expired keys are keys with activation dates older than the Live key's activation date.

In terms of a timeline, imagine the future extending off to the right, the past trailing off to the left, and key activation dates marked along the length. As the current date sweeps past an activation date, that key becomes Live. All the keys to the right of it are Pending, and all the keys to the left of it are Expired. Figure 5.1 illustrates this timeline.

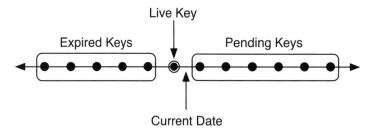

Figure 5.1: A timeline indicating the relationship between key states and activation date

The engine column indicates how the key can be used. It combines the notion of the physical engine and the encryption scheme. For instance, an engine entry might be Local-AES-CBC-128, meaning that the local engine is to be used with the AES algorithm in CBC mode with 128-bit keys.[4] The key vault does not need to

---

4. *It is not uncommon to also specify the type of padding used. Because our design has a default padding scheme, we don't explicitly specify it. If we later added other padding schemes, we would require the manifest's engine field to indicate which nondefault scheme was used.*

be specifically identified because an engine interacts with only a single key vault. By specifying the engine, we also implicitly specify the vault.

The key management system needs to provide functions to manipulate each of these attributes. The functions should ensure that the state model outlined in Figure 3.6 is preserved as well as the rules outlined in this chapter regarding status and activation dates.

We'll assume that the manifest is a table in the database. It's possible, of course, that the manifest is a file on the application server, but that presents problems with keeping the file synchronized across possibly several servers. Because it's a database table, all the application servers have easy access to the manifest, as do any back-office processes that also need access to the encrypted data.

Unfortunately, this convenience means that the manifest is more exposed to attack. While the keys themselves are locked up in the vault, the manifest is stored in the same database as the data. For offline attacks, this isn't much of a concern. Nothing that could significantly aid in attacking the cryptography is stored in the manifest.

Online attacks, though, are a different story. An online attack could alter the manifest. Generally, this isn't a significant concern. Tampering with the manifest could corrupt data and force a restore from backup, but this risk is faced by databases even without encryption. The threat of an online attacker corrupting data always exists with a database, and we are not designing our cryptographic system to thwart this threat.

However, two attacks introduced by the manifest could compromise the system's security. The first attack is to terminate or delete all the keys in the manifest. In such a case the cryptosystem would not have a valid key with which to encrypt the data. Rather than simply not encrypting the data (which is what the attacker hopes), we rely on a *default* key.

The default key is a special key that is used in the case of partial system failure. A corrupt manifest is one such case. Loss of connectivity to an HSM or key server would be another. The default key should be used in a local engine and should be stored split into two files (much like the master key of a key store). As soon as the default key is invoked, the system should alert the security team that something is amiss.

The second attack against the manifest is to set a compromised or Terminated key to Live. In the case of a Terminated[5] key, the error from the engine should prompt the system to try again, but this time with the default key.

---

5. Recall that Terminated means that the key has been deleted from the vault.

In the case where a compromised key is set to Live, the attacker has three types of keys to work with: Pending, Expired, and Retired. The best defense against this attack is to limit the number of keys in any of these states. In principle, the most vulnerable keys, based on how long they've been in existence, are the Retired keys, followed by the Expired, and finally the Pending. As soon as possible, Expired keys should be Retired, and Retired keys Terminated. Pending keys should not be created too far in advance—a few months at most.

5.3 Key Managers

When a key administrator needs to create, delete, or alter a key, she uses the key manager. The key manager interacts with both the key vault and the key manifest. Because many changes to a key require changes to both the vault and the manifest, the manager ensures that transactions are complete in both places.

The key manager is a very sensitive component. A compromise quickly translates to a compromise of the entire cryptosystem. Not only does access to the key manager need strong controls, but because the manager itself accesses many vaults and manifests, those access credentials must also have strong protection. Our design encrypts these credentials and has a dedicated engine, key manifest, and key vault (ideally the engine and vault reside in an HSM).

5.3.1 Key Zones

To keep the distribution of keys from becoming too complex, the key manager defines *key zones*. A key zone is a self-contained collection of keys and aliases: no alias may reference a key outside its zone, and no alias or key may belong to more than one zone. Any operation performed by the manager occurs in a single key zone. If a key is created, it is created in a particular zone.

In practice, this implies that manifests may belong to only a single zone, and all the manifests in a zone contain the same set of aliases. Vaults, however, may contain keys for different zones so long as each key in a vault is assigned to one and only one zone. Because engines and vaults are always linked in a one-to-one relationship, any zone that uses multiple vaults will have manifests that contain aliases for keys using different engines.

In Figure 5.2, vault 1 contains only keys for zone A, while vault 2 contains keys for both zones A and B. Manifests in zone A reference the two engines that work with vaults 1 and 2. Manifests in zone B contain only aliases that reference vault 2. Partitioning, in vaults that support it, can be used to dedicate sections of the vault's memory to specific zones. In such cases the partitions can be thought of as an extension of the key zones.

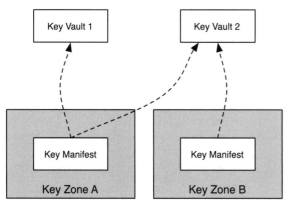

Figure 5.2: Key zones

Cryptographic providers work directly with manifests and often access manifests in multiple key zones. Access to a manifest in a key zone implies that the provider may also issue cryptographic requests to any engine/vault pair also in that key zone.

An application, then, through its provider, may use keys in several key zones. The key zones themselves are invisible to the application and are really relevant only to the key manager. Typical key zones include zones for e-commerce, finance, and human resources.

Not only do key zones help keep keys manageable, they also provide an additional layer of security. Key administrators can be assigned to specific zones. Should an administrator account be compromised, only the keys in the zones assigned to that administrator are at risk.

Figure 5.3 shows the core subcomponents of the key manager and illustrates the relationship between the key manager and key zones. Note that the cryptographic engine used by the manager is either included with the key vault in the case of an HSM or is integrated into the manager itself as a local engine. The manager exists in its own zone, which contains only the vault and manifest used by the manager itself.

When an administrator logs into the key manager, the manager notes the zones for which the administrator is authorized. The administrator selects one of those zones and can then invoke commands. To execute a command in, say, zone A, the manager identifies the manifests for zone A and then pulls the appropriate encrypted credentials and the encryption receipt from the credentials repository.

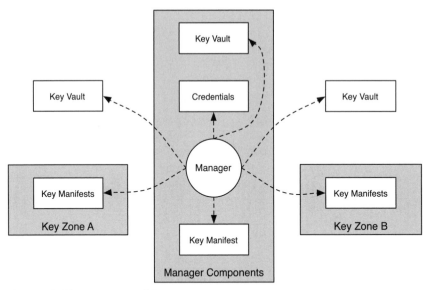

Figure 5.3: Key manager and key zones

As per our specified design, the manager then uses its own manifest and vault to decrypt the credentials. At this point, the manager can use the credentials to access the zone *A* manifests, which typically reside in one or more databases.

If the command requires vault access, the administrator must indicate which vaults need to be included. This can be done either by explicitly listing to the affected vaults or by programming the manager to know which keys should be placed in each vault. Once the vaults have been identified, accessing them follows the same process as accessing the manifests.

While the design supports multiple manifests in a zone, it is rarely necessary to do so. Simple zones are preferable. Simple typically means a single manifest and, if possible, a single set of engines and vaults that are not shared across zones. If simplicity is to be broken, attempt to keep a single manifest in each zone, but allow vaults to be shared.

5.3.2 Managing Keys

From the key administrator's perspective, the key manager provides essential functions:

- Create key
- List keys
- Set key family

- Set activation date
- Set key ID
- Retire key
- Terminate key
- Back up keys

These functions are the foundation for guiding keys through the key life cycle. They have the downside of requiring the administrator to remember how all the zones and vaults are configured. A mistake could render a key unavailable and trigger the default key. While these "primitive" operations need to be available, hopefully the manager will supply more-advanced functions.

These more-advanced or custom functions remove the need for remembering zone configuration and instead focus on the relevant data. Examples include "create e-commerce credit card key" and "create HR PII key." The adminstrator simply selects the data and the operation, and the manager takes care of the rest.

The principle mentioned in section 3.3.1, "Key Separation," that a key should be used for a "single purpose," is relevant here. Keys with a single purpose are more easily managed.

5.4 Summary

This chapter covered the three components that handle cryptographic keys in one sense or another. The key vault protects keys. Although an HSM is recommended, key servers and key stores are discussed as replacements. A key manifest tracks a key's state and provides a safe alias that the rest of the system can use rather than referencing the actual key. Finally, the key manager was discussed. Key administrators use the key manager to create, manipulate, and destroy keys.

In our tour so far, we've covered engines, algorithms, and keys. The next chapter turns to the two remaining components—the cryptographic provider and the consumer.

Chapter 6

Cryptographic Providers and Consumers

Consumers need cryptographic operations performed on the data they manage, and providers supply an easy-to-use interface for those operations. A consumer must know which family of keys to use for the protected data. It must know about striping and scopes, and it must know how to handle receipts. An application's business logic interacts directly with the consumer. Providers know about keys and algorithms, modes and engines, receipts and padding schemes. Essentially, consumers know how to handle data, both raw and encrypted, but they know nothing about how to encrypt or decrypt that data; providers know about encrypting and decrypting data, but they know nothing about how to handle the data itself.

The provider is generic and supplies common services to all consumers. It needs to be changed only when fairly fundamental alterations are made to the cryptosystem itself. Consumers, on the other hand, must be configured for each database table that stores encrypted data. Whenever a database schema changes such that new columns need encryption, the consumer or consumers must be updated.

Figure 6.1 illustrates the components discussed in this chapter. It is an exploded view of Figure 3.2 and focuses only on components directly relevant to the consumer and provider. Interactions with the provider have been labeled simply "Request" and "Result" to conserve space. The exact nature of the request and the response depends on whether the request is for encryption or decryption as well as the mode. For instance, if the consumer needs data encrypted, the provider's request to the encoder is for encoding.

If the consumer had data it needed decrypted, the provider would request decoding from the encoder.

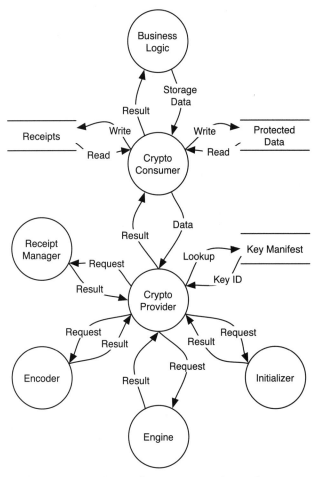

Figure 6.1: Detailed view of a consumer and provider

6.1 The Provider

The cryptographic provider is the hub of the system. It takes data from the consumer, finds the appropriate key in the manifest, and engages the engine to perform the operation. The engine returns the data to the provider, which, in the case of an encryption operation, prepares a receipt and then passes the data and receipt back to the consumer.

Typically the provider is a component that resides on the application server. It consists of several subcomponents:

- Service interface
- Manifest interface
- Initializer
- Engine interface
- Encoder
- Receipt manager

Of these, only the service interface is exposed for use by other components.

The service interface allows the consumer to request a cryptographic operation. This API generally just allows encryption and decryption requests. For an encryption request, the consumer passes the plaintext data and the key family to the provider. For a decryption request, the consumer passes the encrypted data and the encryption receipt to the provider.

The provider uses the manifest interface to interact with the manifest. Because the manifest typically resides on a database, the manifest interface must be able to make database connections. This interface allows the manifest to ask for the key alias, engine, key ID, and algorithm for a given family's currently Live key. It also can return the engine, key ID, and algorithm for a given key alias.

The initializer has dual functions: it supplies initializing values such as an IV or a counter, and it handles padding where necessary. The initializing function is needed only during encryption requests. The padding function may be needed for encryption requests (to add padding) and decryption requests (to strip the padding added during encryption). Recall from Chapter 4 "Cryptographic Engines and Algorithms," that CBC mode needs an initialization vector and padding while CTR mode needs only an initial invocation counter value.

The engine interface allows the provider to pass data to the engine and specify the key and any initialization parameters. In the case of an HSM, the engine interface is typically simply a bridge between the provider and a libary supplied by the HSM vendor. As mentioned in Chapter 4, this interface (and any library it calls) should only allow cryptographic requests and not facilitate any key management calls. Because this is often not the case, the provider's engine interface should at least only invoke cryptographic operations. A separate component should be developed for key management.

The encrypted data returned by the engine is in the form of an apparently random string of bits. These bits do not map neatly into values that can be stored in most database columns, which are generally text or numeric types. Unless the receiving columns are equipped to handle raw binary data, the encrypted data must be encoded for database storage. We'll use hex encoding, which takes binary data and turns it into text that can be stored in a database. The provider performs the encoding on any encrypted data passed to the consumer, and it de-encodes any encrypted data passed to it from the consumer prior to handing the data to the engine.

For an encryption request, the provider must assemble and return a receipt to the consumer. For a decryption request, the provider must open the receipt and extract the necessary decryption information. The receipt manager handles these functions for the provider. The receipt is a data structure that generally consists of just the key alias and the initialization vector or invocation counter value used for the request.

Attacks against the provider would generally take the form of subverting one of its subcomponents. Perhaps the most dramatic of these would be an attacker outright substituting components with her own replacements. For instance, an attacker could replace the engine interface so that instead of calling an HSM, the provider calls encryption code installed by the attacker. The data would still look encrypted and would even decrypt correctly,[1] but the data would still be compromised.

Other types of subversion include typical application attacks such as buffer oveflows, injection attacks, and race conditions. For instance, imagine an engine interface that invokes a shell script to interact with the engine, and the encryption command supports a -v flag to turn on verbose debug logging. In such a case (admittedly somewhat contrived), it might be possible for an attacker to append -v to the key ID in the manifest in such a way that when the encryption command were executed, the -v would be interpreted as the debug logging flag. The logging might dump the unencrypted text into a directory to which the attacker has access.

This example indicates the kind of out-of-the-box thinking that is necessary for securing applications. Protecting against these attacks requires strict adherence to secure coding practices. Thoroughly sanitizing all inputs (reading the key ID from the manifest *is* an input to the provider), strong release-to-production controls, and frequent verification of production code all contribute to securing an application.

---

1. *The attacker would have to be somewhat clever to ensure that the code handled decryption requests for data encrypted prior to the installation of the malicious code, but it could be done—especially by an insider. Besides, relying on the hope that attackers are not clever is not a good strategy.*

6.2 The Consumer

When business logic needs to store or process protected data, it engages the cryptographic consumer. The consumer, then, manages the cryptographic data and is closely integrated into the business logic. Because the consumer must be available wherever the business logic accesses the encrypted data, the consumer is typically located on the application server. In applications that provide separate components for business logic and database interactions, the consumer would likely be integrated into the database interaction code.

The data managed by the consumer includes not only the business data, but also the receipts necessary for decryption. The receipts can be stored in the same table as the encrypted data or in a separate *receipt table*. If a receipt table is used, each table containing encrypted business data (known as a base table) would have its own receipt table. This discussion assumes a receipt table, but the analysis remains essentially the same if the receipt table is integrated into the base table.

The receipt table contains columns for key aliases, initializers, and a foreign key back to the base table. The exact structure of a receipt table depends on how keys are scoped in its base table. Each scope in the base table has its own key alias column in the receipt table, while each encrypted column has a matching initializer column.[2] The foreign key ties each row in the receipt table to a single row in the base table.

Under this scheme, a table covered by narrowly scoped keys has at least $2n + 1$ columns when the base table has n encrypted columns. Each encrypted column has its own initializer column, and given the keys are narrowly scoped, each column has its own scope, so a separate key alias is stored for each column. This gives us the $2n$ columns. The additional column comes from the foreign key. More columns may be desired to hold creation or update dates or even receipt IDs.[3]

Internally, the consumer must be able to resolve the key family and scope to which a column belongs. Determining the family typically requires just the column name, but if striping is used, other data may need to be provided as well. Because all columns in a scope must be encrypted with the same key, the consumer must link all the columns that share a scope.

To decrypt a field, the consumer first determines which scope contains the field's column. It then searches the receipt table for the foreign key corresponding

---

2. *The algorithms and modes used in this book always require a single initializer, either an initialization vector or a counter. If other algorithms or modes are used, a different number of initializers may be necessary.*

3. *Receipt IDs are unique for each receipt generated in the cryptosystem and can be used to tie encrypted data to specific entries in a log.*

to the field's row and extracts the key alias for the field's scope and the initializer for the field's column. It passes the encrypted data, the alias, and the initializer to the provider in a decryption request. The provider works its magic and returns the decrypted data to the consumer.

When new data arrives for a protected column, the consumer first determines which family owns the column and which other columns, if any, belong to the same scope. If other columns are in scope, the consumer first decrypts the appropriate fields for those columns. Next, the data for each field in scope is passed to the provider along with the family. For each field, the provider returns the encrypted data and a receipt. If three columns were in scope, the consumer would make three requests to the provider and end up with three encrypted items and three receipts.

Finally, the consumer writes the encrypted data to the appropriate columns and updates the receipt table. Each receipt should have the same key alias,[4] and that alias should be written to the appropriate field for its scope. The initializer in each of the receipts should then be extracted and written to the appropriate fields.

In some cases, the base table may not support storing the encrypted data. This is especially true if the base tables are part of a third-party application and any alterations would break the application, void support, or compromise future upgrades. In such cases, it is possible to store the encrypted data in special columns in the receipt table. Programs that access the original column will need to be altered, but they will need to be altered regardless in order to deal with the encryption.

Attacking the consumer is equivalent to an attack against the application's business logic. Defending the consumer is no different than protecting the provider: Both require secure coding practices.

6.3 Summary

The division of labor between consumers and providers is designed so that the consumer is the only element in the cryptosystem that needs to know anything about the encrypted data. The provider and every other component function generically regardless of the structure of the data itself. Key families and cryptographic receipts form the common language that enables the consumer and the rest of the cryptosystem to communicate.

---

4. *If they don't, which can happen if a key state transition occurred after the first encryption but before the last, the entire process should begin again.*

This encapsulation enables the majority of the system to remain unchanged as new requirements emerge for encrypting information within the database. Only the consumer has to change, given that it must work directly with the data in its natural habitat.

This chapter concludes the design coverage of the cryptosystem. The following chapters provide guidance on how a team might best approach a project for building a database cryptosystem. If you're familiar with the methodology of secure application development, these chapters may not be surprising. However, secure application development is not widely practiced. Security, when building a cryptosystem, must be a primary concern of the development team.

PART III

THE CRYPTOGRAPHIC PROJECT

Chapter 7

Managing the Cryptographic Project

At their beginning, projects storing information in a database might not have any particular security requirements for protecting that stored information. People generally assume—incorrectly, as we've discussed—that the database is secure enough. Over the course of the next several chapters, we'll take a project from this state of primordial innocence, determine if the information in the database needs cryptographic protection,[1] and then examine how to implement that protection using the infrastructure we've already discussed.

These chapters focus on integrating secure implementation practices into the development process. Such integration is crucial to the security of any application. For software on which other applications depend for security, integration of security practices is paramount to success. Unfortunately, security is generally not well integrated into most project methodologies, and as a result, most applications end up riddled with vulnerabilities. While such a fate is bad enough for most applications, it is especially disastrous should the vulnerabilities appear in security infrastructure. Every application that depends on the infrastructure for protection is suddenly vulnerable.

Because a vulnerability in the cryptosystem is so damaging and because secure development methods are rarely understood or followed, this book would be incomplete without coverage of this critical subject. Hopefully, in the future, the necessity of

---

1. We assume, of course, that the information does need cryptographic protection, although that need may be unknown at the beginning of the project.

prioritizing security in each phase of an application project will be widely recognized and second nature. In such a future, these chapters would be unnecessary. Until then, though, these chapters provide guidance on securing the development process and implementation so that cryptographic projects are truly successful.

Such a security-enhanced project methodology can in fact lead to requiring cryptography. That is, if the project methodology emphasizes security in each component, it is likely that any information needing cryptographic protection in the database will be identified.

A security-enhanced project proceeds much like any other software project: Requirements are gathered, a design is made, coding is followed by testing, and finally the application is released and monitored. Unsurprisingly, an intense focus on security in each of these phases differentiates our approach from most.

Most project managers today know that security should be a priority. Often this translates to a last-minute round of security patching that leaves plenty of exploitable flaws. Slowly, more and more projects are taking those first steps of integrating security into the overall project plan, but it is still far from a common practice. The project methodology discussed here is slanted toward database cryptography, but it can be extended to other projects as well.

Because computer security and cryptography in particular are still somewhat esoteric subjects, the project manager needs to take the initiative in ensuring that security is considered in each stage of the development process. The project manager's best ally in this task is to instill in the development team a culture of security.

7.1 A Security Culture

Security, like quality, cannot be externally imposed on a system. It must permeate the design and seep into every line of code. This requires a culture that prioritizes security. Architects, analysts, programmers, testers, and management must all be committed to security and keep a critical eye on all they do. Security weaknesses are often introduced from unlikely sources, and unless constant vigilance is maintained by people who understand security, these weakness may be revealed only during a post-attack forensics examination.

A process, including the one outlined here, cannot change a development culture. That change must come from an understanding of the seriousness of security and a dedication to eradicating weaknesses. Case studies are very useful in showing a team how weaknesses are introduced, how they are found, and how they are exploited. This exposure, coupled with vulnerable source code for analysis and experimentation, can quickly lay the foundation for building a security culture.

Once the foundation is in place, a process can be helpful to cultivate the security culture. By providing a sequence of deliverables throughout the software life cycle, the process gives a team focused on security a tangible road map to address security concerns. No one wants his or her system to be the next team's case study for what not to do.

In the long term, developing a culture of security depends on looking at security as an opportunity to provide extra value to the customer. If security is viewed merely as a series of checklists and practices put in place to hamper development, the game is lost. To keep security in constant view of the team, it is best if the customer emphasizes security.

A customer who explicitly demands security gives the team clear motivation, and the project manager should make a point of ensuring that the customer gives as much consideration to security as he does functionality.

7.2 Engaging the Customer

As software professionals concerned with security, we want customers to give the security of their applications as much importance as the functionality. Attempting to convince a customer focused on the near-immediate delivery of functionality that time needs to be spent on the security of that functionality is often a thankless task. Including the customer in the team's security culture should be included in the project manager's agenda.

The legislation and regulations discussed in the first part of this book work in the project manager's favor. Because compliance is generally the customer's responsibility, these requirements help raise the level of security awareness. On the downside, though, these requirements are often seen as hindrances, and customers often focus on meeting the letter of the requirements rather than ensuring that the system is truly secure.

When working with customers at the beginning of the project, our goal is to understand how much security risk they are willing to accept from the new functionality. In practice, this question becomes how much effort the project should spend on reducing the risk posed by the application. This is not an easy question to answer, and unfortunately customers are typically the least equipped to answer it.

Ideally, an internal information security team acts as a surrogate for the customer by providing the necessary security expertise. In such cases, a mature information security team will have already worked out with the customer what is acceptable risk and what is not. Based on this, the information security team can provide a set of policies, procedures, and requirements covering security. At the very least, the team, especially if new to application security, should be able to act as a consultant to the customer and advise on the risks and possible mitigation strategies to reduce the risks to an acceptable level.

If an information security team isn't available to act in this capacity, the development team needs to determine what the customer considers an acceptable degree of risk. Our approach is to first evaluate what is at risk and then determine how much mitigation is appropriate. We direct the customer's attention to a set of common risks:

- Denial of access
- Unauthorized access
- Unauthorized modification

For each of these risks, we ask the customer how much damage, on a scale from 1 to 5 (with 5 indicating the most damage), would occur if an event exposed the risk. This analysis is applied to all the data the project touches. The rating is subjective, but it should consider the effects on reputation, competitiveness, regulatory compliance, efficiency, and, in some cases, safety. A project handling the personally identifiable information of customers or their credit card numbers should see ratings of 4 or 5, while a project processing part numbers will not generate much that is higher than a 3.

Once the customer has a clear understanding of how much is at risk, the next step is to determine how much that risk should be mitigated. Essentially, this question centers around how much security should be applied to the application. This too can be rated from 1 to 5, with 5 requiring the most security.

The amount of security specified should reflect how much the customer is worried about the given risk. Lower numbers indicate that the customer does not want to devote many resources to preventing the risk, while higher numbers show that the customer wants to make security a priority. As the number increases, so should the stringency of the requirements, the depth of the security analysis, and the coverage of the penetration testing.

For applications and data, it is frequently useful to rate the amount of security needed to protect against general attacks separately from what is needed for privileged attacks.[2] This allows the security classification to reflect other security

---

2. A privileged attack is an attack carried out by an attacker with heightened privileges, such as a system administrator.

measures that might be present (such as extensive screening when hiring system administrators and robust logging) as well as the size of the threat. If the ratings for privileged and general attacks differ, the assumptions that account for that difference should be explicitly documented.

The result of engaging the customer should be a customer that understands his security needs and has a desire to ensure that those needs are met. In addition, the customer should have some idea of what plans are in place to provide the appropriate security and how that security will be tested.

This effort sets the stage for further security discussions later in the project. There isn't a magic rating at which cryptography becomes necessary. Cryptography is more likely at higher ratings, but it could be deemed appropriate at lower ratings as well.

7.3 Project Scope

In some cases, cryptography is a known requirement from the very beginning. Perhaps the project is purely a cryptography project, or encrypting the data might be a regulatory requirement imposed on a larger project. In other cases, the need for cryptography is revealed only during the requirements hardening phase. Either way, the scope of the cryptography must be determined.

This book discusses a cryptographic infrastructure. Up to this point, it has assumed that once built, other applications merely integrate with the infrastructure. In this scenario, the key manager is built once, and several applications take advantage of the same set of providers and engines. Perhaps individual applications will need to introduce new engines, but generally the infrastructure is static and all the components are heavily reused.

However, this need not be the case. The cryptography could be implemented entirely from scratch for each application. The infrastructure presented in this book would then be a blueprint that would be implemented repeatedly as necessary. In such a case, code might be reused through "copy-and-waste" rather than object reuse.

Given that no components are shared, lots of duplicated functionality exists, but should the security of one component fail, it likely won't lead to an immediate compromise of the entire system. Of course, the duplicated functionality means that more modules could fail.

Most implementations fall somewhere in between. A strong argument, based on security, consistency, and manageability, can be made for a single, centralized key manager or at least as few as possible, but the degree to which the other components are duplicated depends on the local environment.

The project's scope should be made clear as near to the beginning as possible. Is the cryptosystem narrowly targeted and streamlined, providing services to just a single suite of applications, or is the system to be an actual infrastructure that will be used for applications both current and future? The more infrastructure-like, the more effort will need to be applied to securing the system because it will likely have more entry points, and those entry points will be more exposed.

7.4 Project Roles

The roster of our project is typical, but we'll define who's who so as to avoid confusion. The project manager oversees the entire project and coordinates schedules to ensure that all the deliverables arrive on time and within budget.

The business analyst acts as a bridge between the development team and the business users. If not an actual user, the business analyst should at least be intimate with the user's needs. Because the business analyst is responsible for the requirements document, the more familiar he or she is with the user's job, the better the requirements will be.

The systems analyst reads the requirements document and then designs software that will meet those requirements and fit within the local environment. The design is typically captured in some type of written software specification. These specifications are often very informal, and many of today's agile methodologies deemphasize them (to the point of doing away with them entirely in some cases). These challenges are looked at in greater detail in Chapter 9, "Design Hardening."

Because security is as much an indicator of quality as functionality, we'll refer to the traditional quality assurance team as functional testers. Their responsibility is to test that the system delivers what the requirements state. In many cases, security can be tested under this perspective as well. If 128-bit AES encryption is required, the functional testing team can devise tests to validate that the system performs as expected. Security testing, though, also includes penetration testing, discussed next.

While not strictly part of the development cycle, operations monitoring is an important, if often overlooked, component of the system's life cycle. For our purposes, the monitoring team watches the application for security events and alerts the incident response team when necessary.

The final two roles we'll discuss are the application security analyst and the application penetration tester. While the other roles discussed here are common in most projects, these two are typically missing. The application security analyst examines the system for vulnerabilities from a risk perspective and is often the point person in engaging the customer. The analysis starts with the requirements and continues through the design and implementation.

The application security analyst is a specialist in application security and should be experienced in application development. The analyst needs to know how to "read between the requirements" in a requirements document to identify relevant security concerns. Similarly, the analyst needs to be familiar with typical application design documents, including use cases and abstraction techniques such as the Unified Modeling Language's class and interaction diagrams. The security analyst need not be a cryptographer in the sense of a researcher who designs new algorithms, but the analyst should understand cryptography and be experienced in cryptographic implementations.

All this knowledge allows the security analyst to analyze an application for potential vulnerabilities, work with the customer to determine where the risk is unacceptable, and then work with the development team to securely mitigate the risk.

The application penetration tester attempts to find actual vulnerabilities in an application. Often using information discovered by the security analyst, and a variety of tools, the penetration tester attacks the software, looking for weaknesses. This typically occurs during the testing phase and is as critical for security as normal quality assurance testing is for functionality.

The application security analyst and the application penetration tester may be the same person. This is common when application security teams are still young. More mature teams separate the analyst from the tester for several reasons. First, penetration testing can be time-intensive. New automated testing tools are great for finding the low-hanging fruit, but the more subtle vulnerabilities require a clever and persistent mind to ferret out.

Secondly, the separation mirrors the separation between developer and functional tester. A security analyst who has worked on the requirements, wrote the threat analysis, and contributed to code hardening is too closely involved with the application to objectively test it. A set of fresh eyes is needed to discover weaknesses in unexpected areas.

Finally, the skills needed by each, while similar and somewhat overlapping, are ultimately different. This difference in skills arises from the difference in objectives. The analyst is focused on identifying and reducing risk and does a significant amount of work before any code is written. The penetration tester is focused on finding vulnerabilities in the actual software and does most of that work after the software is written.

7.5 Summary

The next several chapters provide guidance on securely navigating a cryptographic project. The chapter sequence follows a typical project flow. Chapter 8, "Requirements Hardening," covers requirements and how to insert security requirements into a requirements document. Chapter 9 looks at what needs to be done during the design phase to ensure that the design addresses the security requirements and that the design itself doesn't contain any security flaws. Chapter 10, "Secure Development," discusses best practices for writing secure code. Chapter 11, "Testing," looks at the role of the application penetration tester and investigates ways to breach applications. The final chapter of this part, Chapter 12, "Deployment, Defense, and Decommissioning," looks at what it takes to defend an application while it is in operation.

Chapter 8

Requirements Hardening

One of the first steps in most projects is creating a requirements document that specifies what the project needs to accomplish. It is typically written by the business analyst and consists of a numbered list of statements such as "The system will take the customer's credit card number as an input on the Web page." Different teams operate with different levels of detail. In some cases the requirements are very high-level and simply sketch what is desired. In others, the requirements are thorough and detailed and describe every aspect of the system that the analyst considers relevant.[1]

Requirements hardening is the process of ensuring that the requirements document includes the necessary security requirements. The necessary security requirements are those that reduce the system's security risk to an acceptable level. For example, during this phase, several items must be identified: the information that needs cryptographic protection, the locations where the business needs that information, and who or what needs access.

Security requirements are statements that indicate the types of security the system must posses. At a high level, these requirements might simply state the class of protection necessary: This data must be encrypted, access controls must protect that asset, this communication must be tamper-proof. If the application designer happens to also be a security expert, such a high-level description may be all that is needed. However, because most application designers are not security experts, a high-level description, such as is found in most security policies, is not enough. Detailed security requirements indicate

---

1. *An unfortunate reality of requirements-gathering is that they are* never *complete. Necessary details are always left out. Hopefully these missing details are caught during the design phase, but often they are caught only during programming or even testing. Recognizing this fact is part of what drove the development of the modern agile methods of development.*

specifically what type of protection is necessary: What type of encryption, coarse or finely-grained access controls, can the tamper-proofing rely on in an established trust relationship?

Security analysts generally consider two types of security requirements: functional and defensive. Functional security requirements are like typical requirements and state in a positive manner what security must be in place. Clear testing criteria are typically characteristics of functional security requirements. For instance, "Use 128-bit AES in CBC mode" would be a functional security requirement. It states what must be done, and it is clear how to test the requirement.

In contrast, defensive requirements state what the system must not do, or, more accurately, what the system must resist. These requirements are generally stated in the negative: "Resist SQL injection attacks." In many cases these types of requirements can be rephrased as functional requirements such as "Filter all input that is to be used in a SQL statement," but such rephrasing can obscure the underlying requirement (resist the attack) and can potentially leave out a better approach to mitigating the attack. Testing defensive requirements is more difficult because the tester is looking to show that something cannot happen. Defensive requirements typically require a trained penetration tester for validation.

The security requirements applied to a given project depend on the specifics of that project's business requirements. If the business requirements don't call for storing sensitive data, database encryption is not likely to be a requirement for the project. In the same way, the design itself influences the security requirements. The requirements may not call for a particular item to be stored in the database, but the system's designers might realize an efficiency somewhere else if the item is stored. Should that piece of information need encryption, suddenly a new requirement is introduced during the design.

This sort of requirement-design feedback can be a source of frustration on projects where the requirements are supposedly fixed before design begins. Technically, the requirement isn't *new* because a policy that requires encryption of certain information should already exist. Prior to the design, though, that policy wasn't relevant to the project. Now that the project is handling sensitive information, the policy is relevant, so it appears that a new requirement has been introduced.

There's no real way to avoid this situation completely. The best that can be done is to ensure that the application security policies are available to the design team and that everyone is aware that the design itself can bring to bear new security policies and through those policies introduce new requirements.

8.1 Security Requirements, Policies, and Standards

Security policies specify the organization's security goals. As mentioned earlier, they are written at a high level and are typically too vague to be of much use to an application designer. A typical policy might state "All stored, classified data must be encrypted." At first glance, this policy looks like a requirement, but it lacks detail: what sort of encryption, how long the key should be, or how the key should be protected.

The answers to these questions are typically found in a *standard*. A standard describes *how* the goals in the policy should be met. Where a policy is vague and high-level, a standard is specific and detailed. The standard relevant to the policy "All stored, classified data must be encrypted" might say "Use 128-bit AES in CBC mode and store the key in an HSM."

The statements in a standard are far closer to detailed requirements than what exists in a policy. In a sense, standards are prepackaged bundles of requirements. When you specify that a standard applies to a project, the project automatically inherits all the requirements dictated by the standard. If a relevant standard exists, the project's requirements should state that adhering to the standard is a requirement.

In some cases, the standard may not fully apply to the project. Perhaps the standard requires narrowly scoped keys, but the business has decided that the overhead for narrowly scoped keys is too great for the project, and security has agreed that a wider scope is sufficient. In other cases, the standard may not be seen as providing enough protection; perhaps the business desires 256-bit encryption instead of the 128-bit required by the standard. In either of these cases, the security requirements should reflect the modifications to the standard.

Standards are often more than just documented requirements. The environment might contain a set of accepted components or infrastructure already in place that meets the standard. For instance, the cryptographic infrastructure we've discussed can supply the necessary components for new projects to meet the cryptographic standard. The project's requirements might simply state that the system must integrate with the existing infrastructure to meet the cryptographic policy.

If a policy or other security goal applies to a project but a relevant standard doesn't exist, the requirements must themselves specify the necessary security practices. This situation often occurs when the project introduces new technology. The security analyst must research the technology and come up with a set of requirements to bring the technology into line with security policy. If the new technology is likely to be used in future projects, the analyst may decide to create a new standard.

In the end, the security requirements must clearly communicate the specific types of security controls the designer needs to implement. The requirements should not state how those controls should be implemented,[2] just that they should exist and function in a particular way.

8.2 Common Requirements

A handful of high-level requirements tend to apply to nearly every project. These five requirements reflect fairly straightforward security policies and, once documented, should become very familiar to most everyone involved in project development. While other requirements also apply, most notably integrity and availability requirements, the ubiquity and importance of these five call for a brief discussion of each. The purpose is to simply present a sketch of what these requirements entail. In practice, the detailed requirements necessary for development are far more expansive than what is presented here.

8.2.1 Access Controls

Access control requirements cover how users are authenticated and authorized for access to systems and data. Authentication is the process of a user's proving his identity. It occurs every time the user logs into a system. Typically, the user presents credentials such as a password or a retina for scanning as proof of identity. After he is logged in, every time the user attempts to access a resource, the system checks to see if he is authorized for that access. If the authorization check finds a privilege or permission that explicitly allows the access, the user is allowed to continue. If an explicit permission is not found, the access should be denied.

The requirements should not only cover how the system must carry out these tasks but also should detail how accounts are to be administered and reviewed for accuracy. The administration section of the standard should seek to enforce the principle of least privilege and separation of duties.

A single-sign-on system is an example of an access control mechanism in which the user must authenticate only once. Requirements involving a single-sign-on system might specify that each application must be changed to integrate into the single-sign-on system, or the single-sign-on system might need to be integrated into each new application.

---

2. *Organizations that have standardized on particular technologies or infrastructures may very well include implementation details in the requirements.*

In the database cryptosystem presented in this book, access controls are necessary in several places. The key vault is perhaps the most obvious component in need of strong access controls, but the key manager must also exhibit strong controls considering that it interacts directly with the key vault and handles sensitive key functions. Finally, any application proving access to the decrypted data must have a strong access control system lest an attacker simply use it to access the data.

In this last case, it is interesting to note that encrypting information in the database at the application level provides a way of specifying fine-grained access controls for the encrypted data. Only individuals authorized by the application can view the decrypted information. Other users, including database and system administrators, cannot by default read the information.

8.2.2 Data Sanitization

Systems are most frequently attacked through entry points such as input fields. Data sanitization standards describe what sorts of filtering and verification must be in place to protect those entry points. While probing a system, the attacker carefully examines the system's output to see what effects different types of input cause. To limit the usefulness of this information, data sanitization standards also describe the types of filtering and validation that must be applied to output.

Data sanitization requirements generally specify that inputs must be checked for length, data type, and known, acceptable values. The requirements should not say "Do not accept the characters < or >" but instead should require something like "Accept only letters and numbers."

The types of output filtering can range from prohibiting verbose error messages to checking that what is going out looks correct. If the output is supposed to be a simple confirmation message of a few dozen bytes, but the system detects a few hundred bytes streaming out, output filtering might block the output and instead display a generic error.

In terms of application security, data sanitization is perhaps the one thing that will drastically improve an application's resistance to attack. Most known attacks will be stopped by robust data sanitization. Input sanitization goes a long way toward producing a more secure application environment.

Input sanitization is appropriate in several places in our cryptosystem. Referring to Figure 3.2, you can see where data flows into processes. Although each of these inflows is a candidate for data sanitization, the highest priority are the external entry points. The "data input" and "key admin" interactions should be given the most scrutiny. Following these, in priority, are the inflows from data stores. Successful integrity attacks against these data stores could insert malicious data that would eventually be processed by the cryptosystem. Finally, in accordance with defense in depth, flows between components should be sanitized.

Output sanitization is most appropriate where information is returned to a user. As mentioned, this occurs in two locations. Output read by the key administrator and the end users should be scrubbed for appropriateness.

8.2.3 Logging and Monitoring

Extensive and appropriate logging and monitoring are necessary for a good defense strategy. Defense is covered in more detail in Chapter 12 "Deployment, Defense, and Decommissioning." If requirements for logging and monitoring security events are not specified and followed, defending the system from attacks is very difficult.

Logging requirements should define what types of events should be logged and how they should be logged. Security events include all authentication attempts, all authorization requests, and security-related exceptions. A security-related exception should occur any time a program finds itself in a suspicious state. For instance, a request to decrypt data using a terminated key is suspicious.

Most logs are either files resident on the local machine, files sent across the network using syslog, or both. The requirements should define what mechanisms must be used and what information should be gathered. Included among the gathered information should be the nature of the event, the application response, the date and time, and the IP address of the event's source.

Ideally, security events are collected at a centralized location where possible patterns can be examined across applications and, if necessary, alerts issued. In this area, the logging and monitoring standards need to be tied into the incident response plan. The standard should require documentation of the significance of different security events so that the operations center will have a better idea for evaluating events. Also if the incident response plan requires certain information to be available, the logging standard should require that it be gathered.

Logging requirements, as applied to our database cryptosystem, should mandate, at the very least, logging of encryption and decryption requests and any key management activity. All key management access events should also be logged. Failures generally should be given higher priority. A cryptographic operation that fails because the key has been terminated should be given a very high priority. There should be no data in the system referencing a terminated key.[3] The

---

3. *This is true of a Retired key as well, but we allow for more possibility of a key being Retired incorrectly.*

attempted use of a terminated key (or a nonexistent key) is likely to indicate a compromise.

8.2.4 Common Threats

As discussed, the two types of security requirements are functional and defensive. The standards we've talked about so far have been functional. The common-threats standards are defensive. These requirements list threats that are common enough to warrant special treatment.

Requirements for mitigating common threats should be listed for each project. Such threats often include SQL injection, command injection, buffer and integer overflows, format string overflows, session hijacking, and cross-site scripting. The exact nature of the listed threats depends on the type of application. Web applications might have one standard and database applications another.

Because these requirements are defensive, they don't proclaim what must be done to avoid these attacks. Instead, they require the system analyst to include in the design a discussion of the mitigation strategies specified for each of these attacks. This discussion need not be extensive—a few sentences indicating what was done (such as sanitizing inputs and encrypting stored data) and where it was applied.

If a technology or infrastructure has been specified to address a certain class of threats, the system analyst's job is much easier. In such cases, all that is necessary is a line or two stating that the standard input sanitization library or the enterprise cryptosystem was used.

Because common threats are specific to the technology in use, it is difficult to apply them generically to our cryptosystem. It is possible that the key manager and consumer are Web applications, and it is likely that the manifest is in the same database as the protected data. All of these should meet the appropriate common threats requirements.

8.2.5 Information Confidentiality

Nearly all organizations eventually deal with information that needs to be kept confidential. This might be operational information, competitive plans, or employee or customer information. We discussed confidentiality at length earlier in this book in the context of cryptographic protection. Now we'll look at what a standard should cover to protect confidentiality.

One of the primary goals of the previous security requirements was to keep information confidential. Beyond those topics, several other steps should be taken to ensure confidentiality. Encryption is, of course, among the most important confidentiality safeguards available. However, careful consideration of how to store the confidential data offers perhaps the best protection.

This consideration should begin with storing confidential information only where there is a clear business need. Storing confidential data just because it *might* be useful later increases cost and risk for no discernible reason. If a business need is identified, the next question should be how long the business needs the data. As soon as the explicit need for the information has passed, the information should be deleted.

Finally, storage of that data must be limited to locations where the business absolutely needs it. Confidential information should not be stored with convenience as a priority. It should be stored in a single location surrounded by strong security. Under no circumstances should confidential information be placed in test or development environments.

Encryption must be accompanied by a holistic approach to securing data's confidentiality. This book focuses on cryptographic protection, but that is just one facet of a complex process. The data must be secured in transit, it must be protected by strong access controls, and decommissioned media must be thoroughly wiped. The machine hosting the data must be hardened, and the applications handling the data must be secure.

In regards to our cryptosystem, we don't move confidential information any more than is necessary. Every effort is made to keep keys in the vault and engine. Unencrypted data that is passed across a network to an online engine, for instance, must be temporarily encrypted while it traverses the network.

8.3 Requirements Review

Now that we've examined the role of security requirements in a project, we turn to the process of actually hardening a requirements document. We'll cover who is involved, when the review should occur, and what steps should be followed.

During requirements hardening, the primary players are the business analyst and the security analyst. When requirements gathering begins, the business analyst spends considerable time with the end users, determining exactly what is desired. The business requirements can change considerably from day to day during this early stage. Once the requirements solidify somewhat, the security analyst should be involved.

The security analyst works with the customer and business analyst to understand the business requirements. Then, based on that review, the security analyst outlines the risks those requirements introduce and what mitigation techniques are available. As a result of this discussion, the customer may decide to modify the requirements to remove the risk, or he might simply accept the risk and do nothing. Most likely, he will ask the security analyst to specify requirements to reduce the risk. This pattern continues throughout requirements specification and application design.

For instance, a business requirement might state that credit card numbers are to be stored. The security analyst, upon review, explains that storing credit card information introduces quite a bit of risk and that encrypting the stored credit card numbers would be an effective mitigation technique. The customer may then decide that the limited benefit of storing credit card numbers isn't worth the cost of protecting them and strike that requirement from the list. Or the customer might decide to approve the encryption requirement.[4]

Security analysis often begins with an overview of the application so that the analyst can gain an understanding of the outlines and better understand where security applies. The security analyst might ask the business analyst to address the following questions:

- Who (users and other applications) must have access to the application and data?
- What sensitive information will be handled or stored?
- When will the sensitive data be removed from the system?
- Where will the application and data reside (existing or new hosts and networks)?
- Why does the sensitive data need to be stored?
- How will the system and data be accessed?

The answers to these questions will give the security analyst a better context in which to review the requirements. Because these questions are asked during the requirements phase of the project, some of the answers may not be known or may be known with only the vaguest of details.

With the overview in hand, the security analyst reviews the requirements and looks for items that have security implications. These include requirements for storing and handling confidential information, accepting input from users,

---

4. *Of course, the worst case is that the customer decides that the risk isn't actually that severe and is willing to accept it. That is the customer's choice, of course, but in most organizations, that decision may need to be reviewed by executive staff given that it could open the organization to legal penalties.*

interfacing with other systems, providing access to important resources, and network exposure (especially Internet exposure).

As the security analyst finds these elements, she includes the appropriate security requirements. These security requirements might be, as we've already discussed, a single item stating that a particular standard must be met, or they might be a listing of several items detailing specific security practices.

One difference, hinted at earlier, between business and security requirements is that while business requirements are to some degree fixed prior to application design, security requirements continue throughout the design phase as well. The design itself is likely to uncover additional requirements. In particular, as covered in the next chapter, an assessment of the threats against a system should be translated into additional security requirements to mitigate those threats.

In an environment that has built the cryptographic infrastructure described in this book, any requirements for storing confidential information would be candidates for cryptographic protection through integration with the existing cryptosystem. In environments without an available cryptosystem, such requirements may lead the security analyst to refer to a cryptographic standard or to include a set of cryptographic requirements.

8.4 Specifying the Cryptographic Standard

Requirements for cryptography are much more complex than simply stating an algorithm and a key length. As you've seen, the security provided by a cryptosystem depends on many implementation details, and the specification of these details depends on the threats driving the use of cryptography. Here are some of the details that a database cryptography standard must address:

- What are the accepted algorithms, modes, and key lengths?
- Will HSMs be required?
- How will key families be assigned?
- In what ways, if any, is striping allowed?
- What key scoping is appropriate?
- How long can keys remain in each phase of the key life cycle?
- How are keys to be backed up?

In addition, if HSMs are not used, the standard must supply details on how the local engine and the key vault should be implemented and how the keys and master keys will be protected throughout their life.

In approaching these details, it is often useful to classify the type of attackers against which the cryptography must defend. The following questions can help in this effort:

- Does the attacker have elevated privileges?
- Can the attacker browse the database? As a legitimate user?
- Can the attacker download the database file?
- Can the attacker read the file system on which the database resides?
- Can the attacker launch repeated attacks against the system?
- Can the attacker invoke the decryption function?

Each "Yes" indicates a type of attacker the cryptography implementation should resist. Conversely, each "No" indicates that the cryptography may be vulnerable to that type of attacker. To ensure that the appropriate security is in place, each "No" should also be justified with a list of other security measures that mitigate the risk of that type of attacker.

For instance, if the cryptosystem needs to protect the data from only attackers who are browsing the database, the cryptographic specification will not be as stringent as it would if resistance were needed to all the attackers just described.

The answers to these questions, coupled with consideration of the points brought up in the infrastructure portion of the book, should provide enough information for a security analyst to define a cryptographic standard or set of requirements for protecting databases.

8.5 Data Classification

While not strictly part of the cryptographic standard, knowing when data must be encrypted is essential. Most security-conscious organizations already classify data. Often a simple three-tier system is used: public, confidential, and highly confidential. Unfortunately, such a system does not always clearly indicate which data should be encrypted. Inevitably, once one of the classifications is tagged with encryption requirements, data in that classification is found for which encryption is deemed too expensive, and data in a lesser classification is found that should be encrypted.

To avoid this situation, the security analyst can use the *sensitive* tag to indicate that the data needs encryption. This tag can be applied to information in any of the classification levels. It is more likely that highly confidential data will be tagged as "sensitive," but it is not mandatory.

Another consideration is the location the data is stored. It is possible that encryption is required for information stored in databases in the extranet, but not for databases buried deep in a secure intranet data center. To capture this distinction, the analyst might use a hierarchy of network zones.

At the bottom of this hierarchy would be the most secure zone—say, offline data stored in a vault. At the top would be the least-secure zone—perhaps a server connected directly to the Internet. Between these extremes would be zones such as the data center; the general-purpose intranet; and the extranet's data, application, and presentation tiers.

Sensitive data would be graded based on zone. Whenever the data was stored in a zone equal to or greater than its grade, the data would need to be encrypted. Table 8.1 shows possible sensitivity grades. These grades depend on how the organization's network is segregated and protected.

Table 8.1

Data sensitivity grades		
Grade	**Zone**	**Network Description**
AAA	None	When not in use, remove the encrypted drive from the machine and store it in a vault
AA	Offline	The machine should be kept off any network and protected with adequate physical security
A	Internal enclave	Highly secured data center network
B	Intranet	General-purpose company network
C	Extranet database tier	Database servers
D	Extranet application tier	Application servers
E	Extranet presentation tier	Web servers

For instance, data with a sensitivity grade of B must be encrypted when it is stored on a machine in the intranet or anywhere in the extranet (grades C, D, and E), but it does not need to be encrypted if it is stored in the data center (grade A).

These grades may be overkill for some organizations. They may prefer to either encrypt the data or not, especially if their networks are not highly segregated. Just using the sensitive tag is sufficient in those cases. However, even a simplified form of the sensitivity grades is likely to prove useful where networks have been segregated and secured according to their use.

Ultimately, whoever is responsible for the information must decide if the data is sensitive and assign it a grade. Often regulations and privacy concerns drive the owner to consider encryption, and it may be necessary for the security analyst to bring up appropriate regulations if it looks like a violation may occur. Once the information is tagged and graded, the analyst will find it easier to specify encryption requirements for that data.

8.6 Summary

This chapter covered security requirements, statements that indicate the types of security the system must possess. Given that security expertise is not yet common among application designers, security requirements should be quite detailed. A security analyst should be responsible for generating these detailed requirements based on reviews of the business requirements, relevant policy, the threats posed to the system, and an understanding of the risks the customer finds acceptable.

The last part of the chapter looked at requirements relevant to a database cryptosystem. The degree of security, key handling, and the threats that the security must mitigate were all considered. An information classification system was discussed at the end of the chapter. A classification scheme can be used to identify information that needs to be encrypted. The classification can be based on the impact to the organization if compromised, on a tag based on other criteria such as regulatory compliance, on where in the network the data is stored, or on some combination of all three.

Application designers specify security controls based on the security requirements, and quality assurance staff later validate that those controls actually fulfill the security requirements. Failure to specify requirements significantly weakens the team's ability to produce a secure application because the designers won't know which risks need additional mitigation, the developers won't know which controls are appropriate to implement, and the testers won't know what to test.

Chapter 9

Design Hardening

After the requirements are agreed on, a system to meet those requirements is designed. System designs can range from a specification detailing every logical branch the system must implement to a quick sketch on a whiteboard showing only the major components. The goal of the design phase is to let everyone know how the team intends to meet the requirements.

Each role looks for something different in the design. The users and business analysts review the design to ensure that their requirements have been understood and addressed. Programmers must thoroughly understand the design and adhere to it as they write their code. The quality assurance staff examines the design to inform their testing plans, and the security analyst reviews the design for two things: whether the design meets the security requirements and whether the design itself is secure.

If the security requirements state the need for 128-bit AES encryption, the analyst looks for that support in the design. The analyst digs as deep into the design as possible and checks that the implementation details are correct. For instance, when reviewing a cryptographic consumer component, the security analyst checks to ensure that the receipt-handling capabilities match the specified key scope. Generally, this is detail-oriented work in which the design is carefully compared to appropriate security standards.

Checking the design's security ensures that the design does not introduce any security weaknesses that weren't accounted for during the requirements gathering. This type of analysis is what uncovers the additional security requirements we discussed earlier. For instance, the requirements might specify that the system accept and process user input from the Web. From the letter of the requirements, a single synchronous system might be assumed, but the design might actually store the data in a database where it is processed asynchronously by another component.

In this case, the design introduces additional data entry and storage points. While the requirements may be explicit about protecting the current input handling, protecting the database components is not likely to be covered. The security analyst must uncover these types of situations and ensure that they are secure.

When securing a system design, the security analyst can approach the problem at three levels of detail. A *guideline* approach focuses on reflecting security best practices in the design. *Threat modeling* approaches the design at a more detailed level and focuses on determining the threats to which the system might be vulnerable. At the most detailed level, the analyst can focus on applying *security patterns* to the weak spots in the design. While these three approaches are presented as separate, in practice they are typically blended, and bits of each are used, with emphasis placed on one.

A commonality between these approaches is the need for the analyst to have a firm understanding of the design. Security analysts working with teams using minimalist designs, such as those used by agile development processes, face a challenge in this area. To overcome this difficulty, and to give some degree of uniformity to the wide range of design methodologies, we'll look at how the analyst can use data flow diagrams to get a clear picture of the application.

This chapter covers subjects to which whole books have been devoted. While enough information is provided to proceed, the interested reader is encouraged to read [12], [21], [10], and [20] in the Bibliography. These books all provide excellent coverage of design hardening, and most deal with the rest of the security life cycle as well.

9.1 Data Flow Diagrams

Data flow diagrams (DFDs) are a way for the security analyst to understand how a system works at a high level. Other types of process diagrams could fill this need as well, but a data flow diagram is preferred because it shows inputs to the system, interfaces between systems, and data stores that hold sensitive information. The diagram doesn't need to comply with any strict formalism so long as it communicates accurately.

Figure 9.1 is reproduced from Chapter 3, "An Overview of Cryptographic Infrastructure," and is an example of a data flow diagram that shows the major features of a system.

Rounded rectangles, such as the one at the top labeled "Data Input," show user interaction with the system. Circles indicate processes that handle data, and double circles such as "Crypto Provider" indicate a process composed of subprocesses.

These compound processes can be broken into their constituent components, as Figure 6.1 does for the Crypto Consumer and Provider.

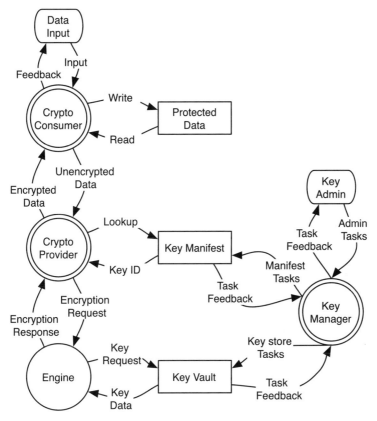

Figure 9.1: A data flow diagram

Rectangles with no sides are data stores. They might be databases, or they could be flat files. Because data stores are mostly passive entities that can't initiate actions, always place a process between two data stores when data flows between them. This clarifies that some type of process manages the exchange.

The arrows linking these components show the direction and kinds of data flows. Labels identify which data is exchanged. In many diagrams, boundaries between machines or networks are illustrated with dotted lines. This can be useful to the security analyst because processes that cross these boundaries may be susceptible to network-based attacks.

At the highest level of abstraction, a data flow diagram often shows just the primary users interacting with a single compound process and the main data stores. This *context diagram*, as it is called, can then be expanded into a series of increasingly detailed diagrams. The level of detail used to diagram our cryptographic infrastructure and its compound processes is generally as detailed as a security analyst needs.

If the design team does not and will not produce a data flow diagram, the security analyst should draw it. Ideally, the analyst reads a design document, draws a preliminary diagram, and then sets up a meeting with the lead system analyst to confirm the diagram. The books referenced earlier also contain more detail on drawing a DFD.

9.2 Design Guidelines

An approach to design hardening centering on design guidelines can seem abstract and theoretical, but for projects with limited resources to apply to design hardening, it may be the most practical approach. The security analyst specifies guidelines but leaves most of the execution details to the system analyst. The risk is that the system analyst, lacking the experience of the security analyst, will miss crucial details in the implementation.

To minimize this risk, the security analyst can ask that the design explicitly describe where the guidelines were applied in terms of the data flow diagram and how the guidelines were followed. This need not be excessively detailed but should convey enough information so that the programmers will understand how the designer wants a guideline implemented.

When reviewing the design, the security analyst evaluates how well it adheres to the guidelines and if enough details are provided to enable the programmer to proceed securely. For instance, if the design mentions that filtering should be implemented on all inputs, the analyst should make sure that the white list of acceptable characters is also specified. Clearly, application development experience is a great help to the analyst during the review.

We'll discuss each guideline in the following sections, covering why the guideline is important and what a designer needs to consider when following it.

9.2.1 Minimize the Attack Surface

Applications are nearly always attacked through their entry points, which include input from form fields and command lines, configuration files, database reads, RMI calls, and SOAP objects. Any time an application accesses or processes external data, an entry point is involved. Because processing external data is the purpose of most applications, entry points are absolutely necessary. However, we want the application to resemble the entrances to a bank, not a park.

An entry point can be thought of as having a size based on how permissive it is in accepting inputs: Large entry points accept nearly all inputs, and small entry points filter input based on such characteristics as size, data type, and composition. This filtering makes smaller entry points more difficult to successfully attack. The ubiquitous buffer overflow is due to entry points that are too large. The size of the attack surface is the aggregate size of all of an application's entry points.

Each input field on a Web form, for instance, is an entry point, as are any hidden fields, URL parameters, and cookies. For each of these, the designer should specify what type of data is allowed and its minimum and maximum length. In the case of text data, a list of permitted characters should be specified. Any character not on that list should be rejected. In some cases, such as with an e-mail address or credit card number, the designer knows the format of the data as well. For this data, the designer should describe the format so that the input can be validated by comparing it to the format.

Data output is also included in the attack surface, although it is not stressed as much. Output should contain the minimal amount of information that is necessary and appropriate. The most common target of this principle is error messages. Error messages that are shown to potential attackers should be brief and offer only enough information so that a legitimate user knows what options are available. The classic example are the errors for failed authentication. These errors should only state that the login failed and not indicate which of the username and password was incorrect.

9.2.2 Assign the Least Privileges Possible

No user or application component should be able to access more than the absolute minimum required to do its job. If access is not a necessity, it should not be granted. This principle helps contain the damage should a compromise occur. If the compromised component can only write to the database, confidentiality is preserved even though the attacker might be able fill up the database with junk.

Account permissions are the most obvious and well-known application of this, and an application designer should strive to ensure that the application's components require only the least-necessary privileges. A design that meets the requirements and requires the fewest privileges should almost always be preferred over one that requires additional privileges. Nothing should run as root without extensive review and confirmation that it is absolutely necessary, and even then, the application should drop those permissions as soon as possible. Any access that the designer does not explicitly call out should be prevented through strict permissions and techniques such as `chroot`.

While account permissions are critically important, the principle of least privilege extends into other areas of application design. For instance, one of the security benefits of many object-oriented programming languages is that access to data and functions can be limited to specific sets of other components. By default, an object's members should be tagged so that no other components can access them. Where possible, the design, if it reaches this level of detail, should specify which members may provide additional access.

Any time a component can be accessed by others, the designer should ensure that the component provides as little access as possible. However, if you have just a single component, least privilege can't be applied because that one component must do everything. For least privilege to be the most effective, the system must also exhibit a thorough separation of duties across multiple components.

9.2.3 Separate Duties

Separation of duties is a security principle typically applied to job responsibilities: The auditor shouldn't also manage the bank vault. Duties are generally separated to limit the ability of any one person to commit fraud or otherwise abuse his or her privileges. Essentially, separating duties enables a system to limit privileges.

Separation of duties has a long history in software. The common organization of having separate staff for application design, programming, and QA is one example. Such separations may not have initially sprung from security requirements, but their security implications are certainly a contributor to their persistence.

When specifying components, the designer should attempt to split components based on transaction and privilege. Different types of transactions should be handled by different components. Placing an order should not be handled by the same components that allow account status to be checked. Separation by privilege keeps components requiring greater privileges separate from those that require less.

The designer has several ways of separating components:

Separation by programmer Programmers should work on different components, especially for the most security-sensitive components.

Separation by administrator System administrators should be responsible for different components.

Separation by network tier Components should be distributed through each tier as each is exposed to different degrees of attacks.

Separation by functionality Only functionality absolutely required should exist in any component.

Separation by user No single user should be able to originate and complete a sensitive transaction without other users offering validation.

Ideally, each transaction crosses each of these boundaries at least two or three times.

For example, components for ordering and checking account status could be separated by functionality and programmer.[1] In terms of functionality, the different transactions will need to read from a similar set of tables but likely will differ in the tables to which they need to write.

Components of different privileges are more likely to be separated along all the lines. Consider the separation of functionality between the presentation and application tiers. Generally, the presentation tier contains less privileged code than the application tier. For instance, code on the presentation tier typically cannot directly access the database, while application tier code can. This separation could be further enhanced by requiring one team to write the presentation code and a different team to implement the code on the application servers. In addition, different administrators can be specified for the different tiers.

User separation is often formalized in a security model that specifies the users or user roles that may have various levels or types of access to information assets. While this matrix of roles and privileges is defined by the customer, the designer must ensure that the access control system provides the appropriate capabilities to meet the customer's needs.

These schemes allow privileges to be fine-tuned and granted only where necessary. If a component becomes compromised, the damage is tightly contained to just the privileges that component possesses. To effectively split components, the designer must balance a healthy paranoia with the need to keep the design simple by avoiding an excessive proliferation of components. Simplicity also keeps the maintenance burden introduced by multiple components with fine-grained permissions manageable. Achieving this balance requires experience.

9.2.4 Defend in Depth

Functionality split into separate components also allows security to be applied in layers so that if one control fails or is avoided, other controls maintain security. This principle is known as defense in depth, and a designer should look for opportunities to protect the system with multiple security "shells." At the very

---

1. *In practice, the sensitivity of these particular transactions may not warrant too much effort to ensure that different programmers build these components.*

least, the designer should find and fix any controls that represent a single point of failure.

As discussed earlier, database cryptography is an example of defense in depth. Databases are typically protected by access controls, firewalls, and server hardening. Should those fail, or should an attacker find a way to simply avoid them, perhaps by virtue of being an administrator, database cryptography acts as a last line of defense.

9.2.5 Fail Securely

When an application component fails, it should do so such that security is maintained. For instance, if a hardware encryption module is unavailable, a temporary software system could kick in to protect the data until the hardware comes back online. If the authentication system fails, access should be refused. Attackers have been known to deliberately target particular components if, when those components fail, security is reduced.

The designer should consider what happens if any component or sequence of components fails and include coverage for these cases in the design. While defense in depth addresses how security components should be layered, designing for secure failure focuses more on what behavior the system should perform if a failure is detected.

For instance, a failure in an online ordering component might result in just an alert if other defenses are maintaining security. However, if the failure is significant, the application might switch to a different subsystem or shut down the order functionality altogether.

A key concept in failing securely is that the application should degrade gracefully and predictably in the face of failure. The system should monitor itself, and when problems are detected, it should alter its behavior so that security and as much functionality as possible are preserved.

9.2.6 Default to Secure

An application's default behavior should be secure. For example, by default all input should be refused unless specifically allowed, and all authorization requests should be denied unless specifically allowed. Any behavior that could potentially introduce a security issue (accepting input or allowing access) should be allowed only if specific criteria are met.

Whenever a design has a decision tree, the default branch should result in the most security. This approach ensures that if an attacker discovers a way to avoid the expected branches, perhaps through some specially constructed input, the reward will only be increased security.

9.2.7 Plan a Defense Strategy

An application's defense plan describes the security events that the application generates, how to identify an incident or possible breach from a collection of security events, and, in the case of an actual breach, what actions should be taken to defend the application and resources. These actions might include checking the logs of related severs and applications, blocking IP addresses, turning on additional protections, and even shutting down the application or calling in a forensics team.

The design should specify when security events should be generated and how they should be handled. A mechanism for alerting appropriate personnel should be in place, and any special defensive systems must be specified. A key capability for a solid defense plan is the ability to check the application's logs and current behavior. This functionality should be included in the design.

The designer should consider the sorts of exceptional states in which the application might find itself, and the application should generate security events if the state is suspicious. Suspicious states include attempts to decrypt data with terminated keys or access tables that don't exist. Another example of suspicious behavior is when the length of the delivered output drastically exceeds what is expected. A failed authentication attempt, while not necessarily suspicious by itself, should still generate a security event. If a certain threshold of failed authentications is met, the aggregate might indicate that an attempt to guess passwords is under way.

After identifying security events, the designer must decide what response is appropriate. Typically this involves close coordination with the Information Security team and alignment with the incident response plan if available.

9.3 Threat Modeling

Threat modeling is the process of determining the threats to which each component of the DFD might be vulnerable. The threat model itself is a listing of these threats, categorized and prioritized. The categories indicate the type of threat, and the prioritization is based on the threat's severity rating, which reflects the damage potential, the location, and the exposure.

The threat model has several uses. For the system analyst, the model provides a clear picture of where security is essential to the design. For the security tester, the model shows where testing should be focused. For the Information Security team and the customer, the model captures the system's security profile and plays a key part in determining if the system's security is acceptable.

The application designer and the security analyst work together to build the threat model. Building the model should begin after the design is fairly well sketched out, but with enough time remaining to fix any weaknesses revealed by the process. Depending on the project's complexity, the threat model could take anywhere from a few hours to a few weeks. Most projects would likely need a day or two to produce a useful model.

Creating a threat model consists of looking at each component in the DFD and determining if it is a target for the following:[2]

- Confidentiality breaches
- Integrity violations
- Availability denials
- Repudiation attempts
- False authentications
- Unauthorized access

While the first three were discussed earlier in this book, the rest haven't had as much coverage. A repudiation attack enables someone who initiated or approved a transaction to later deny his or her involvement. A false authentication is any situation in which the component interacts with an entity it believes to be some other entity. For instance, if the component interfaces with another across the network, a potential false authentication exists because an attacker could attempt to masquerade as that other system.

An unauthorized access occurs when an attacker gains access to data or systems to which he lacks explicit permissions. Systems where assets are protected by privileges are, of course, prime candidates for unauthorized access. While a false authentication generally implies unauthorized access as well, the reverse is not true. In some cases it is possible to gain unauthorized access without masquerading.

Often, components are targets of multiple types of attacks. For each identified type, though, the analysts should consider the attack's specific target or targets. For instance, a confidentiality breach against the database might be described as a

---

2. *These categories are similar to the STRIDE categories in [12] and [20] in the Bibliography but reflect the terminology used in this book.*

"disclosure of a customer's personal data" or "exposure of sensitive marketing campaign material." As you can see, a given class of attack may very well have several specific threats.

These specific threats comprise the threat model. They should be listed, along with their category, and then rated. The ratings provide a rough measure of the threat's severity. While many formulas and techniques exist for estimating threat severity, a simple three-parameter formula is generally sufficient for our needs. Each parameter is rated from 1 to 3, and the overall severity is the average. High numbers indicate higher severity.

Damage is the relative degree of damage that would be incurred: (1) little damage, (2) moderate damage, (3) major damage.

Location is where the component resides: (1) secured data center, (2) intranet, (3) extranet.[3]

Exposure is how exposed the component is to attack: (1) little exposure due to the presence of other security controls, (2) moderate exposure, (3) high exposure due to the lack of compensating security controls.

These ratings, of course, are subjective. More mature security organizations may have metrics and more objective risk assessments to use in estimating the severity of these threats. In any case, the goal is to create a ranking of threats.

Once the threats have been rated (or in parallel with the rating effort), the designer and security analyst must determine which threats present more risk than the customer will accept. While it is best if the customer also reviews the final assessment to ensure its accuracy, customers often have a poor sense of the severity of threats, and the security analyst should be prepared to explain in depth why the risk of any given threat was deemed too high. Based on this assessment, either additional security requirements should be added to the requirements document and appropriate controls specified in the design, or the designer should revise the design so as to eliminate the threat.

9.4 Security Patterns

Patterns, common solutions to recurring design problems, have become a staple of modern application design. Major works in software patterns include [9] and [3].

---

3. *This rating is geared to projects implementing applications in a corporate-like network rather than for individual products.*

The core of a pattern is its context, the problem, and the solution. A pattern strives to be flexible, and its description considers the typical constraints that an implementation might face.

Security patterns provide specific guidance on how to secure a design from particular threats. In pattern terms, the threat is the recurring design problem. A threat model certainly helps identify where a security pattern is applicable, but familiarity with a good library of security patterns should be sufficient considering a pattern's context and problem statement should include information on the pattern's applicability.

The field of security patterns is still growing, but references include [2] and [6]. A Web search will also yield a variety of locations worth investigating. The patterns we're referring to here can be viewed as the "defense" versions of the "attack patterns" described in [11].

Ideally, an organization standardizes on a set of patterns to cover the common threats encountered in its environment. Frequently used patterns are best implemented as infrastructure so that new projects avoid implementing the pattern from scratch. Indeed, this book is, in a sense, an elaborate pattern for implementing cryptography to protect a database.

Consider a "User Authentication Across a Network" pattern as an example. The context is that of an application whose users must be identified before they can use the application. The problem description would include preventing impersonation, protecting credentials in transit and in storage, and safeguarding against attempts to guess the credentials.

The solution might go into using passwords, biometrics, and two-factor authentication schemes. It could cover the use of SSL and hashes to protect the password. Account lockouts and complex pass phrases could be discussed as a means of reducing the threat of password guessing. In terms of caveats, a highly useful feature of many patterns, account denial-of-service attacks (exploiting lockouts) and overly verbose error messages might be explained.

When working with patterns, a designer first selects a pattern that addresses the threat. The pattern will likely provide options, and the designer needs to specify the appropriate configuration. Good patterns provide enough detail that a programmer can implement the pattern without extensive notes from the designer. In this way, patterns can streamline and reduce ambiguity in a design even while securing it.

9.5 Designing the Cryptosystem

Turning the design presented in this book into a detailed production design should include extensive hardening. The basic data flow diagram (Figure 9.1) is included and can be modified to reflect design changes for a given environment.

The design as presented in this book is already aligned with many of the guidelines covered in this chapter, but as more detail is added and actual technology specified, the guidelines need to be revisited and validated. The inputs to the system are well known and have been kept to a small number, but the particulars of accepting only good values depends on the actual environment.

The system is modularized, and the privileges and duties of each module have been limited and separated. Our provider should only have the privileges to encrypt and decrypt; the key manager should only be able to manage keys. User separation, in the context of key management, allows the use of key zones to limit what changes a given key administrator can introduce. The specific permissions matrix remains to be specified, of course. Administrator separation was also addressed given that the database itself cannot decrypt data, so database administrators cannot view confidential information. System administrators may have access to all the information necessary to view confidential information, but the defense-in-depth guideline offers further protection.

Not only is the encrypted data an example of defense in depth, but the cryptosystem itself offers several different layers of defense. Strong protections around the key vault lie at the center of our defense strategy. Both direct and indirect access to keys have been covered in the design. The next layer of defense is the cryptographic routines themselves. We called them "choke points" earlier. While this may seem frightening from a performance perspective, in terms of security they allow us to focus our monitoring and auditing on a small set of well-defined calls. Abuse in such a situation is much easier to detect. Finally, input sanitization, access controls, and modularization form the outer perimeter of our defense.

We've discussed what should happen if the engine fails, and the possibility of including a backup local engine was introduced. Failure responses for each component remain to be developed so as to comply with local policy. The central question is, in the event of a failure, should unencrypted data be written to the database, or should processing stop until the cause of the failure is resolved? In the first case, we have the potential for a confidentiality breach. In the second we have a denial of service. An organization's answer to this question will guide the failure response plan for the rest of the system.

Of all the guidelines presented, the defense plan depends the most on an individual organization's policies. The degree of monitoring, alerting, and incident response varies significantly. At the very least, the detailed design should specify the security events and require a security log to be written. Even if it isn't regularly monitored, the logs will be ready as the organization's security posture matures.

Once a detailed design that includes technology specifications is available, the threat model should be developed. Each component of the data flow diagram should be evaluated with regard to the type of threats covered in section 9.3, "Design Hardening." Once the threats are understood, the designer and the security analyst should rate and review the model with the customer driving the encryption project. Any threats posing risks the customer is not willing to accept should be mitigated through additional security controls.

To date, few organizations have assembled a library of security patterns. The design of the cryptosystem should be seen as an opportunity to begin collecting relevant security patterns. The resources mentioned in the previous section should be mined for patterns that apply to the security problems uncovered in the DFD and threat model. In addition, the team should not be shy about documenting their own patterns as they mitigate each high-risk threat.

9.5.1 Searching and Profiles

Searching for information that has been encrypted is a common problem with database cryptography. Because the encryption transforms meaningful information into apparent gibberish, searching becomes very difficult to do quickly. The fundamental problem with attempting to increase the performance is that any information used to optimize the search can also be used by an attacker to compromise the encryption's security. Striking a balance is often very difficult, and the general rule is to design the data model to minimize the need to search on encrypted data.

For instance, don't use a customer's credit card number or social security number as an identifier. Instead, use information that isn't considered sensitive enough to encrypt—perhaps a person's name, e-mail address, or phone number.[4] Even if such information isn't enough to uniquely identify the exact row, it is likely to reduce the number of rows enough so that decryption of each of the candidates is reasonable.

---

4. *The use of name, e-mail, or phone number in this example isn't meant to imply that they aren't sensitive enough to encrypt.*

In some cases, sensitive data contains some nonunique element that is considered nonsensitive. We'll call such data a *profile*[5] of the information. Examples might include a person's initials, the last four digits of a credit card number or social security number, or a phone number's area code. These can often be combined with other nonunique identifiers to further limit the number of rows that need to be decrypted.

When sensitive data does not have a well-known profile, such as the last four digits of a social security number, one can easily be created. A simple method of accomplishing this is to hash the data with SHA-1 and retain only the first 10 bits. This produces a profile for the data in the form of a number between 0 and 1023.

Use only one profile for each item of data. For instance, don't store unencrypted the last four digits of a credit card number and the first 10 digits of the SHA-1 hash. It is possible that a sophisticated attacker can use interactions between multiple profiles to recover the encrypted data. One way to think of this is to imagine that the encrypted data is a person's face and that each different data profile is a profile of that face from a different angle. As more profiles are accumulated, the easier it becomes to determine what the actual face looks like.

Guarding against such interactions is very difficult, and it is best to use just a single profile. If the SHA-1-based profile doesn't provide enough granularity, the number of retained bits could be increased. For instance, if one million credit card numbers are profiled, each possible profile value would match about 1,000 of the stored credit cards. In other words, about 1,000 credit cards would have a profile value of 0, about 1,000 would have a profile of 1, and so on. If we increased the number of bits retained to the first 16, each profile value would have about 16 possible values. This is a far more reasonable number of fields to decrypt for a definitive search. If it's combined with generic information such as a zip code, the criteria has a good chance of identifying a single row.

Care must still be taken when considering which data should be profiled and how it is profiled. As implied earlier, every profile leaks some knowledge about the encrypted information. Obviously, any profile that consists of some segment of the sensitive information, such as initials or first or last digits, leaks explicit knowledge. Information leaked by other profiles may not be as explicit, but it can still be damaging.

For instance, if the SHA-1-based scheme just discussed was applied to first names, attackers attempting to determine which row contained information about a

---

5. *Technically, what we're calling a profile is known as a noncryptographic hash. We'll use the term profile to avoid confusion.*

particular person would also be able to determine which set of rows was a candidate. The attacker could then use additional information discovered through other sources to further isolate the desired row. Let's say that once the attacker identifies the correct row, the next target is to determine the value of a field that contains a value from a rather small range of possibilities—say, the person's weight. If this information is profiled, an attacker could create a table of the first 10 bits of the SHA-1 hash of every weight between 1 and 500 pounds. The attacker then compares the value in the profile to the table and determines the person's weight. This attack is successful despite strong encryption on the data itself.

9.6 Summary

Design hardening is the process of specifying security controls necessary to meet the security requirements. While some security requirements will have been identified before design begins, a significant portion of the final security requirements will be revealed only as the design is developed in detail.

This chapter looked at three approaches to design hardening. By relying on guidelines, the team specifies controls based on security principles, experience, and best practices. Unfortunately, such an approach is more likely to miss necessary controls because the threats against the system aren't given a rigorous analysis. To counter this weakness, a threat model can be used to assess the threats against a system. Threat modeling is perhaps the most important activity during design hardening because it is used and referenced throughout the rest of the system's development life cycle. Security patterns help the team determine the most appropriate controls for particular threats. Organizations should develop their own repositories of patterns that apply to their environments.

Finally, this chapter looked at the issue of searching in an encrypted database. Encryption and fast searching are antagonistic at a fundamental level. The provided guidance is to design the system so that searches on encrypted data are not necessary. When it is necessary, try to use nonsensitive data to limit the range of possible rows, and then decrypt each of these possibilities until the desired row is found. As a last resort, encrypted data could be profiled, and searches could use the profile to limit the number of rows to be decrypted.

Chapter 10

Secure Development

Development covers all aspects of implementing an application according to the design. In most cases development includes actual programming, but it can easily refer to assembling prefabricated components with a little scripting glue or configuring an application platform. The goal of secure development is to ensure that the implementation, whatever form it takes, produces a secure application.

Two characteristics of the development phase cause it to be security-intensive. The first is that development is the last chance to take the offense when building an application. Once development is complete and the application released, security becomes reactive and defensive.

The second characteristic is that development is also extremely detail-oriented. In many cases, every behavior the application can perform must be transformed into specific instructions by the developer. This work often uncovers conditions the application can encounter that the designer did not foresee. Every instruction the developer implements needs to be evaluated in terms of security.

Paradoxically, while development is among the most security-intensive phases, the security analyst does not have a large role in this effort. Most projects require the work of at least several developers, and many projects involve several large teams of developers. Development security depends on these individuals. They must be able to recognize the security implications of their work, know the appropriate techniques to implement security, and tirelessly secure those dark corners of program behavior—the places where a lesser developer becomes sloppy because "this would never happen."

Before this phase begins, the security analyst should ensure that a security guidebook is available. This guidebook should cover general secure development practices as well as provide specific actions for the relevant languages and platforms with which the team will be working. The analyst should also help identify training that would help the team understand and implement current security techniques. Like the guidebook, trainings should range from general principles of application security to strategies for securing a given language or platform.

During the development phase, the analyst's primary goals are to provide guidance on security-related issues and to keep security in the minds of the developers. Development is often a high-pressure activity, and it is very tempting for a developer to postpone researching security issues and to simply allow security concerns in general to fade into the background. To counter these tendencies, the analyst can adopt a workshop approach.

Every couple of weeks or so, the analyst should host a workshop covering some aspect of secure development. These workshops provide a forum for questions and concerns, allow the analyst to present the latest security techniques, and keep the team thinking about security. Depending on the topics covered and the amount of time the team has available, the workshops can range from a couple of hours to a full day. Possible topics include any of the guidelines listed next, security patterns, security-related APIs, secure use of development tools, and case studies.

10.1 Guidelines for Secure Development

The rest of this chapter covers general guidelines for secure development. Occasionally specific languages or platforms are mentioned, but these guidelines apply to nearly any development effort. Several other books go into much more detail on many of these guidelines. See [12], [21], and [10] in the Bibliography for more information.

10.1.1 Sanitize All Inputs and Outputs

This guideline is the development counterpart to "Minimize the Attack Surface" in the preceding chapter. The first thing a program should do when presented with input is to scrub it to ensure that it is of the correct type, size, and composition. Where possible, the input should be validated as well if the form of the data is known.

Ideally, any variables containing input data should be marked and reexamined prior to use in any security-sensitive context. For instance, if a variable containing user input is about to be used as part of an SQL query, that variable should be cleansed of any potentially harmful characters.

In some cases, variables can be constructed so as to support sanitization flags. These flags indicate what sort of sanitization has already been applied to the variable's contents. Variables known to be safe for SQL, e-mail, or shell scripts would be marked as such. This allows the program to check that the variable has been appropriately sanitized and eliminates the overhead of multiple sanitization runs. Of course, each time the variable's data changes, all the flags would need to be reset.

Sanitization, with or without the flags, should be applied to *all* inputs. Direct user input such as form fields and command-line parameters definitely must be sanitized. Other, more subtle inputs should also be scrubbed. These often-overlooked inputs include URLs, values read from files (including configuration files), objects sent via protocols such as RMI or SOAP, and data read from a database. All these represent paths leading into the program's internals. A clever attacker will find weaknesses and exploit them.

When a program returns with output, that output should also be sanitized. The same approach of examining type, size, and composition applies here as well. If the program should return an ID number of up to 10 digits, output sanitization will prevent it from returning 16 digits (say, a credit card number) should the program become subverted.

10.1.2 Execute with the Least Privileges Possible

This guideline is also a parallel to a design principle: "Assign the Least Privileges Possible." Too often an application runs with excessive privileges not because those permissions are required but because the developer didn't make the extra effort of limiting the privileges.

A restricted privilege environment is often frustrating to developers when they frequently encounter errors due to obscure (and not so obscure) permission issues. To avoid this, developers often work within highly privileged accounts (in an environment lacking sensitive information). Unfortunately, this leads to "privilege inflation."

Frequently developers plan to first get the code working and then go back and fix permission issues. In practice, though, schedule pressures squeeze what little time is typically allocated to the permissions rework. Even when the rework has begun, it is often abandoned when it is discovered that a fair amount of other code has taken advantage of the relaxed environment.

To avoid privilege inflation, the development environment should be configured with the same permissions scheme as production. Although a developer sandbox is often appropriate and necessary, the code should run in the production-configured account before QA accepts it.

Privilege management is often an overlooked skill when interviewing developers. A skilled developer can accomplish more within limited privileges than a less-skilled developer. Lead developers, especially security leads, should build a deep knowledge of how privileges work in their enviroment and seek out techniques for accomplishing tasks with the least privileges. For instance, when selecting database connection drivers, the developer should select the one requiring the least privileges, all other things being equal.

The skilled developer also knows exactly how long elevated privileges are necessary. This knowledge is essential to ensure that when the program must run with additional privileges, it does so for the shortest amount of time. As soon as the privileges are no longer necessary, the program should shed the new privileges and return to the baseline.

In terms of privilege management, the developer must also ensure that within the program, access to data and function calls is as restricted as possible. The goal is to limit any given execution thread to just the access it needs to accomplish its tasks and deny everything else. Because languages vary in their support of internal access controls, the project's security goals should be considered when selecting the implementation language.

For example, in Java, variables should all be private and final; accessor methods should be used to set and alter variables. Methods should also be private and classes final unless there is an explict reason to do otherwise, and then the access should be no more permissive than is absolutely necessary. Comments in the source code should contain the rationale for exceptions.

10.1.3 Wipe Sensitive Data from Memory

When a program is finished handling sensitive data, it should wipe that data from memory as thoroughly as it can. This reduces the risk of an attacker scanning memory and extracting the data. While easily stated, carrying out this guideline is often difficult because the locations where a computer places a program's data are often inaccessible by most programming languages. Fortunately, the risk posed by such hard-to-reach registers is generally small, so targeting variables stored in primary memory is often sufficient.

The notable exception is the situation posed by swap files. The operating system uses swap files to manage memory. These files can contain all the data accessed by your program, and they are written to disk as the OS needs. Programmatic control over what data gets written is very rare. After the data is written to disk, it can stay there indefinitely. Wiping sensitive data from memory as soon as possible minimizes the likelihood of its capture by the swap file, but it cannot eliminate the risk.

Languages offer differing capabilities for wiping memory. The standard strategy is to "zero" the memory by writing zeroes to the memory locations where the data was stored. Unfortunately, not all languages allow the necessary access in all cases. Once data has been cast as a String type in Java, for instance, the data enters the string pool, where it stays until it is no longer referenced and the Java garbage collector decides to delete it. If at all possible, sensitive data should not be cast as a String type in Java.

The more sensitive the data, the greater the urgency to wipe it. Among the most important data to wipe is key data. An attack that extracts data from a program's memory is bad, but the damage is limited to just what happens to be in memory at the time. However, if a key is extracted, the protection rendered by that key vanishes and the information is vulnerable. Unless the encryption occurs on highly secure dedicated hardware, the key should be accessed for each cryptographic job, then used, and then wiped. These steps should follow each other as quickly as possible.

10.1.4 Log All Security Events

The ability to monitor security events is critical to an application's operational security. Few banks install a vault and then forgo other security precautions such as alarms, cameras, and guards. Software should be the same, and the software equivalents of these other precautions depend on security event logging.

We discussed security events in the context of planning a defense strategy (section 9.2.7, "Plan a Defense Strategy") and indicated that the application designer needs to include a logging mechanism and specify security events. However, developers, focused as they are on the details of the application, are likely to discover conditions that have security implications but that are not covered by the designer's event specifcations. The developer should bring these cases to the designer's attention so that an appropriate event can be specified and accounted for in the defense plan.

A security event should contain enough information to enable the response. Generally, the developer should include the date and time of the event, the source IP address, the nature of the event, and any appropriate information regarding the event's context. For instance, a failed authorization in an attempt to access an encryption key might result in a log stating "Event ID 123, failed authorization: key ID 56789," and then, as context, give details on the account used.

Because many applications generate a great many low-priority security events, the logging mechanism may provide a way of removing those low-priority events from the log so as not to needlessly consume valuable space. Only events that correspond to a possible security incident need to be kept for a significant amount of time.

10.1.5 Inspect Code and Binaries

This section covers both manual inspections and automated inspection scans. In both cases, the aim is to identify implementation flaws early, before they become "institutionalized" in the program. The flaws we are concerned with are security-related. In particular, security inspections need to look for violations of security guidelines and practices.

Manual inspections are typically conducted by a small group including the developer, a moderator, a lead developer, and, in our case, a security lead. Because manual inspections are labor-intensive, they are generally reserved for just the most security-sensitive pieces of code. The threat model is an excellent indicator of which code should be considered for manual inspections.

For best results, the code should be distributed to the inspection team a week or so before the inspection meeting. Prior to the meeting, the team should review the code and match it to the design. They should also evaluate the code against security requirements, guidelines, and standards. Deviations should be noted. During the meeting, the deviations are discussed to determine which need remediation. The moderator documents the decisions, and any remediations are scheduled.

Because manual inspections cannot cover the entire codebase, automated tools should be used to complete the coverage. Inspections done by automation can look for programming errors or bad practices, such as uninitialized variables and array bounding issues, as well as more obvious potential security conditions such as risky use of input and lax access control specifications.

Some automation examines the actual source code files, while other tools run against the compiled binary produced from the source code. The quality of these tools and the types of imperfections targeted vary considerably from tool to tool, and it is worthwhile to experiment to find a tool that meets a particular team's needs.

10.1.6 Unit Test Security

A unit test is a developer-conducted test, often automated, of a specific component. Generally, these tests don't validate high-level functionality so much as confirm that the low-level individual components that produce the high-level functionality perform as expected.

The "units" are typically functions and procedures, and the tests input a variety of data and then check that the output matches the specifications. In most cases, the code under test is not directly accessible through the user interface, so only other code can exercise the tests. This leads to the extreme programming advocacy of suites of automated tests that can be run against the program after any change.

Security unit tests need to try the program's security features. Unreasonably long and other pathological inputs should be given to the units under test. If the code accesses resources based on input, a test should attempt to access a denied resource.

Unit testing frameworks are available for many languages. In some cases it might be possible to construct a unit-testing utility that generates a wide variety of traditionally bad inputs. This utility could then be applied to test the boundary conditions of input. This practice is commonly known as "fuzzing." The utility would need to be developed only once, and each use might require just a minimum amount of configuration.

A fuzzing utility not only reduces the overhead associated with security unit testing, it also gives a baseline against which applications can be compared. Because no code should be released to QA until it passes all unit tests, the fuzzing utility provides relatively objective metrics that a security analyst can look at when evaluating the program's security. Failed (or skipped) security unit tests are a cause for concern.

Unit tests can also be used for focusing code inspections. A cursory inspection of the actual code with a more detailed inspection of the unit test conditions and their results is often enough to estimate the code's robustness. Code that is not thoroughly unit-tested or fails its unit tests should be inspected with more detail (and undergo reworking so that it passes thorough unit testing).

10.1.7 Use a Language or Platform Security Guide

A security guide, of the kind we're discussing here, describes an organization's accepted secure development practices. They are typically targeted at a specific language or platform. Java and C would have distinct guides, as would the organization's enterprise resource planning and customer relationship management platforms.

These guides typically contain a mixture of "how to" and "should/should not" information. The "how to" guidelines address common scenarios such as checking authorization, handling path names, and building SQL queries. If infrastructure for access controls or cryptography has beeen standardized, the guidelines should include instructions on how to best use them.

The "should/should not" sections present coding and configuration standards. Such guidelines as "Always mark object members as private unless there exist clear reasons otherwise" and "Never load a key as a String" should find their home in these sections. Naming conventions and configurations such as "Always check the 'Use strong authentication' box" should also be included.

When building these guidelines, an excellent place to start is the Internet. A wealth of secure coding practices for nearly every language is available online. Practices for platforms are a little harder to come by, but they exist, particularly for large, common platforms such as Oracle Applications and Lotus Notes. The platform vendor is also a good place to start when collecting guidelines.

Security analysts should use these found practices as a base and work with the respective developement teams to refine the list. The goal is to remove items that don't apply to the given environment and tailor those that do to fit as well as possible.

10.2 Summary

This chapter is short because it is so heavily dependent on the technology used in an implementation. A development team building a database cryptosystem should take the time to thoroughly understand the security implications of the chosen technologies. The guidelines presented here can help shape the discovery process, but in the end, each technology and language should have a documented set of rules the team has adopted to ensure the consistency and security of the final product.

Chapter 11

Testing

Traditional software development methodologies often describe two phases of testing. Quality assurance testing verifies that the required functionality exists and meets specifications. User acceptance testing verifies that the functionality actually fulfills the user's needs.

Software security testing also consists of these two phases. Functional testing verifies that security controls exist and meet specifications. Application penetration testing checks that those controls are effective and sufficient. Typically, penetration testing follows functional testing, and the two types of testing are carried out by different teams.

Splitting the testing between two teams is not only another case of separating duties, but it also recognizes that the skills needed for each phase are different. Functional security testing is often carried out by the quality assurance team as part of their typical testing. Penetration testing, though, should be done by security experts, just as traditional user acceptance testing is done by actual business experts rather than QA staff.

The security analyst assists with both types of testing but shouldn't engage in either. The reasoning for this separation mirrors the reasoning behind having a separate QA staff perform testing rather than relying on the developers and designers. The security analyst knows what to expect and brings a set of preconceptions regarding the application's operation. These generally act as unconscious blinders and keep the analyst from trying truly novel approaches.

Keeping the security analyst out of the actual testing helps keep the tests objective and encourages more creative thinking when developing test cases. However, the analyst does need to make sure that the testing sufficiently challenges the application's security. Not every test should focus on obscure edge cases. The analyst should review the test plans and keep testing on track and relevant.

11.1 Functional Security Testing

Functional security testing is based on the security requirements identified at the beginning of the project. Each requirement should be covered by a set of test cases to reveal how well the application meets the requirement. The test cases should test the stated functionality as well as test edge cases and boundary conditions that include scenarios where other parts of the system fail.

Consider the requirements we discussed in Chapter 8, "Requirements Hardening":

- Access controls
- Data sanitization
- Logging and monitoring
- Common threats
- Information confidentiality

We'll briefly look at possible test cases for each of these common requirements, which should be present in most projects. The focus of these tests isn't to discover clever means of circumventing the security. That's what penetration testing does. This testing simply verifies that the security controls exist and work as specified.

11.1.1 Access Control

Test cases for access controls should include authentication and authorization checks. For authentication, both valid and invalid usernames and passwords should be tried. If an account lockout mechanism and criteria have been specified, they should also be tested.

The tests must confirm that authentication checks exist where specified. It is not enough to simply check that the user is authenticated at one point and then assume that all the other points are adequately protected. For instance, often initial login and access to basic functionality require a single authentication. However, should the user decide to change the account's password, another authentication is often specified. Testing should ensure that the access controls work in both cases.

Authorization test cases require a set of protected resources that the tester attempts to access via accounts that should have access and accounts that should not. It is often impossible to test all potentially accessible protected resources in the allotted time, so testers need to prioritize and at least attempt to test all the different kinds of resource access, such as file, database, and functionality access.

The access controls used by the key manager and the consumer should be strenuously tested. Weaknesses in these areas, especially in the key manager, can quickly lead to a compromise of the entire cryptosystem.

11.1.2 Data Sanitization

Data sanitization test cases need to subject application inputs to a variety of data, both expected and pathological. The general constraints for data sanitization include size, type, and composition. Test cases should cover each of these constraints as well as points where the design specifies format validations.

These test cases should probe every entry point. These include input fields, command-line parameters, input files, configuration files, database reads, distributed function calls, and object input whether through protocols such as SOAP or techniques such as serialization.

The goal of these tests is to check that the sanitization occurs and that bad inputs are identified. In some cases the input is denied, and in other cases it is accepted but filtered so that the bad data is either removed or rendered harmless.

It is worthwhile to create test cases that resemble the types of inputs typically used by common attacks. For instance, cross-site scripting often uses JavaScript tags, so test cases targeting URLs and Web fields would benefit from including such data. Similarly, inputs used in the construction of SQL queries should be subject to a few different types of SQL constructs, including comment tokens, union statements, and quote characters.

If a sanitization flaw is found during this phase of testing, no effort should be made to construct an exploit.[1] A failure indicates that the application failed to meet the requirements, and it should be treated as such. The flaw should be logged and evaluated along with the other flaws. The security analyst plays a significant role in this evaluation and prioritization. Of course, any flaw that passes through this phase unfixed becomes a prime target during penetration testing.

The key manager and the consumer are again the primary test targets. Secondary targets include data read from the database and, if relevant to a given environment, the key vault. Finally, if these inputs are found to be clean, the tester can move on to attempting to craft input that slips past the initial filters but causes problems in a later process in a different component. For instance, an input might be acceptable to the consumer, but when the data is finally passed to the engine, a problem occurs.

---

1. *This applies to all testing during this phase, but the temptation to find actual exploits is strongest with entry point flaws given that such flaws are paths into the application's internal functioning.*

11.1.3 Logging and Monitoring

The goal of log testing is to ensure that the logs capture the specified events. Tests should cover every action for which the design specifies an event. Not only should the existence of the log entry be verified, but the accuracy of the contents should also be checked. Are the time, IP address, event, and context correct? The tests should try variations to make sure that they are captured faithfully.

One of the challenges in testing log functionality is to create conditions that generate the more obscure log entries. Authentication and authorization activities are easy to check. Logs generated when a particular subset of lookup data is unavailable are more difficult to test, and conditions involving atypical behavior from multiple systems are even more difficult. Nevertheless, testers should make every effort, especially with security-related events, to look into every nook and cranny of the application's behavior and check that logging occurs appropriately.

If the design specifies any response capabilities for the application, whether manual or automated, those should be extensively tested. This functionality often goes unused for long periods and then, during an incident, must be used under pressure. It is critical that everything works as needed. Testing generally requires that an incident be simulated and then the response capabilities engaged. Any flaw discovered in this functionality must either be fixed or documented and incorporated into the defense plan. No one wants to rediscover an overlooked flaw in an application's defense capabilities during an attack.

In a database cryptosystem, generating events that trigger security logging can often be done by manually updating receipt information in the database. By placing references to keys in various states, you can generate a variety of log entries. In addition, testers should attempt both valid and invalid authentications and authorizations with the key manager. Other security events, as specified in the design, must also be tested.

11.1.4 Common Threats

To address the common-threats requirements, the designer must include documentation of the mitigation strategies in the design. The goal of these requirements is to ensure that common attacks are considered during the design. The common-threats requirements might result in specifications of new external controls such as an application firewall, reliance on existing security controls, integration with existing security infrastructure, or an explanation of why the threat is irrelevant.

No general testing approach covers all these situations, so the functional tester must carefully consider the design's discussion of the threats and create additional test cases where appropriate. In many cases, testing should be deferred to the penetration testing phase, where the effectiveness of external controls can be evaluated in the context of the new application.

If the design does specify new functionality to address the risk posed by a common threat, that functionality should be tested. The testing should follow the approach taken with the other types of requirements. The test cases should determine if the control works and if it is implemented as specified. The control's effectiveness will be targeted during penetration testing.

11.1.5 Information Confidentiality

While many different types of security controls help protect the confidentiality of information, such as access controls and data sanitization, the focus in this section is primarily on encryption.

Testing encryption during this phase includes verification that all the cryptographic components are implemented as specified. Test cases should include checks to ensure that the algorithm used is the one specified, that IVs are not reused, that keys are protected appropriately, and that the receipts are handled as specified.

Encryption tests should check the encryption performed by the application against a known-good implementation of the algorithm. These tests require that the same plaintext, key, and IV be used with the reference implementation. The resulting ciphertext should be identical to the ciphertext produced by the application.

The algorithm's reference implementation should be verified as well. This verification requires the use of test vectors. These are sets of data that contain the plaintext, the ciphertext, the key, and the initialization vector and are typically published along with the algorithm's specification. The test vector data should be encrypted and decrypted with the reference implementation, and the results should match the expected results.

11.1.6 Inspecting Instead of Testing

In some cases, it is very difficult to test specified functionality. For instance, determining whether data has been wiped from memory or if the use of known, weak APIs has been avoided are difficult to expose with tests.[2] To validate that the

---

2. *These things are difficult to test for in the limited amount of time typically available, but given enough time, they are certainly discoverable. If they weren't, they would not likely be the source of security issues.*

application meets these sorts of specifications, testing needs to rely on a mixture of manual and automated code inspections.

Inspections used for testing follow the same guidelines as when used during development. However, during the testing phase, individuals should take the time to use the inspection tools more thoroughly than is generally possible during development. In some cases this may allow the use of additional tools and techniques.

The goal is not to surprise development with the results from a "secret deep inspection weapon." Development should know what tools and settings will be used during testing so that they have the opportunity to discover and fix any deficiencies themselves. A prime advantage of this approach is that it helps developers identify any bad habits or misunderstandings early, before much code embodies the problem.

11.2 Penetration Testing

The goal of application penetration testing is to evaluate the effectiveness of the application's security. When penetration testing begins, functional testing has already verified that the specified controls are present and that they operate correctly (or, at least, the testing has identified any deficiencies). Penetration testing checks that those controls provide adequate protection.

Functional testing reveals flaws in the software: points where the specified functionality does not exist or does not behave as specified. A flaw, even in security functionality, may or may not be a vulnerability. Vulnerabilities are points in the application that are susceptible to manipulation beyond the specified behavior. Application penetration testing evaluates the application and any flaws to determine if vulnerabilities are present.

Vulnerabilities by themselves don't cause any harm. An exploit is an action or sequence of actions that take advantage of a vulnerability to cause harm. An attack occurs when someone attempts to apply an exploit to a piece of software. An attack is successful only if the exploit targets an actual vulnerability in the software.

In most cases, penetration testing goes so far as finding vulnerabilities but stops short of developing actual exploits for those vulnerabilities. Building exploit code takes time, and the penetration tester's time is best spent finding vulnerabilities. The mere existence of a vulnerability, even without live exploit code, should be enough to trigger an investigation into the source of the problem.

If there is reluctance to fix an issue, because few arguments are as persuasive as an actual exploit, it might make sense to devote time to building an exploit. But building an exploit is as much an art as a science. Just because a particular penetration tester (who is best at finding vulnerabilities) might be unable to construct an exploit for a vulnerability in the allotted time doesn't mean that the vulnerability can't be exploited.

Vulnerabilities should be treated as bugs. Every attempt should be made to fix the problem, even if an exploit is unavailable. However, when trade-offs must be made, perhaps due to schedule pressures, the potential damage and exploitability must be considered in prioritizing which vulnerabilities are fixed first.

In most cases, high-damage, easily exploitable vulnerabilities should have the highest priority, and those that lead to little damage and are difficult to exploit should have the lowest. The prioritization of vulnerabilities that are difficult to exploit yet carry a high risk of damage or flaws that are easy to exploit but won't cause a great deal of damage need to be evaluated on a case-by-case basis.

Application penetration testing typically begins with an analysis of the application to understand the attack surface and sensitive resources. Ideally, a threat model produced during the design stage is available. Otherwise, the penetration tester needs to take the time to acquire this knowledge independently.

Some organizations believe the use of a threat model or other "inside" knowledge invalidates the penetration test. Instead, these organizations often prefer "red teaming" the application, in which the penetration testing team has the same information an attacker would have.

The problem with this approach is twofold. First, while it is true that a threat model gives the penetration tester up-front knowledge that many attackers would not initially have, this helps balance the limited amount of time the tester has when compared to an actual attacker. A real attacker often has an extended amount of time to work on the application and effectively build his or her own threat model; a penetration tester might have a few weeks.

The second problem with the use of "red teams" is that many attacks, especially the more damaging ones, originate from insiders. Insiders often have extensive knowledge of the environment and may very well have access to detailed information about the application—perhaps even the application's threat model.

Relying just on red teams ignores the threat posed by knowledgeable attackers and is in danger of failing when, say, a malicious insider applies any effort. When building security, assume the worst. Cultivate paranoia, and presume a clever and knowledgeable attacker. If the application is secure under such conditions, it will still easily resist the more common, less taxing attacks.

When constructing a test plan, the penetration tester should also draw on any information produced from functional testing regarding unfixed flaws. These are likely to be the weakest links in the application's "security chain" and should be thoroughly investigated for vulnerabilities.

Once the preliminary information has been assembled, and test cases built, testing begins. The primary targets are the application's inputs and outputs, but other targets such as swap files, program memory, and covert channels may be examined as well. Communication between components is also fair game. Penetration testers also consider what effect chaining together several attacks might have. This helps discover those cases where individual attacks are not serious on their own, but when combined, the attacks become devastating.

Application penetration tests attempt to slip bad data past the input sanitization filters. They attempt to access resources by avoiding or fooling authentication and authorization checks. Network communication is examined for leaks and injection points. Application output, from error messages to the hidden comments on Web pages, is closely examined for any sensitive information. All text data is extracted from binaries. Debuggers and specialized tools are used to determine precisely what the application does. Most developers are amazed at the amount of information a skilled penetration tester can discover.

Once the penetration testers have assembled a listing of discovered vulnerabilities, the security analyst and customer should review it and verify the prioritization. Ideally, the analyst can match each vulnerability to a security pattern or a requirement that the developers can use as a reference when fixing the problem. Development, in turn, also reviews the vulnerability list and looks for any false positives, behavior that the penetration tests identified as vulnerable but that is entirely appropriate and secure, or vulnerabilities that are felt to be prioritized incorrectly due to other mitigating factors.

A useful tool for determining priority is the vulnerability matrix, as shown in Figure 11.1. This matrix ranks the degree of exploitability on the vertical axis and the amount to work to mitigate on the horizontal. Vulnerabilities are then drawn into this matrix as rectangles such that the height of the rectangle indicates the severity. Taller rectangles indicate more severe vulnerabilities. The severity ranking described for threats in section 9.3, "Threat Modeling," can be used as a basis.

Vulnerabilities in the first quadrant are easy to exploit and easy to fix, so it makes sense to fix them first. The fourth quadrant contains vulnerabilities that are difficult to fix, but at the same time difficult to exploit. In most cases, these are addressed last. Vulnerabilities in the second and third quadrants require more careful consideration. Just because a particular vulnerability is easily mitigated, it shouldn't be prioritized ahead of others that are more severe or more easily exploited. The letters in Figure 11.1 indicate a possible ordering, with A as the first vulnerability to be addressed, B the second, and so on.

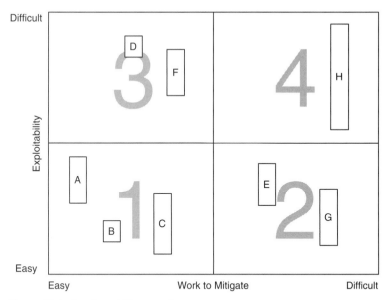

Figure 11.1: A vulnerability matrix

Once everyone has agreed to the prioritized list of vulnerabilities, they should be scheduled for mitigation. If the application must be released with remaining vulnerabilities, each vulnerability should be documented along with the potential impact of any exploits and the rationale for releasing despite the vulnerability. This documentation along with a vulnerability matrix should be closely reviewed by all the application's stakeholders to ensure that the risks are understood and accepted. Mitigating the remaining vulnerabilities should still be scheduled to occur after the initial release.

In the context of our cryptosystem, most application penetration tests should occur against the key manager, the consumer, and the key vault and engine. Even if a third-party HSM is used, it is still worthwhile to conduct penetration tests against it to ensure that it provides appropriate security. The tests should be made as an unauthenticated and unauthorized user, as well as an authenticated and authorized user. Even users allowed access to one key zone, for instance, may attempt to gain access to another zone.

11.3 Summary

Testing security is one of the most important steps in securing a system. Effective testing, though, relies on complete requirements and a thorough design. A deficiency in either of these will lead to missing or inappropriate tests. To paraphrase Robert Frost, testing without security requirements is like playing tennis without a net.

Security testing consists of two types functional testing and application penetration testing. Functional testing, as we saw, verifies that controls exist and that they operate as specified in the design and as mandated by the requirements. Application penetration testing verifies that those controls are effective. Both types of testing are necessary to build confidence in an application's security, and a threat model serves as an excellent source for prioritization of both types.

As a project's deadline approaches, the prioritized list of vulnerabilities should be presented to the customer. After the customer appreciates the risk each poses, the schedule or budget might be modified to ensure that the most severe, as determined by the customer, are fixed, while the remaining are placed in a plan for mitigation as soon as possible.

Chapter 12

Deployment, Defense, and Decommissioning

To paraphrase Paul Valery, "Software is never finished, only released." Most software released into production contains known defects and vulnerabilities. In the end, schedules prove less yielding than the desire for perfection, and a great deal of effort goes into making the software simply good enough to release.

This chapter discusses security considerations for released software. This includes deploying an application, defending it, and decommissioning it when it is no longer needed.

12.1 Deployment

Deployment covers all aspects of placing an application in a production environment where users have access. A deployment might be as simple as changing an existing application's configuration files or as complex as building new networks, servers, and applications. The goal of security during deployment is to ensure that the application that is released is identical to what was designed, programmed, and tested.

The deployment of a large application is a carefully choreographed dance involving dozens of persons in many roles. Build and network engineers, system and database administrators, project and application managers all play a role in most deployments. Some may be involved for a single, brief task, while others have tasks that take hours and are distributed throughout the deployment.

Given this complexity, a deployment is an ideal time for an insider to attempt to sneak malicious code into the release. An extra Java class or stored procedure or an altered version of existing code might go unnoticed. This code could easily offer backdoors into the system and allow the insider access to sensitive data and functionality.

At the heart of secure deployment, we again find separation of duties. The team that deploys an application into production should be separate from the design, programming, and testing staff. The process followed for deployment should at no point allow anyone who can declare code to be authentic to touch the deployed components without a system of checks and balances to verify the component's integrity.

This verification depends on cryptography in the form of hashes. The final versions of each component should be hashed by the programming team and included in the application's documentation (the application's defense plan is an ideal location). These hashes form part of an application's deployment profile, which also includes a list of all files and components and their deployed locations.

The deployment profile must be confirmed at each development phase. This confirmation includes checks that the hashes match and that no additional files or components are present and that none are missing. Quality assurance should check this periodically during testing and must conduct a final verification prior to approving the application for release.

The deployment profile must also be checked as part of the release process. Whomever performs the profile verification should not be involved with any other aspect of the release. At the very least, no component should be verified by the same individuals who deployed the component.

In some cases, a deployment auditor verifies the deployment's integrity. This auditor has no other role in the release and has only the least privileges needed to list and hash components. Often a member of the Information Security team is the deployment auditor.

Ensuring the integrity of deployed software is not the only role of security during a release. Configuring the newly deployed application so that it is in a secure state is a key task of the deployment team. This configuration, though, should already be documented as part of the release instructions, and the configuration should have been extensively tested during the testing phase. Every effort should be made to discover and fix configuration problems during testing. The deployment team should watch for any insecure or questionable configuration specifications but should not implement any untested or unspecified configurations.

Deploying a cryptographic application also requires setting up keys, and, in the architecture we've discussed, configuring the manifest. Generally, this is done by members of the Information Security team. However, in some cases, operations or deployment personnel have limited access to the key management application and can install new keys.

12.2 Defense

Once an application has been deployed, the operations team must defend it. Defending an application is a matter of constantly monitoring mostly innocuous security events, with occasional moments of swift response when an incident occurs.

To enable the operations staff to adequately defend an application, its designers should put together a defense plan. The defense plan describes the security events an application produces, outlines what constitutes an incident, and lists procedures for dealing with incidents.

A security event indicates that the application detected suspicious behavior. While some events are serious enough that they qualify as an incident without corroborating evidence, many other events are mundane and give rise to an incident only when they've been correlated with other events. For instance, a failed login attempt is a security event; a thousand failed logins for one account within a few minutes is an incident.

The first stage of defending an application is to ensure that the application itself is not altered. This requires monitoring, which checks the released application against the deployment profile. Any unexpected change, different hashes, and new or missing files should immediately generate an incident.

Ideally, security events from many applications and sources are fed to a centralized manager that can be configured with rules spanning several applications. This allows security events originating from a key store to be treated more seriously when followed quickly by events indicating suspicious database access.

Responding to incidents is a process of investigation, containment, eradication, and recovery. At the onset of an incident, the goal of investigation is to confirm the incident. Often incidents turn out to be false positives, and nothing further is required. Investigation is also necessary to monitor the incident's progression. Detection of an incident generally triggers additional scrutiny of the application's behavior, much like a security floodlight activates when it detects motion.

The additional scrutiny might take the form of turning on a more verbose level of logging or increasing the sensitivity of the monitoring rules. This could mean that additional rules come online or that the scope of standard rules is expanded.

The aim of this phase of investigation is to ensure the success of the other response stages by gathering all the relevant information for analysis.

Containing an incident keeps the damage from growing or spreading. At the most extreme, containment entails shutting down the system. Less extreme tactics could involve isolating the affected network or switching the application into a static mode where dynamic content is no longer processed and database connectivity is shut down or strictly limited. The application design should include functionality to enable containment, and because the defense plan is drafted during design, the plan can influence the containment strategy.

Once the incident is contained, the next step is to eradicate any remaining malicious activity. Eradication includes shutting down or blocking the source of the incident and killing unauthorized processes. The complexity of the eradication stage depends on the nature of the attack. A network-based attack might be eradicated simply by blocking the attacking machine. An attack that has managed to install a worm or virus might require significant effort to remove the malicious code from all the infected systems.

Recovery returns the system to its normal operating configuration. This stage begins with cleaning up any lingering artifacts from the incident, such as improper accounts or compromised code. A comprehensive recovery procedure might require that the system be rebuilt from the ground up to verify the integrity of all its components. Also during the recovery stage, monitoring and logging are reset to their normal degree of watchfulness.

Recovery should include mitigating the vulnerability that led to the incident. Because mitigation often requires a change that will take some time to implement and test, returning the application to operation while the fix is in development requires careful consideration of the risk. If the vulnerability is on an application accessible from the Internet, the risk is much higher than if the application is accessible only from within a corporate intranet. If the application must be operational prior to the fix, if possible you should consider turning off the vulnerable functionality. At the very least, extensive monitoring should remain in place to immediately detect further exploitation.

The defense plan should list, for each incident, appropriate investigation, containment, eradication, and recovery procedures. The plan should also provide a way for the response team to weigh the incident's relative severity so that the incident can be prioritized correctly. Because procedures are often reused, it is useful to develop a catalog of standard procedures. The defense plan can then indicate for each incident the appropriate procedure for each stage by referencing the standard.

The defense plan should be periodically tested both on paper and through mock incidents. In a paper test, the coordinator describes a scenario to the participants, who then indicate what they would do. All of this occurs verbally—no action is taken. The coordinator of the paper test might add unexpected twists to the scenario, but the goal of paper testing is to ensure that everyone on the response team is familiar with and understands the procedures.

A mock incident, on the other hand, is designed to test that the procedures are accurate. The mock incident is "hands-on" in that the participants act on the procedures. If an application is to be reconfigured, connectivity reduced, or firewalls given more restrictive rules, the response team enacts those changes within the test environment.

In extreme versions of mock incidents, actual attacks are launched against the test environment. These tests, which not only help ensure the accuracy of the procedures but also help measure their effectiveness, are also more difficult to coordinate, especially if the attack involves many machines acting in concert. Still, if such tests are practical in an environment, the feedback regarding the procedures' effectiveness is worth the effort.

Defending the cryptography of a database application is primarily a matter of defending the keys and the decryption routines.[1] Monitoring should cover calls to decryption routines, and incidents based on unexpected spikes should be investigated. The key vault should also be closely watched for unauthorized access and key manipulation.

A cross-application event manager can provide additional depth to the monitoring. Correlating decryption requests with authorized jobs and user requests helps highlight anomalous requests. Incidents arising from the installation of a new key followed by the launching of a key replacement job should be investigated to ensure that the replacement is legitimate.

12.3 Decommissioning

When an application is no longer needed, it is decommissioned, and any sensitive data must be removed from the hardware. Decommissioning ranges from simply reusing the hardware for a new application, to thoroughly erasing the media using a variety of techniques, to physically destroying the media. The precise methodology followed in a particular case depends on the data's sensitivity and the hardware's fate.

---

1. *This assumes that the cryptography was specified to protect the data's confidentiality.*

Hardware to be reused within the organization that held encrypted sensitive information might not require any special treatment. However, if that information were more sensitive, a regimen of erasure might be appropriate prior to reuse.

Erasing data securely involves much more than simply deleting files from the file system. Much like we discussed for wiping sensitive data from primary memory, securely erasing data from drives (also known as "purging") often involves writing zeroes or some other binary pattern across the entire disk. Some schemes specify several cycles of such overwriting, or require degaussing, subjecting the drive to a strong magnetic field.

The more thorough schemes should be seriously considered for any hardware destined to leave the organization. Once a drive has been sold or donated to a third party, it can be analyzed at leisure with a variety of sophisticated tools to recover any lingering data. For extremely sensitive data, the best course of action may very well be a thorough erasing, followed by degaussing, followed by destruction of the disk itself. The U.S. government has specified standards for data erasure, which can be found at [4] in the Bibliography.

12.4 Summary

Deployment, defense, and decommissioning are often overlooked in the rush to get an application out the door. Unfortunately, from a security perspective, an application needs the most attention during its operational life. Applications, like networks, should be monitored for intrusion or subversion attempts. While logging and alerting mechanisms are necessary, an adequately trained and sized monitoring staff is just as important and perhaps even more neglected in most organizations.

Bracketing the application's operational life, deployment and decommissioning may seem like unimportant and unexciting events, but as this chapter discussed, these periods are especially vulnerable to attack. An application's deployment must be carefully guarded to keep unauthorized code from contaminating the release. The checks that validate the deployment's authenticity should be carried out throughout the application's life. Decommissioning an application must include thoroughly erasing media that contained sensitive data.

PART IV

EXAMPLE CODE

Chapter 13

About the Examples

This part of the book provides practical implementations of the design and methodology presented earlier. The approach taken assumes that an organization that handles sensitive information has decided that a cryptographic infrastructure is warranted. The security goal is to protect the confidentiality of the information when it is at rest in the database. The threat model includes both external attackers and insiders with privileged access.

The next several chapters present detailed examples of the cryptographic infrastructure, along with the reasoning that led to the particular implementation. The examples begin with storing, tracking, and managing keys and then move outward to the engine, provider, and finally the consumer. Exceptions used in the examples are covered in their own chapter for ease of reference. Concluding the examples is a "demonstration" of the system at work.

The code is presented using version 1.4.2 of Java. Database structures are detailed in mostly vanilla SQL and were tested with MySQL. Translating the code to another language should be fairly straightforward. The cryptographic APIs may present some translation difficulties depending on the features of the library used, but even that should not be too strenuous because only basic features of the Java Cryptography Extension are used.

The Java code is developed in the `cryptodb` package and the `cryptodb.core` subpackage. The core package is like a virtual HSM in that unencrypted keys should never leave it. Bytes comprising keys are zeroed prior to execution returning to methods outside the core. The general rule is that any public method in the core package must zero keys in any object before the method returns.

While this rule is effective for key references embedded in core objects that eventually end up outside the core package, it does not protect key data that is never destined for delivery outside the core. To address this, the appropriate corollary to our first rule is to zero keys in any object that becomes dereferenced by the end of the method. If during the course of a method's execution key data is placed in an array and an active reference to that array is not maintained when the method completes, you need to zero that array before the method ends.

These practices help guard against key data remaining in memory even after the need has passed. Unfortunately, it does not guarantee that the key data is removed. It is possible that the actual engine has created a clone of the key data array for internal use. If this is the case, zeroing the array to which our reference points will not affect the clone. However, if the engine worked with the reference we passed to it and did not create a clone, because our reference and the engine's reference both point to the same array in memory, zeroing the array through our reference will effectively wipe the data from memory.

The examples prioritize clarity over performance and are meant to show how to implement the primary functionality of the various components discussed so far. Secondary functionality is glossed over. For instance, robust exception handling and logging are important and must be present in every production application. However, these examples do not present a production-quality exception handling system, and exceptions that would generally be handled and logged are simply ignored. Database tuning and multithreading are other examples of important topics the examples do not dwell on.

These examples convert binary data, such as encrypted data and keys, into hexadecimal strings and store those strings in the database. This is done for demonstration purposes so that it is easier for someone exploring the code to look at the binary data and see it change as different operations are conducted. In a production environment, raw binary data is typically used because it generally takes up less space in the database than an encoded representation. An example of working with raw binary data is included in the key encrypting key example.

13.1 Utilities and Common Services

This section covers the data conversions and database connectivity code that are used thoughout the system but are not part of any particular component. The data conversion code is housed in the `Utils` class. The `bytes2HexString` converts an array of bytes to a string containing the hexadecimal representation of those bytes. For instance, the byte array `{0x01,0x02}` becomes the string `0102`.

```
package cryptodb;

final public class Utils {

  public static String bytes2HexString(
    byte[] theBytes ) {
    // Note that input is not filtered or validated
    // because this method is simply used in this
    // demo code and would not be present in
    // production.
    StringBuffer hexString = new StringBuffer();
    String convertedByte = "";

    for ( int i = 0; i < theBytes.length; i++ ) {
      convertedByte =
        Integer.toHexString( theBytes[ i ]  );

      if ( convertedByte.length() < 2 ) {
        convertedByte =
          "00".substring( convertedByte.length() ) +
          convertedByte;
      }
      else if ( convertedByte.length() > 2 ) {
        convertedByte =
          convertedByte.substring(
            convertedByte.length() - 2 );
      }
      hexString.append(
        convertedByte.toUpperCase() );
    }
    return hexString.toString();
  }
```

The inverse is `hexString2Bytes`. It takes the hexadecimal string and converts it to an array of bytes: `0102` becomes the array `{0x01,0x02}`.

```
  public static byte[] hexString2Bytes(
    String hexString ) {
    // Note, again, that input is not filtered or
    // validated because this method is simply used
    // in this demo code and would not be present in
    // production.
    byte[] theBytes = new byte[ hexString.length()/2 ];

    byte leftHalf = 0x0;
    byte rightHalf = 0x0;
    for(int i = 0, j = 0;
        i < hexString.length()/2; i++, j=i*2 ) {
      rightHalf = (byte)(Byte.parseByte(
```

```
      hexString.substring(j+1,j+2), 16 ) &
        (byte)0xF);
    leftHalf  = (byte)((Byte.parseByte(
      hexString.substring(j,j+1), 16) << 4) &
        (byte)0xF0 );
    theBytes[i] = (byte)(leftHalf | rightHalf);
  }
  return theBytes;
  }
}
```

These utility methods are provided to help explore the system but would not likely be needed in most production environments. Because they are not critical, we won't spend any more time on these "throw-away" methods.

Database connections are a common need throughout the system, and the DbManager represents a simple way of getting a connection to the database whenever one is needed. The code is presented here for completeness, but database connectivity is not our subject, so we won't spend any more time discussing it. If you want more depth on Java's database support, [19] in the Bibliography is recommended. For information on Java and MySQL, refer to the MySQL site at [1].

```
package cryptodb;

import java.sql.*;

public class DbManager {

  static {
    try {
    String driver = "com.mysql.jdbc.Driver";
      Class.forName(driver).newInstance();
    }
    catch (ClassNotFoundException e) {
      // handle exceptions
    }
    catch (InstantiationException e) {
      // handle exceptions
    }
    catch (IllegalAccessException e) {
      // handle exceptions
    }
  }

  public static Connection getDbConnection() {
    Connection conn = null;
    try {
      // The hardcoded password is only used
```

```
    // for demonstration. Hardcoded passwords
    // should never be used in production
    // apps.
    conn = DriverManager.getConnection(
      "jdbc:mysql://localhost/cryptodb?" +
      "user=cryptusr&password=password");
  }
  catch (SQLException ex) {
    // handle exceptions
  }
  return conn;
  }
}
```

The examples in this book use a single database, but in a production system, at least two databases would be used. The first database would be the business database and would store the encrypted business data. The other database (or repository) would be part of the key vault and would hold the actual keys. If an HSM is in use, this other database would be embedded within it. Otherwise, the database should reside on its own highly restricted server.

13.2 The Example Engine and Key Vault

The design presented in this book favors HSMs because keys locked in HSMs are generally much more secure than keys located on the application server that processes user input. However, as of Java 1.4.2, there is not a standard Java interface for working with HSMs. Rather than limit the examples to a proprietary interface, we'll instead use a local engine: the AES support that comes bundled with Java 1.4.2.

Because we won't be using an HSM, we'll implement our own key vault to go along with our local engine. Our key vault, as written, is a key store in that it resides on the same hardware as the engine. However, the addition of some network code and an appropriate security model could turn the example key store into a key server.

Java supports a "KeyStore" as part of its security package. The default, file-based implementation isn't suitable for our needs because its support for symmetric keys and a remote key manager is weak. It is possible to build a custom KeyStore class that would use our database key store, but such a solution would be very Java-specific, while the code presented is more generic and easier to translate into another language.

Using a local engine and key store is also likely to prove more practical for a great many organizations that do not want to deal with the additional burden and expense of operating and maintaining a set of HSMs. The design and example code are modular enough so that when the situation does warrant an HSM, it will be relatively simple to plug in the new engine.

If you don't want to use an HSM, the next chapter won't be terribly relevant. Chapter 17, "The Engine," though, does contain general information about interfacing with an HSM. The specifics of the key management chapter will change with the use of an HSM, but the general functionality should, for the most part, remain the same. Refer to the HSM's documentation, though, for information on how to best use the hardware.

13.3 Summary

While the examples in the following chapters rely on the utility functions presented in this chapter, these functions are not covered in detail because their direct relevance to the topic of database cryptography is limited. The guidelines surrounding how keys must never leave the core "virtual HSM" are pursued throughout the examples. Finally, the reasoning behind the presentation of a local engine and key store is discussed. Perhaps a future addendum might cover a standard HSM API (plans for Java 1.5 include support for PKCS 11), but for now our examples don't cover HSMs.

Chapter 14

A Key Vault

As mentioned in the previous chapter, our key vault is a key store used to supply keys to the local engine. More specifically, the local key store is a table in a database. The key database should be dedicated to cryptography, and access to it should be severly restricted. The table is kept to bare essentials in this example, but it could contain other information, such as the engine to which a key is dedicated or handling specifications, if needed.

```
CREATE TABLE local_key_store
(
  key_id     INTEGER PRIMARY KEY AUTO_INCREMENT,
  key_data   VARCHAR(32),
  kek_id     INTEGER
);
```

The `key_id` is the primary key we'll use to identify keys in the key store. The encrypted bits of the key are placed in the `key_data` column. The keys in the key store are encrypted with a key-encrypting key, and the `kek_id` column indicates which key was used to encrypt the key.

The key encrypting keys are stored in another table. These keys are stored in a `TINYBLOB` column. This binary column is the one example in the book in which the raw bytes of the key are stored. Compare the `key_data` column in the `key_encrypting_keys` table with the `key_data` column in the `local_key_store` table. In the latter table, the key is stored as a hexadecimal string.

```
CREATE TABLE key_encrypting_keys
(
  kek_id            INTEGER PRIMARY KEY AUTO_INCREMENT,
  key_data          TINYBLOB NOT NULL,
  activation_date   DATETIME NOT NULL
);
```

The `activation_date` column determines when a key encrypting key becomes Live and available for use. Keys are always encrypted with the Live key-encrypting key, and the key-encrypting key that has the most recent activation date is the Live key. The state model for the key-encrypting key is a simplified version of the model discussed for regular keys. There is only one Live key-encrypting key, and every key is encrypted with it.

14.1 The Local Key

The `LocalKey` class represents a cryptographic key for protecting business data (as opposed to other keys). It resides in the core package and contains a variety of information regarding the key, including the actual key, its encrypted version, and the key-encrypting key.

```
package cryptodb.core;

import cryptodb.*;
import java.security.*;
import javax.crypto.*;
import javax.crypto.spec.*;
import java.sql.*;

final public class LocalKey {
  private String keyData = null; // encrypted key
  private byte[] kek = null; // key encrypting key
  private String keyId = null; // encrypted key id
  private String kekId = null; // key encrypting key id
  private byte[] rawKey = null; // unencrypted key

  public LocalKey( String keyId,
                   String keyData,
                   byte[] kek ) {
    this.keyId = keyId;
    this.keyData = keyData;
    this.kek = kek;
  }

  public LocalKey() {
  }
```

Once a `LocalKey` has been created, it can be used for encryption and decryption. Internally, though, any cryptographic operation with the key requires that we first decrypt the key.

Decrypting the key requires that we create a `SecretKeySpec` from the key-encrypting key. A cipher object does the actual cryptographic operations. We specify that we want it to use the AES algorithm in ECB mode and no padding. Using ECB mode in this case is fine because we are working with other keys that are essentially random bits. We also don't need padding because the keys are exactly 128 bits long.

After the cipher has been initialized to perform decryptions with the SecretKeySpec of the key-encrypting key, the key is finally decrypted. The method getKeyBytes simply returns a byte array containing the encrypted key. It's detailed further next with the rest of this class's accessors. The decryptKey method returns with a byte array containing the decrypted key.

```
final private byte[] decryptKey() {
  SecretKeySpec key = null;
  try {

    SecretKeySpec kekSpec
      = new SecretKeySpec( kek, "AES" );
    Cipher cipher =
      Cipher.getInstance("AES/ECB/NoPadding");
    cipher.init(Cipher.DECRYPT_MODE, kekSpec );
    rawKey = cipher.doFinal( getKeyBytes() );
  }
  catch (NoSuchAlgorithmException nsae) {
    System.out.println( "Algorithm not found." );
  }
  catch (NoSuchPaddingException nspe ) {
    System.out.println( nspe );
  }
  catch ( InvalidKeyException ike ) {
    System.out.println( ike );
  }
  catch ( IllegalBlockSizeException ibse ) {
    System.out.println( ibse );
  }
  catch ( BadPaddingException bpe ) {
    System.out.println( bpe );
  }
  return rawKey;
}
```

As shown, a SecretKeySpec is necessary to initialize cipher objects. The getSecretKeySpec method is a convenience method allowing the LocalKey to return a SecretKeySpec version of itself. This method has package scope, so other objects in the core can invoke getSecretKeySpec, but the method cannot be invoked outside the core.

```
final SecretKeySpec getSecretKeySpec() {
  byte[] rawKey = decryptKey();
  SecretKeySpec key = new SecretKeySpec(rawKey, "AES");
  return key;
}
```

As soon as a `LocalKey` object is no longer needed for cryptographic operations, the actual key bytes within it need to be zeroed. These methods allow the data key, the key-encrypting key, or both to be wiped.

```
final public void wipe() {
  wipeRawKey();
  wipeKek();
}

final public void wipeRawKey() {
  if (rawKey != null) {
    for (int i = 0; i < rawKey.length; i++) {
      rawKey[i] = (byte)0x00;
    }
  }
  rawKey = null;
}

final public void wipeKek() {
  if (kek != null) {
    for (int i = 0; i < kek.length; i++) {
      kek[i] = (byte)0x00;
    }
  }
  kek = null;
}
```

The following methods are accessors to the class's private variables. Most of the accessors are public, with the exception of those that handle the unencrypted key. Because the unencrypted key should exist only in the core, we limit access to within the core package.

```
final public void setKeyData( String key ) {
  this.keyData = key;
}
final public byte[] getKeyBytes() {
  return Utils.hex2ByteArray( keyData );
}
final public String getKeyData() {
  return keyData;
}
```

```
  final public void setKekId( String kekId ) {
    this.kekId = kekId;
  }
  final public String getKekId() {
    return kekId;
  }
  final public void setKeyId( String keyId ) {
    this.keyId = keyId;
  }
  final public String getKeyId() {
    return keyId;
  }
  final void setRawKey( byte[] rawKey ) {
    this.rawKey = rawKey;
  }
  final byte[] getRawKey() {
    return keyData == null ? rawKey : decryptKey();
  }
}
```

This discussion, particularly the key decryption example, assumes that the LocalKey object has already been created and populated. The LocalKeyStore handles the interactions with the key store database and creates populated LocalKey objects.

14.2 Local Key Store

The LocalKeyStore class represents the key store and provides the functionality necessary for the key store to function. Like the LocalKey, this class is located in the core package.

```
package cryptodb.core;

import cryptodb.*;
import java.security.*;
import javax.crypto.*;
import javax.crypto.spec.*;
import java.sql.*;
import java.util.ArrayList;
import java.util.Iterator;

final public class LocalKeyStore {
```

14.2.1 Generating a Key–Encrypting Key

Generating a new key-encrypting key is done through the `generateNewKek`
method. It takes no arguments and returns the ID of the newly created
key-encrypting key. This is a public method, so it can be invoked by objects
outside the core when it is necessary to create a new key-encrypting key.

```java
final public String generateNewKek() {
  byte[] rawKey = new byte[16];
  String kekId = null;
  PreparedStatement pstmt = null;

  try {
```

A `SHA1PRNG` secure random-number generator is used to generate the
key-encrypting key. The `rawKey` array ends up containing 128 pseudo-random bits.

```java
    SecureRandom kekGenerator =
      SecureRandom.getInstance( "SHA1PRNG" );
    kekGenerator.nextBytes( rawKey );
```

The newly generated key-encrypting key is inserted into the database, and the
automatically generated ID is returned into `kekId`. The key's activation date is set
to the current time. Whenever a key-encrypting key is created, it becomes available
for use immediately. Any older key-encrypting keys are still available for
decryption, but they aren't used to encrypt new keys.

```java
    String sqlStmt =
      "INSERT INTO key_encrypting_keys " +
      "values ( NULL, ?, now() )" ;

    Connection conn = DbManager.getDbConnection();
    pstmt = conn.prepareStatement(sqlStmt,
      Statement.RETURN_GENERATED_KEYS);
    pstmt.setBytes( 1, rawKey );
    int rows = pstmt.executeUpdate();
    ResultSet rs = pstmt.getGeneratedKeys();
    if (rs.next()) {
      kekId = rs.getString( 1 );
    }
  }
  catch (NoSuchAlgorithmException e) {
    System.out.println( e );
  }
  catch (SQLException e) {
    System.out.println( e );
  }
```

After any exceptions are caught, we close resources. Then, because this is a public method, we overwrite the raw key with zero bytes. Finally, we return the key-encrypting key ID to the method's caller.

```
finally {
  if (pstmt != null) {
    try {
      pstmt.close();
    }
    catch (SQLException sqlEx) {
      // ignore
    }
    pstmt = null;
  }
  if (rawKey != null) {
    for (int i = 0; i < rawKey.length; i++) {
      rawKey[i] = (byte)0x00;
    }
  }
}
return kekId;
}
```

When the method finishes, the newly created key-encrypting key has been written to the `key_encrypting_keys` table in binary form.

We can check that the key-encrypting key exists:

```
mysql> select count(*) from key_encrypting_keys;
+----------+
| count(*) |
+----------+
|        1 |
+----------+
1 row in set (0.00 sec)
```

The key-encrypting keys are not themselves encrypted. Because they exist only to obfuscate the actual keys and are also stored within the restricted key store database, the risk is somewhat mitigated. However, we could certainly increase security by splitting the key-encrypting key and storing one half in the table and the other half on the file system. In a production system, this would be a worthwhile control. For our example, though, we'll stick to existing controls and recognize that an HSM still provides the best protection for the keys.

14.2.2 Generating a Key in the Local Key Store

Now that we can encrypt a key with a key-encrypting key, we need a way to create an actual data key, a key that will be used to encrypt business data. The generateKey method creates such a key. It takes no parameters and returns a LocalKey object containing the key ID, the encrypted key, and the ID of the key-encrypting key used to encrypt the key. In short, the returned LocalKey object contains everything needed to be used immediately.

The following code generates the key using the SHA1PRNG technique we saw earlier. Much of the actual work of creating and preparing the LocalKey object is done by the encryptKey and saveKey methods. Because this is a public method, we zero any unencrypted key data in the LocalKey object prior to returning.

```
final public LocalKey generateKey() {
  LocalKey localKey = new LocalKey();
  byte[] rawKey = new byte[16];
  try {
    SecureRandom ivGenerator =
      SecureRandom.getInstance( "SHA1PRNG" );
    ivGenerator.nextBytes( rawKey );
    localKey.setRawKey( rawKey );
  }
  catch (NoSuchAlgorithmException e) {
    System.out.println( e );
  }
  encryptKey( localKey );
  saveKey( localKey );
  localKey.wipe();
  return localKey;
}
```

14.2.3 Encrypting a Key

The encryptKey method takes a LocalKey object containing an unencrypted key and encrypts it using the current key-encrypting key. The LocalKey object is then updated with the encrypted key and the ID of the key-encrypting key.

```
final private void encryptKey( LocalKey localKey ) {
  PreparedStatement pstmt = null;
  ResultSet rs = null;

  byte[] encryptedKey = null;
```

The query used to retrieve the key-encrypting key from the key store selects all the key-encrypting keys and then sorts them by activation date, with the newest at the top. It then simply grabs the top key considering it is the current live key-encrypting key (there are no Pending keys given the code to create the keys activates them immediately).

```
try {
  String query =
    "SELECT * " +
    "FROM   key_encrypting_keys " +
    "WHERE  activation_date <= now() " +
    "ORDER BY activation_date DESC";

  Connection conn = DbManager.getDbConnection();
  pstmt = conn.prepareStatement(query);
  rs = pstmt.executeQuery();

  byte[] keyData = null;
  if (rs.next()) {
    keyData = rs.getBytes( "key_data" );
    localKey.setKekId(
      rs.getString( "kek_id" ) );
  }
  else {
    System.out.println(
      "KeyEncryptingKeyNotFoundException" );
  }
```

The encryption code follows the same pattern we saw earlier in the decryption example. The primary difference here is that the Cipher object is initialized for encryption. Note that the encrypted key is formatted as a hexadecimal string. In a production system, the key would remain an array of bytes, but we use the hexadecimal string here to allow easy inspection of the contents of the database tables while gaining familiarity with the system.

Just before the method returns, we zero the sensitive key data. First we call wipe in the LocalKey object to delete the business data key. Next, we manually wipe the byte array containing the key-encrypting key.

This manual zeroing represents a bit of asymmetry between the encrypt and decrypt methods for keys. When decrypting the key, we use the wipe method in the LocalKey class to zero both byte arrays. The difference, though, is that when decrypting, the code is operating on a populated LocalKey object that was produced by a LocalKeyStore. As we'll see later in this chapter, the LocalKeyStore writes the key-encrypting key into the LocalKey. So wipe affects both arrays after a decryption operation.

When encrypting the key, though, the LocalKey object is not populated with the key-encrypting key. References to the array exist only within the encryptKey method, so calls to the wipe method of LocalKey do not affect it. Hence, we must manually zero the array that contains the key-encrypting key.

```
      SecretKeySpec kekSpec =
        new SecretKeySpec(keyData, "AES" );
      Cipher cipher =
        Cipher.getInstance("AES/ECB/NoPadding");
      cipher.init(Cipher.ENCRYPT_MODE, kekSpec);
      encryptedKey =
        cipher.doFinal( localKey.getRawKey() );
      localKey.setKeyData(
        Utils.bytes2HexString(encryptedKey,""));
    }
    catch (SQLException ex) {
      // handle any errors
      System.out.println(e);
    }
    catch (NoSuchAlgorithmException nsae) {
      System.out.println( "Algorithm not found." );
    }
    catch (NoSuchPaddingException nspe ) {
      System.out.println( nspe );
    }
    catch ( InvalidKeyException ike ) {
      System.out.println( ike );
    }
    catch ( IllegalBlockSizeException ibse ) {
      System.out.println( ibse );
    }
    catch ( BadPaddingException bpe ) {
      System.out.println( bpe );
    }
    finally {
      if (rs != null) {
        try {
          rs.close();
        }
        catch (SQLException sqlEx) {
          // ignore
        }
        rs = null;
      }
      if (pstmt != null) {
        try {
          pstmt.close();
        }
```

```
      catch (SQLException sqlEx) {
        // ignore
      }
      pstmt = null;
    }
    localKey.wipe();
    if (keyData != null) {
      for (int i = 0; i < keyData.length; i++) {
        keyData[i] = (byte)0x00;
      }
    }
    keyData = null;
  }
}
```

14.2.4 Saving a Key to the Key Store

After the key has been encrypted, we must save it to the key store. The database
assigns the new key an ID, which is returned to our code and placed in the
LocalKey object.

```
final private void saveKey( LocalKey localKey ) {
  PreparedStatement pstmt = null;
  ResultSet rs = null;
  try {
    String sqlStmt =
      "INSERT INTO local_key_store " +
      "values ( NULL, ?, ? )" ;

    Connection conn = DbManager.getDbConnection();
    pstmt = conn.prepareStatement(sqlStmt,
        Statement.RETURN_GENERATED_KEYS);
    pstmt.setString( 1, localKey.getKeyData() );
    pstmt.setString( 2, localKey.getKekId() );
    int rows = pstmt.executeUpdate();
    rs = pstmt.getGeneratedKeys();
    String keyId = null;
    if (rs.next()) {
      keyId = rs.getString( 1 );
    }
    localKey.setKeyId( keyId );

  }
  catch (SQLException e) {
    // handle any errors
    System.out.println(e);
  }
```

```
finally {
  if (rs != null) {
    try {
      rs.close();
    }
    catch (SQLException sqlEx) {
      // ignore
    }
    rs = null;
  }
  if (pstmt != null) {
    try {
      pstmt.close();
    }
    catch (SQLException sqlEx) {
      // ignore
    }
    pstmt = null;
  }
}
}
```

14.2.5 Replacing the Key-Encrypting Key

At this point we can generate a key-encrypting key, and we can generate a data key that will be encrypted with the key-encrypting key and placed in the key store. To be useful, though, we must be able to replace the key-encrypting key either as part of a periodic key replacement schedule or because of a key compromise.

Replacing a key-encrypting key is a matter of decrypting all the keys encrypted with the old key-encrypting key and re-encrypting them with a new key-encrypting key. The replaceKek method takes the ID of the new key-encrypting key as a parameter and then carries out the re-encryption.

```
final public void replaceKek( String newKekId ) {
  LocalKey key = null;
  String keyString = null;
  String keyId = null;
  byte[] kekBytes = null;
  PreparedStatement pstmt = null;
  ResultSet rs = null;
  ArrayList keys = new ArrayList();
  try {
    String query =
      "SELECT * " +
      "FROM   local_key_store lks, " +
      "       key_encrypting_keys kek " +
      "WHERE  lks.kek_id = kek.kek_id";
```

```
Connection conn = DbManager.getDbConnection();
pstmt = conn.prepareStatement(query);
rs = pstmt.executeQuery();

while (rs.next()) {
  keyId = rs.getString( "lks.key_id" );
  keyString = rs.getString( "lks.key_data" );
  kekBytes = rs.getBytes( "kek.key_data" );

  key = new LocalKey( keyId,
                      keyString,
                      kekBytes );
  keys.add( key );
}
```

The `keys` object contains a list of all the `LocalKeys` in the key store, each with its respective key-encrypting key. The following `Iterator` cycles through each of these, decrypting, re-encrypting, saving, and then zeroing the key data from memory. Should an exception be thrown, the `Iterator` in the `finally` clause ensures that the key data is still safely zeroed.

```
Iterator iterator = keys.iterator();
while( iterator.hasNext() ) {
  key = (LocalKey)iterator.next();
  key.setRawKey( key.getRawKey() );
  encryptKey( key );
  updateKey( key );
  key.wipe();
}
keys = null;
}
catch (SQLException e) {
  // handle any errors
  System.out.println(e);
}
finally {
  if (rs != null) {
    try {
        rs.close();
    }
    catch (SQLException sqlEx) {
      // ignore
    }
    rs = null;
  }
  if (pstmt != null) {
    try {
      pstmt.close();
```

```
      }
      catch (SQLException sqlEx) {
        // ignore
      }
      pstmt = null;
    }
    if (keys != null) {
      Iterator iterator = keys.iterator();
      while( iterator.hasNext() ) {
        key = (LocalKey)iterator.next();
        key.wipe();
      }
    }
  }
}
```

The replaceKek method uses updateKey to save the newly encrypted key back to the database. This method takes a key already in the key store and updates it with its new encrypted representation and the ID of the key-encrypting key used.

```
final private void updateKey( LocalKey localKey ) {
  PreparedStatement pstmt = null;
  try {

    String sqlStmt =
      "UPDATE local_key_store " +
      "SET    key_data = ?, " +
      "       kek_id = ?"  +
      "WHERE  key_id = ?";

    Connection conn = DbManager.getDbConnection();
    pstmt = conn.prepareStatement(sqlStmt);
    pstmt.setString( 1, localKey.getKeyData() );
    pstmt.setString( 2, localKey.getKekId() );
    pstmt.setString( 3, localKey.getKeyId() );
    int rows = pstmt.executeUpdate();
  }
  catch (SQLException e) {
    // handle any errors
    System.out.println(e);
  }
  finally {
    if (pstmt != null) {
      try {
        pstmt.close();
      }
```

```
      catch (SQLException sqlEx) {
        // ignore
      }
      pstmt = null;
    }
  }
}
}
```

14.3 Accessing a Local Key

Finally, we look at how a `LocalKey` is retrieved from the key store. The `getLocalKey` method simply reads the necessary data from the key store tables and populates a `LocalKey` object with that information.

```
final LocalKey getLocalKey( String keyId )
throws KeyNotFoundException {
  LocalKey key = null;
  String keyString = null;
  byte[] kekBytes = null;
  PreparedStatement pstmt = null;
  ResultSet rs = null;

  try {
    String query = "SELECT * " +
              "FROM  local_key_store lks, " +
              "     key_encrypting_keys kek " +
              "WHERE  lks.key_id = ? " +
              "AND    lks.kek_id = kek.kek_id";

    Connection conn = DbManager.getDbConnection();
    pstmt = conn.prepareStatement(query);
    pstmt.setString( 1, keyId );
    rs = pstmt.executeQuery();

    if (rs.next()) {
      keyString = rs.getString( "lks.key_data" );
      kekBytes = rs.getBytes( "kek.key_data" );
    }

    if ( keyString == null ) {
      KeyNotFoundException e =
  new KeyNotFoundException( keyId, "LocalAES" );
      throw e;
    }
```

```
        key = new LocalKey( keyId,
                      keyString,
                      kekBytes );
      }
      catch (SQLException ex) {
        // handle any errors
        System.out.println("SQLException: " + ex.getMessage());
        System.out.println("SQLState: " + ex.getSQLState());
        System.out.println("VendorError: " + ex.getErrorCode());
      }
      finally {
        if (rs != null) {
          try {
            rs.close();
          }
          catch (SQLException sqlEx) {
            // ignore
          }
          rs = null;
        }
        if (pstmt != null) {
          try {
            pstmt.close();
          }
          catch (SQLException sqlEx) {
            // ignore
          }
          pstmt = null;
        }
      }
      return key;
    }
```

14.4 Summary

This implementation of a key vault consists of two classes: `LocalKey` and
`LocalKeyStore`. A `LocalKey` object contains the actual cryptographic key and
provides a variety of methods to access and manipulate data members. One of the
most important methods in the class is `wipe`, which zeroes the key material in
memory. `LocalKeyStore` manages the key material stored in the key store
database table. It provides methods to generate and save new keys in the store as
well as encrypt them with a key-encrypting key.

As mentioned earlier, the `LocalKeyStore` class presented here could be rewritten as a `java.security.KeyStoreSpi` subclass and extended to allow management across the network. This is nontrivial and is beyond the scope of this book. However, for an organization already relying on Java's security mechanisms for JAR signing, it might be worthwhile to integrate the database encryption key store into an existing enterprise-wide key management infrastructure. See [15] in the Bibliography for a discussion of such a key management scheme.

Chapter 15

The Manifest

We now leave the keys in the `core` package and examine the manifest, which resides in the base `cryptodb` package. The database table that holds the manifest information should be located somewhere other than in the database that holds the key store. A likely place for the manifest is the database that holds the business data.

The `key_manifest` table is as follows:

```
CREATE TABLE key_manifest
(
    alias_id             INTEGER        NOT NULL PRIMARY KEY
                                            AUTO_INCREMENT,
    key_alias            VARCHAR(30)    NOT NULL,
    key_family           VARCHAR(30)    NOT NULL,
    engine               VARCHAR(30)    NOT NULL,
    key_id               VARCHAR(30)    NOT NULL,
    key_activation_date  DATETIME       NOT NULL,
    status               VARCHAR(30)    NOT NULL
);
```

These fields are described in Chapter 5 "Keys: Vaults, Manifests, and Managers." Each row in the table represents a key alias, and a key alias is used by two different components. The provider only reads the alias from the manifest, and the key manager has full read and write access.

15.1 The Key Alias

The `KeyAlias` class represents a key alias. As you can see, the class contains the definitive flags for key states, along with internal variables to hold the manifest attributes.

The constructor takes the ID of the alias and then retrieves the alias attributes from the manifest table through the populate method.

```
package cryptodb;

import java.sql.*;
import java.util.Calendar;

public class KeyAlias {
  public static final String TERMINATED = "TERMINATED";
  public static final String RETIRED   = "RETIRED";
  public static final String ACTIVE    = "ACTIVE";
  public static final String PENDING   = "PENDING";
  public static final String EXPIRED   = "EXPIRED";
  public static final String LIVE      = "LIVE";

  private boolean changed = false;

  private String aliasId   = null;
  private String keyAlias  = null;
  private String keyFamily = null;
  private String engine    = null;
  private String keyId     = null;
  private Timestamp activationDate = null;
  private String status    = null;

  public KeyAlias( String aliasId ) {
   this.aliasId = aliasId;
   populate();
  }
```

A portion of the class is devoted to accessor methods for the various manifest attributes. Each of the "set" methods also trips the changed flag. This flag is used to ensure that when the key state is calculated, the alias is synchronized with the manifest. We'll look at this more closely when we examine the getKeyState method.

```
  public final String getAliasId() {
    return aliasId;
  }
  final void setKeyAlias( String alias ) {
    this.keyAlias = alias;
    changed = true;
  }
  final String getKeyAlias() {
    return keyAlias;
  }
```

```
final void setKeyFamily( String family ) {
  this.keyFamily = family;
  changed = true;
}
final String getKeyFamily() {
  return keyFamily;
}
final void setEngine( String engine ) {
  this.engine = engine;
  changed = true;
}
public final String getEngine() {
  return engine;
}
final void setKeyId( String keyId ) {
  this.keyId = keyId;
  changed = true;
}
public final String getKeyId() {
  return keyId;
}
final void setActivationDate( Timestamp when ) {
  this.activationDate = when;
  changed = true;
}
final Timestamp getActivationDate() {
  return activationDate;
}
final String getStatus() {
  return status;
}
```

The method to set the status is private because setting it arbitrarily can break the state model. Only other methods in this class, which enforce the state model, can set the status. Because status should only be set to ACTIVE, RETIRED, or TERMINATED, and keys are created in the ACTIVE status, these other methods allow the key to be retired or terminated. Each of these methods checks the current state before updating the status. Only an Expired key can become retired, and only a Pending or Retired key can be terminated.

```
private void setStatus( String status ) {
  this.status = status;
  changed = true;
}
final void retireKey()
throws InvalidKeyStateException {
  if ( getKeyState().equals( KeyAlias.EXPIRED )) {
    status = KeyAlias.RETIRED;
```

```
      changed = true;
    }
    else {
      throw (new InvalidKeyStateException(
        "Only expired keys can be retired." ));
    }
  }

  final void terminateKey()
  throws InvalidKeyStateException {
    if ( getKeyState().equals( KeyAlias.PENDING ) ||
         getKeyState().equals( KeyAlias.RETIRED ) ) {
      status = KeyAlias.TERMINATED;
      changed = true;
    }
    else {
      throw (new InvalidKeyStateException(
        "Only pending or retired" +
        " keys can be terminated" ));
    }
  }
}
```

15.1.1 Creating a New Key Alias

A new alias is created with a call to `getNewAlias`. This static method takes the information necessary to create an alias as parameters and then writes the alias to the manifest and returns the ID of the newly created manifest entry.

Note that the date is set as a value that indicates the number of days from now until the key becomes Live. Should we need a key to become Live immediately, we can set this value to zero. We don't want keys to be created in the past, so we explicitly disallow negative values.

```
static KeyAlias getNewAlias( String alias,
String engine, String family, String days_pending,
String vaultKeyId)
throws AliasException {

  try {
    int days = Integer.parseInt(days_pending);
    if (days < 0) {
      throw (new AliasException( "Date in the past." ));
    }
  }
  catch (NumberFormatException e) {
    System.out.println( e );
  }
```

```
String aliasId = null;
PreparedStatement pstmt = null;
ResultSet rs = null;
try {
  // Create manifest entry next.
  String query =
    "INSERT INTO key_manifest " +
    "VALUES ( " +
      "NULL,?,?,?,?," +
      "DATE_ADD(NOW(), INTERVAL ? DAY)," +
      "'ACTIVE')";

  Connection conn = DbManager.getDbConnection();
  pstmt = conn.prepareStatement(query,
    Statement.RETURN_GENERATED_KEYS);
  pstmt.setString( 1, alias );
  pstmt.setString( 2, family );
  pstmt.setString( 3, engine );
  pstmt.setString( 4, vaultKeyId );
  pstmt.setString( 5, days_pending );
  int rows = pstmt.executeUpdate();
  rs = pstmt.getGeneratedKeys();
  aliasId = null;
  if (rs.next()) {
    aliasId = rs.getString( 1 );
  }
}
catch (SQLException e) {
  System.out.println(e);
}
finally {
  if (rs != null) {
    try {
     rs.close();
    }
    catch (SQLException sqlEx) {
     // ignore
    }
    rs = null;
  }
  if (pstmt != null) {
    try {
      pstmt.close();
    }
    catch (SQLException sqlEx) {
      // ignore
    }
    pstmt = null;
  }
```

```
  }

  KeyAlias newAlias = new KeyAlias( aliasId );
  newAlias.populate();
  return newAlias;
}
```

15.1.2 Reading a Key Alias from the Manifest

The populate method does the work of reading the alias from the database. When this call completes, the KeyAlias object contains an accurate representation of what is in the manifest. This method is the only way to keep the KeyAlias up to date with what is in the manifest. The longer a particular KeyAlias object is used, the greater the chance that a change to the manifest or the simple progression of time will cause a change to some attribute or state of the alias. Because of this, if a system keeps a particular key alias around for an extended period of time, perhaps to limit the number of calls to the database, it should periodically call populate.

```
final void populate() {
  PreparedStatement pstmt = null;
  ResultSet rs = null;
  try {
    String query =
      "SELECT * " +
      "FROM   key_manifest " +
      "WHERE  alias_id = ? ";

    Connection conn = DbManager.getDbConnection();
    pstmt = conn.prepareStatement(query);
    pstmt.setString( 1, aliasId );
    rs = pstmt.executeQuery();

    if (rs.next()) {
      setKeyAlias( rs.getString( "key_alias" ) );
      setKeyFamily( rs.getString( "key_family" ) );
      setEngine( rs.getString( "engine" ) );
      setKeyId( rs.getString( "key_id" ) );
      setActivationDate(
        rs.getTimestamp( "key_activation_date" ) );
      setStatus( rs.getString( "status" ) );
    }
```

The changed flag is set to indicate that given this alias was just read from the database, no changes have been made.

```
    changed = false;
  }
```

```
    catch (SQLException e) {
      // handle any errors
      System.out.println(e);
    }
    finally {
      if (rs != null) {
        try {
            rs.close();
        }
        catch (SQLException sqlEx) {
          // ignore
        }
        rs = null;
      }
      if (pstmt != null) {
        try {
          pstmt.close();
        }
        catch (SQLException sqlEx) {
          // ignore
        }
        pstmt = null;
      }
    }
  }
}
```

15.1.3 Reading the Current Live Key

This method, `getLiveKeyAlias`, retrieves the current Live key for the given key family. The query that selects the Live key generates a list of all keys in the given family with a status of ACTIVE and an activation date in the past. It then orders that list from the most recent activation date at the top to the oldest at the bottom. The Live key is the key at the top of the list.

```
public static KeyAlias getLiveKeyAlias(String keyFamily)
throws LiveKeyNotFoundException {

  KeyAlias alias = null;
  PreparedStatement pstmt = null;
  ResultSet rs = null;

  try {
    Connection conn = DbManager.getDbConnection();
    pstmt = conn.prepareStatement(
      "SELECT * "             +
      "FROM   key_manifest " +
      "WHERE  status = 'ACTIVE' " +
      "AND    key_activation_date <= now() " +
```

```
        "AND    key_family = ? " +
        "ORDER BY key_activation_date DESC");
      pstmt.setString( 1, keyFamily );
      rs = pstmt.executeQuery();

      if (rs.next()) {
        String aliasId = rs.getString("alias_id");
        alias = new KeyAlias(aliasId);
        alias.setKeyAlias(rs.getString("key_alias"));
        alias.setKeyFamily(rs.getString("key_family"));
        alias.setEngine( rs.getString("engine"));
        alias.setKeyId( rs.getString("key_id"));
        alias.setActivationDate(
          rs.getTimestamp("key_activation_date"));
        alias.setStatus(rs.getString("status"));
        alias.changed = false;
      }
      else {
        LiveKeyNotFoundException e =
          new LiveKeyNotFoundException(keyFamily);
        throw e;
      }
    }
    catch (SQLException e) {
      // handle any errors
      System.out.println(e);
    }
    finally {
      if (rs != null) {
        try {
            rs.close();
        }
        catch (SQLException sqlEx) {
          // ignore
        }
        rs = null;
      }
      if (pstmt != null) {
        try {
          pstmt.close();
        }
        catch (SQLException sqlEx) {
          // ignore
        }
        pstmt = null;
      }
    }
    return alias;
  }
```

15.1.4 Saving the Key Alias

When a change is made to the alias, it needs to be saved back to the manifest. Once the information is saved, the `changed` flag is set to indicate that this is a clean representation of what is in the manifest. Note that this code does not explicitly track what changes were made or who made them. This information should be tracked and logged as per whatever standards exist in the local environment.

```java
final void save() {
  PreparedStatement pstmt = null;

  try {
    String query =
      "UPDATE key_manifest " +
      "SET    key_alias = ?," +
             "key_family = ?," +
             "engine = ?, " +
             "key_id = ?," +
             "key_activation_date = ?," +
             "status = ? " +
      "WHERE alias_id = ?";

    Connection conn = DbManager.getDbConnection();
    pstmt = conn.prepareStatement(query);
    pstmt.setString( 1, keyAlias );
    pstmt.setString( 2, keyFamily );
    pstmt.setString( 3, engine );
    pstmt.setString( 4, keyId );
    pstmt.setTimestamp( 5, activationDate );
    pstmt.setString( 6, status );
    pstmt.setString( 7, aliasId );
    int rows = pstmt.executeUpdate();

    changed = false;
  }
  catch (SQLException e) {
    System.out.println(e);
  }
  finally {
    if (pstmt != null) {
      try {
        pstmt.close();
      }
      catch (SQLException sqlEx) {
        // ignore
      }
```

```
      pstmt = null;
    }
  }
}
```

15.1.5 Determining the Key State

The `getKeyState` method returns the key's state. This method is called prior to performing any cryptographic operations with the key data to ensure that the key is in the proper state for that operation. The method first makes sure that the alias hasn't been changed with respect to what is in the database. If it has, the alias is saved to the database before continuing.

Most of the logic determines if the key is Live, Pending, or Expired. If the status is `ACTIVE`, the code checks to see if the key is Pending. If it's not Pending, we retrieve the actual Live key from the manifest and check to see if it has the same ID as the key we are working with. If it is, the key state is Live; otherwise, it is Expired.

```
public final String getKeyState()
throws InvalidKeyStateException {
  String state = null;

  if ( changed ) {
    save();
  }

  Timestamp now =
    new Timestamp(
      (Calendar.getInstance()).getTimeInMillis() );

  if ( status.equals( KeyAlias.TERMINATED ) ) {
    state = KeyAlias.TERMINATED;
  }
  else if ( status.equals( KeyAlias.RETIRED ) ) {
    state = KeyAlias.RETIRED;
  }
  else if ( status.equals( KeyAlias.ACTIVE ) ) {
    String family = getKeyFamily();
    try {
      // We assume that the clock in the database
      // and the clock used by the JVM are
      // synchronized
      if ( activationDate.after( now ) ) {
        state = KeyAlias.PENDING;
      }
      else {
        KeyAlias liveAlias =
          KeyAlias.getLiveKeyAlias( family );
```

```
      if ( aliasId.equals(
            liveAlias.getAliasId() ) ) {
        state = KeyAlias.LIVE;
      }
      else {
        state = KeyAlias.EXPIRED;
      }
    }
  }
  catch (LiveKeyNotFoundException e) {
    state = null;
  }
}
if (state == null) {
  InvalidKeyStateException e =
    new InvalidKeyStateException( aliasId );
   throw e;
}
return state;
}
```

15.1.6 Optimized State Checks

The preceding check to see if the KeyAlias is Live introduces an extra call to the database. Unless we specifically need to know the actual state, we can follow a more efficient strategy to ensure that the keys are in the appropriate states for the defined cryptographic operations.

First, for encryption requests, we'll always use getLiveKeyAlias, which returns the correct alias. We don't need to check the state again. If a particular system is modified to cache the alias for the Live key, getLiveKeyAlias should be called periodically to refresh the cache.

For decryption requests, we only need to ensure that the key is either Live or Expired. Decryption is not allowed in any other state. Because both Live and Expired keys have a status of ACTIVE, we check that first. For keys that pass the test, we need to confirm that the key is not Pending. A simple timestamp check resolves this question. If the key passes both tests, it can be used for decryption; otherwise, it cannot.

The same caveats hold true if the alias of an Expired key is cached and reused over a period of time. In such cases, the alias should be refreshed as frequently as comfort allows, knowing that the greater the amount of time between refreshes, the longer an alias might present an invalid state as compared to what is recorded in the manifest.

```
public boolean isValidForDecryption() {
  boolean valid = false;
  Timestamp now = new Timestamp(
    (Calendar.getInstance()).getTimeInMillis() );
  if ( status.equals( KeyAlias.ACTIVE ) ) {
    if ( activationDate.after( now ) ) {
      valid = false;
    }
    else {
      valid = true;
    }
  }
  return valid;
}
```

15.2 Summary

This chapter focused on the key aliases that make up the manifest. Creating and saving aliases along with various methods for determining the current state were covered. Most interactions with the manifest use the methods discussed in this chapter. Decryption requests use an already known alias ID to create a new KeyAlias. Encryption requests use getLiveKey to retrieve an alias to the current Live key for the specified family.

Chapter 16

The Key Manager

A cryptographic administrator creates and manipulates keys using the key manager. The manager, in turn, interfaces with both the key vault and the manifest to configure keys. To do this, the key manager must verify that the cryptographic administrator is authorized to conduct the desired operations, and it must have access to the necessary credentials to access the vault and manifest.

All the information necessary for these tasks would typically be stored within the key manager, perhaps in its own dedicated database. In our examples, though, the manager does not track this information. Ideally, the authentication and authorization information would be integrated into an enterprise-wide identity management infrastructure.

The vault and manifest credentials would be stored with the key manager and must be protected, possibly with a miniature version of the cryptosystem described in this book. This repository could be a small database protected with its own dedicated HSM, as discussed in Chapter 5, "Keys: Vaults, Manifests, and Managers."

Our example key manager is a command-line application called the KeyTool. This is fine for an example but would not be appropriate for a production system. A production key manager should be housed on a server so that access can be centrally controlled and the integrity of the application itself better protected.

16.1 KeyTool

The KeyTool, for the most part, takes user input and then interacts with a KeyAlias, the LocalKeyStore, or a LocalKey as needed. In some cases the KeyTool parses or formats user input before passing it on.

```
package cryptodb;

import cryptodb.core.*;

import java.sql.Timestamp;
import java.util.Calendar;
import java.text.SimpleDateFormat;
import java.text.ParseException;

public class KeyTool {
```

16.1.1 Interacting with the KeyTool

The general command format is

```
KeyTool <command> <arguments>...
```

The commands known by the KeyTool are

- genKek
- load
- print
- printLive
- retire
- terminate
- update

The main method interprets user commands and then calls the appropriate method to carry out the necessary action.

```
public static void main( String[] args ) {

  String usage =
    "KeyTool {load, update, print, printLive, " +
    "retire, terminate, genKek}";

  if (args.length == 0) {
    System.out.println( usage );
    System.exit(2);
  }

  KeyTool tool = new KeyTool();

  if (args[0].equals("load")) {
    if (args.length == 5) {
      String alias = args[1];
```

```
      String engine = args[2];
      String family = args[3];
      String days_pending = args[4];
      tool.loadLocal(alias, engine, family,
        days_pending);
    }
    else {
      System.out.println(
        "KeyTool load <alias> <engine>" +
        " <family> <days_pending>");
    }
  }
  else if (args[0].equals("print")) {
    if (args.length == 2) {
      String keyId = args[1];
      tool.printKey( keyId );
    }
    else {
      System.out.println("KeyTool print keyId");
    }
  }
  else if (args[0].equals("printLive")) {
    if (args.length == 2) {
      String family = args[1];
      tool.printLiveKey( family );
    }
    else {
      System.out.println("KeyTool print family");
    }
  }
  else if (args[0].equals("retire")) {
    if (args.length == 2) {
      tool.retireKey( args[1] );
    }
    else {
      System.out.println("KeyTool retire aliasId");
    }
  }
  else if (args[0].equals( "terminate" ) ) {
    if (args.length == 2) {
      tool.terminateKey(args[1]);
    }
    else {
      System.out.println("KeyTool terminate <alias_id>");
    }
  }
  else if (args[0].equals( "update" ) ) {
    if (args.length >= 2) {
      if (args[1].equals( "date" ) ) {
```

```
      if (args.length == 4) {
        tool.updateActivationDate(args[2], args[3]);
      }
      else {
        System.out.println(
        "KeyTool update date <alias_id> <date>");
      }
    }
    else if (args[1].equals("family")) {
      if (args.length == 4) {
        tool.updateKeyFamily(args[2], args[3]);
      }
      else {
        System.out.println(
        "KeyTool update family <alias_id> <family>");
      }
    }
    else if (args[1].equals("alias")) {
      if (args.length == 4) {
        tool.updateAlias(args[2], args[3]);
      }
      else {
        System.out.println(
        "KeyTool update alias <alias_id> <alias>");
      }
    }
    else if (args[1].equals("engine")) {
      if (args.length == 4) {
        tool.updateEngine(args[2], args[3]);
      }
      else {
        System.out.println(
        "KeyTool update engine <alias_id> <engine>");
      }
    }
    else if (args[1].equals("key_id")) {
      if (args.length == 4) {
        tool.updateKeyId(args[2], args[3]);
      }
      else {
        System.out.println(
        "KeyTool update key_id <alias_id> <key_id>");
      }
    }
  }
  else {
    System.out.println(
      "KeyTool update {date, family, alias" +
```

```
        " engine, key_id}");
    }
  }
  else if (args[0].equals( "genKek" ) ) {
    if (args.length == 1) {
      tool.generateKek();
    }
    else {
      System.out.println( "KeyTool genKek" );
    }
  }
  else {
    System.out.println( usage );
  }
}
```

The following sections describe the KeyTool commands in terms of both their usage and code. The compiled class files are assumed to reside in a subdirectory of the current working directory called out.

16.1.2 Generating the Key–Encrypting Key

To begin using a new key-encrypting key, KeyTool provides the genKek command. If the local key store contains three keys, the output would be

```
$ java -cp out cryptodb.KeyTool genKek
KEK ID: 2
```

As the example shows, genKek creates a new key-encrypting key and re-encrypts the key store with the new key. The generateKek method uses the LocalKeyStore class for both tasks.

```
void generateKek() {
  LocalKeyStore keyStore = new LocalKeyStore();
  String kekId = keyStore.generateNewKek();
  System.out.println( "KEK ID: " + kekId );
  keyStore.replaceKek( kekId );
}
```

16.1.3 Loading a New Key into the Key Store

The load command creates a new key in the key store used by the given engine. The following command creates an alias called 01-2005 in the local key store (the key store used by the local engine) in the family pii, which will become active in 10 days.

```
$ java -cp out cryptodb.KeyTool load
KeyTool load <alias> <engine> <family> <days_pending>
$ java -cp out cryptodb.KeyTool load 01-2005 local pii 10
```

The loadKey method is invoked by the load command. Based on the engine, it creates a new key in the appropriate vault. It then creates a new alias in the manifest using the ID returned from the vault.

```
private void loadKey(String alias, String engine,
String family, String days_pending) {
  String vaultKeyId = null;
  if (engine.equals( "local" )) {
    LocalKey localKey = makeNewRawKey();
    vaultKeyId = localKey.getKeyId();
  }
  else {
    System.out.println("Unknown engine");
  }

  if ( vaultKeyId != null ) {
    try {
      KeyAlias.getNewAlias(alias, engine, family,
        days_pending, vaultKeyId );
    }
    catch (AliasException e) {
      System.out.println( e );
    }
  }
}
```

The makeNewRawKey method calls into the LocalKeyStore to create a new key in our example vault. We looked at the generateKey method when we discussed the LocalKeyStore class.

```
private LocalKey makeNewRawKey() {
  LocalKey localKey = null;
  LocalKeyStore keyStore = new LocalKeyStore();
  localKey = keyStore.generateKey();
  return localKey;
}
```

16.1.4 Viewing Keys

The command print is a simple utility to view all the attributes in the manifest for a given alias. It takes the ID of the alias as a parameter.

```
java -cp out cryptodb.KeyTool print 1
Alias Id:        1
Alias:           05-2005
Family:          pii
Engine:          local
Key Id:          5
Activation date: 2005-05-01 00:00:00.0
Status:          ACTIVE
State:           EXPIRED
```

The printKey method relies on the KeyAlias to read all the information from the manifest. The overridden versions of printKey allow us to easily print a key if we know the alias ID or have a reference to the actual alias. Note that we actually use the getKeyState method here despite the extra database call. Because this is an interactive command, its performance is not critical.

```
private void printKey( String AliasId ) {
  KeyAlias alias = new KeyAlias( AliasId );
  printKey(alias);
}

private void printKey( KeyAlias alias ) {
  alias.populate();
  System.out.println( "Alias Id:        " +
    alias.getAliasId() );
  System.out.println( "Alias:           " +
    alias.getKeyAlias() );
  System.out.println( "Family:          " +
    alias.getKeyFamily() );
  System.out.println( "Engine:          " +
    alias.getEngine() );
  System.out.println( "Key Id:          " +
    alias.getKeyId() );
  System.out.println( "Activation date: " +
    alias.getActivationDate() );
  System.out.println( "Status:          " +
    alias.getStatus() );
  try {
    System.out.println( "State:           " +
      alias.getKeyState() );
  }
  catch (InvalidKeyStateException e) {
    System.out.println( "State:           UNKNOWN" );
  }
}
```

If we simply want to know which key is Live for a given key family, we can use the printLive command. The family is passed as an argument.

```
$ java -cp out cryptodb.KeyTool printLive pii
Alias Id:        8
Alias:           08-2005
Family:          pii
Engine:          local
Key Id:          9
Activation date: 2005-08-01 00:00:00.0
Status:          ACTIVE
State:           LIVE
$
```

The code behind this command uses the **KeyAlias** to create an alias for the current Live key and then passes this information to **printKey**.

```
private void printLiveKey( String keyFamily ) {
  try {
    KeyAlias liveKeyAlias =
      KeyAlias.getLiveKeyAlias( keyFamily );
    printKey( liveKeyAlias );
  }
  catch (LiveKeyNotFoundException e) {
    System.out.println( "Live key not found." );
  }
}
```

16.1.5 Retiring Keys

The commands to retire or terminate a key both take the ID of the alias to be changed. If the key is not in the correct state, an appropriate error is printed.

```
$ java -cp out cryptodb.KeyTool retire 2
```

Given that the key state is purely a function of what is in the manifest (because we never know what capabilities a given vault supplies for tracking state), retiring a key works with a **KeyAlias** to alter the state.

```
final private void retireKey(String keyId) {
  try {
    KeyAlias alias = new KeyAlias( keyId );
    alias.retireKey();
    alias.save();
  }
  catch (InvalidKeyStateException e) {
    System.out.println(e);
  }
}
```

16.1.6 Terminating Keys

Terminating a key is significantly different from retirement. Key termination must remove the key from the key vault. Despite this difference, it is simply invoked.

```
$ java -cp out cryptodb.KeyTool terminate 2
```

Like the `retireKey` method, the status in the manifest is updated via a `KeyAlias` object. However, deleting the key from the key store is not delegated to another object. The `KeyTool` itself contains the ability to delete keys from the store. While this functionality might seem to belong in the `LocalKeyStore` class, it is placed here because of the sensitivity of the operation. A deleted key means that any data encrypted with that key is no longer accessible. The key manager should be protected by very strong access controls, and those controls will keep unauthorized entities from deleting keys.

Had we placed it in the `LocalKeyStore`, the method would need to be `public` in order for it to be accessible by the key manager. Code written by anyone and existing in any package could then delete keys by simply calling the public method. That risk is too severe, so the code is placed here even though it might not seem a good fit in terms of object-oriented design.

```
final private void terminateKey(String aliasId) {
  PreparedStatement pstmt = null;
  try {
    KeyAlias alias = new KeyAlias( aliasId );
    String state = alias.getKeyState();

    if (state.equals(KeyAlias.RETIRED) ||
        state.equals(KeyAlias.PENDING)) {
      alias.terminateKey();
      alias.save();

      String sqlStmt =
        "DELETE FROM local_key_store " +
        "WHERE key_id = ?";

      Connection conn = DbManager.getDbConnection();
      pstmt = conn.prepareStatement(sqlStmt);
      pstmt.setString( 1, alias.getKeyId() );
      int rows = pstmt.executeUpdate();
    }
    else {
      System.out.println( "Key is not RETIRED");
    }
  }
```

```
    catch (InvalidKeyStateException e) {
      System.out.println(e);
    }
    catch (SQLException e) {
      // handle any errors
      System.out.println(e);
    }
    finally {
      if (pstmt != null) {
        try {
          pstmt.close();
        }
        catch (SQLException sqlEx) {
          // ignore
        }
        pstmt = null;
      }
    }
  }
}
```

16.1.7 Updating Pending Keys

The KeyTool offers several commands to update the attributes of Pending keys.
The activation data, alias, key ID, family, and engine can all be changed. They all
follow this form:

```
KeyTool update <subcommand> <alias_id> <new_value>
```

The new_value for changing the activation date must be of the form
YYYY-MM-DD HH:mm:ss in our example. Obviously a production system need not
be so limited. If, instead of a date value, asap is specified, the key is set to become
Live almost immediately. Otherwise, the user has to specify a time that is soon but
that won't be in the past as the command executes.

```
$ java -cp out cryptodb.KeyTool update date \
> 5 '2006-01-01 00:00:00'
$ java -cp out cryptodb.KeyTool update alias 5 test
$ java -cp out cryptodb.KeyTool update family 5 pii
$ java -cp out cryptodb.KeyTool update engine 5 hsm-1
$ java -cp out cryptodb.KeyTool update key_id 5 12
$ java -cp out cryptodb.KeyTool print 5
Alias Id:      5
Alias:         test
Family:        pii
Engine:        hsm-1
Key Id:        12
```

```
Activation date: 2006-01-01 00:00:00.0
Status:          ACTIVE
State:           PENDING
```

The code for these commands is fairly similar, with the exception of `updateActivationDate`, which must parse the date and ensure that the new date is in the future. If you aren't in the `America/Los_Angeles` time zone, you need to change the parameter passed to `getTimeZone`.

```java
private void updateActivationDate( String aliasId,
String dateString ) {
  boolean success = false;
  SimpleDateFormat df = new SimpleDateFormat(
    "yyyy-MM-dd HH:mm:ss" );
  df.setTimeZone( java.util.TimeZone.getTimeZone(
    "America/Los_Angeles") );
  try {
    java.util.Date date = new java.util.Date();
    java.sql.Timestamp  dbTime = null;
    if ( dateString.equals( "asap" ) ) {
      date =
        new java.util.Date(date.getTime() + 5000);
      dateString = df.format( date );
    }
    else {
      date = df.parse(dateString);
    }
    KeyAlias alias = new KeyAlias( aliasId );
    alias.populate();
    String state = alias.getKeyState();
    Timestamp now = new Timestamp(
      (Calendar.getInstance()).getTimeInMillis() );


    if ( state.equals( KeyAlias.PENDING ) &&
        date.after( now ) ) {
      alias.setActivationDate(
        Timestamp.valueOf(dateString) );
      alias.save();
      success = true;
    }
  }
  catch (InvalidKeyStateException e) {
    System.out.println( "Key '" + e.getAliasId() +
      "in unknown state" );
  }
  catch (ParseException e) {
    System.out.println( "Invalid date format." );
  }
```

```
    if ( ! success ) {
      System.out.println(
        "Updated failed. Check key state " +
        "and make sure that activation date " +
        "is a future date." );
    }
  }

  private void updateKeyFamily( String aliasId,
  String keyFamily ) {

    try {
      KeyAlias alias = new KeyAlias( aliasId );
      alias.populate();
      String state = alias.getKeyState();
      if (state.equals( KeyAlias.PENDING )) {
        alias.setKeyFamily( keyFamily );
        alias.save();
      }
      else {
        System.out.println(
          "Only pending keys may be updated." );
      }
    }
    catch (InvalidKeyStateException e) {
      System.out.println( "Key '" + e.getAliasId() +
        "in unknown state" );
    }

  }

  private void updateAlias( String aliasId,
  String aliasLabel ) {

    try {
      KeyAlias alias = new KeyAlias( aliasId );
      alias.populate();
      String state = alias.getKeyState();
      if (state.equals(KeyAlias.PENDING)) {
        alias.setKeyAlias(aliasLabel);
        alias.save();
      }
      else {
        System.out.println(
          "Only pending keys may be updated.");
      }
    }
    catch (InvalidKeyStateException e) {
      System.out.println( "Key '" + e.getAliasId() +
```

```
        "in unknown state" );
  }

}

private void updateEngine( String aliasId,
String engine ) {

  try {
    KeyAlias alias = new KeyAlias( aliasId );
    alias.populate();
    String state = alias.getKeyState();
    if (state.equals(KeyAlias.PENDING)) {
      alias.setEngine(engine);
      alias.save();
    }
    else {
      System.out.println(
        "Only pending keys may be updated.");
    }
  }
  catch (InvalidKeyStateException e) {
    System.out.println( "Key '" + e.getAliasId() +
      "in unknown state" );
  }

}

private void updateKeyId( String aliasId,
String keyId ) {

  try {
    KeyAlias alias = new KeyAlias( aliasId );
    alias.populate();
    String state = alias.getKeyState();
    if (state.equals(KeyAlias.PENDING)) {
      alias.setKeyId(keyId);
      alias.save();
    }
    else {
      System.out.println(
        "Only pending keys may be updated.");
    }
  }
  catch (InvalidKeyStateException e) {
    System.out.println( "Key '" + e.getAliasId() +
      "in unknown state" );
  }
}
```

16.2 Summary

The KeyTool presented in this chapter allows a key administrator to create and manipulate keys. For the most part, the distinction between the key vault (or key store in this particular implementation) and the manifest is invisible to the key administrator using the KeyTool. The administrator can load and alter keys without having to worry about determining which information goes in the manifest and which goes in the key vault.

Chapter 17

The Engine

Because we are striving for simplicity and most environments will not need more than a handful of algorithms, our idea of an engine is tied to the key size, algorithm, mode, and padding. For instance, our EngineWrapper in this chapter implements 128-bit keys for AES in CBC mode with PKCS#5 padding. If we wanted to use a 256-bit key, we'd implement a new engine class similar to `EngineWrapper`, but we might call it `EngineWrapper-256`.

Granted, this is not the most clever strategy. However, clever, at least in this case, means additional complexity. If the key size, algorithm, mode, and padding could all be individually specified, we would have to deal with cases where some or all of the specification were invalid. A general-purpose cryptographic library should handle such things gracefully. Our single-purpose cryptosystem need not be so flexible. By avoiding cleverness, we lessen the chance of configuration mistakes.

17.1 The Local Engine

As of version 1.4.2, the Java Cryptography Extension includes support for AES. The JCE, then, contains our engine, and the `EngineWrapper` class is our interface into the JCE. The class's responsibilities are simple and few: act as a bridge for encryption and decryption calls. Only other classes in the core can create or call methods in the EngineWrapper.

```
package cryptodb.core;

import cryptodb.*;
import java.security.*;
import javax.crypto.spec.*;
import javax.crypto.*;
```

```
public class EngineWrapper {

  EngineWrapper() {}
```

This encrypt method is used to encrypt actual business data, as opposed to the other encryption methods we've seen up to now, which were used to encrypt keys. The flow of logic through this method is similar to what we've seen before, but the details are different.

First, the key is retrieved from the key store and decrypted. The key-encrypting key is wiped from the LocalKey because it is no longer needed, and the IV and the cipher are prepared. The cipher specification is AES/CBC/PKCS5Padding. After the cipher is initialized for encryption with the key and IV, the plaintext is encrypted. Finally, in the finally block, the key is wiped, and a byte array of the ciphertext is returned.

```
byte[] encrypt( byte[] plaintext,
                byte[] rawIv,
                String keyId )
throws KeyNotFoundException {

  byte[] ciphertext = null;
  LocalKey localKey = null;
  try {
    LocalKeyStore keyStore = new LocalKeyStore();
    localKey = keyStore.getLocalKey( keyId );
    SecretKeySpec key = localKey.getSecretKeySpec();
    localKey.wipeKek();

    IvParameterSpec Iv = new IvParameterSpec( rawIv );
    Cipher cipher =
       Cipher.getInstance("AES/CBC/PKCS5Padding");
    cipher.init(Cipher.ENCRYPT_MODE, key, Iv);
    ciphertext = cipher.doFinal(plaintext);

    // Note there is no way to wipe memory with
    // the Sun supplied providers.

  }
  catch (NoSuchAlgorithmException nsae) {
    System.out.println( "Algorithm not found." );
  }
  catch (NoSuchPaddingException nspe ) {
    System.out.println( nspe );
  }
  catch ( InvalidKeyException ike ) {
    System.out.println( ike );
  }
```

```
    catch ( IllegalBlockSizeException ibse ) {
      System.out.println( ibse );
    }
    catch ( BadPaddingException bpe ) {
      System.out.println( bpe );
    }
    catch ( InvalidAlgorithmParameterException bpe ) {
      System.out.println( bpe );
    }
    finally {
       if (localKey != null ) {
          localKey.wipe();
       }
    }
    return ciphertext;
}
```

Decryption follows the same pattern but initializes the cipher for decryption.

```
byte[] decrypt( byte[] ciphertext,
                        byte[] rawIv,
                        String keyId )
throws KeyNotFoundException {

  byte[] plaintext = null;
  LocalKey localKey = null;
  try {
    LocalKeyStore keyStore = new LocalKeyStore();
    localKey = keyStore.getLocalKey( keyId );
    SecretKeySpec key = localKey.getSecretKeySpec();
    localKey.wipeKek();

    IvParameterSpec Iv = new IvParameterSpec( rawIv );
    Cipher cipher =
       Cipher.getInstance("AES/CBC/PKCS5Padding");
    cipher.init(Cipher.DECRYPT_MODE, key, Iv);
    plaintext = cipher.doFinal(ciphertext);

    // Note there is no way to explicitly wipe memory with
    // the providers.

  }
  catch (NoSuchAlgorithmException nsae) {
    System.out.println( "Algorithm not found." );
  }
  catch (NoSuchPaddingException nspe ) {
    System.out.println( nspe );
  }
```

```
catch ( InvalidKeyException ike ) {
  System.out.println( ike );
}
catch ( IllegalBlockSizeException ibse ) {
  System.out.println( ibse );
}
catch ( BadPaddingException bpe ) {
  System.out.println( bpe );
}
catch ( InvalidAlgorithmParameterException bpe ) {
  System.out.println( bpe );
}
finally {
    if (localKey != null ) {
        localKey.wipe();
    }
}
return plaintext;
}
```

17.2 Summary

The engine, in keeping with our recommendation to use only established third-party cryptographic libraries (preferably on an HSM), is the default cryptographic support that ships with Java 1.4.2. While this is rather convenient for these examples, use of other engines would follow the same approach. The library would be initialized with the appropriate key, algorithm, and padding scheme. Then the IV and data would be passed to the library for encryption or decryption. The specifics vary, but, in general, the calls are straightforward.

With an HSM the biggest difference is that the connection to the HSM itself must be initialized and maintained. Typically, the application connects at startup and maintains the connection for as long as the application is running. It is best if each call to a cryptographic routine does not have to reconnect to the HSM.

Chapter 18

Receipts and the Provider

This chapter covers the provider's operation. This includes the `Provider` class itself along with supporting classes such as `EncryptionRequest`, `CryptoReceipt`, and `CompoundCryptReceipt`. Each of these plays a role in giving consumers easy access to the provider's cryptographic services.

18.1 Encryption Requests and Decryption Results

The `EncryptionRequest` interface is used to tag classes that contain the `getPlaintexts` method as needed by the `encrypt` method of the `Provider`. This method returns a `HashMap` containing the plaintexts and the columns that store the plaintexts.

```
package cryptodb;

import java.util.HashMap;

public interface EncryptionRequest {
  public HashMap getPlaintexts();
}
```

The `DecryptionResults` class contains the data returned from a call to `decrypt` in the `Provider`. Note that `DecryptionResults` is also an `EncryptionRequest`, enabling the output of any given decryption call to immediately be sent to an encryption operation. The methods of `DecryptionResults` allow the consumer to access the plaintexts.

```
package cryptodb;

import java.util.*;
```

```
public class DecryptionResults
implements EncryptionRequest {

  private HashMap plaintexts = new HashMap();

  public void addPlaintext( String column,
  String plaintext ) {
    plaintexts.put( column, plaintext );
  }

  public String getPlaintext( String column ) {
    return (String)plaintexts.get( column );
  }

  public HashMap getPlaintexts() {
    return plaintexts;
  }
}
```

The HashMap class provides the glue that binds these two classes. The consumer, as we'll see later, places a plaintext and a label representing the column from which the plaintext was taken into an EncryptionRequest. This is then passed to the encrypt method of the Provider.

The Provider encrypts the plaintext and then returns a DecryptionResult, which also contains a HashMap. This HashMap, though, matches the column label with the ciphertext instead of the plaintext.

The consumer then simply looks in the DecryptionResult for the same labels it used in creating its EncryptionRequest and places the appropriate ciphertext in the correct column. This will be looked at in more detail when we look at the consumer, but it is discussed here to give some context on how these classes are used.

18.2 Receipts

Unencrypted data is passed to the provider as an EncryptionRequest, and the encrypted data is passed back as a CryptoReceipt. Or, more accurately, as a CompoundCryptoReceipt that represents one or more CryptoReceipts, all encrypted with the same key. Then, when the consumer wants data decrypted, the receipt is passed back to the provider.

18.2.1 The Cryptographic Receipt

This class just bundles a ciphertext, an IV, and the alias ID of the encrypting key.

```
package cryptodb;

public class CryptoReceipt {

  private String ciphertext = null;
  private String iv = null;
  private String aliasId = null;

  public CryptoReceipt( String ct,
  String iv, String aliasId ) {
    this.ciphertext = ct;
    this.iv = iv;
    this.aliasId = aliasId;
  }

  final public String getCiphertext() {
    return ciphertext;
  }

  final public String getIv() {
    return iv;
  }

  final public String getAliasId() {
    return aliasId;
  }

}
```

18.2.2 The Compound Receipt

The CompoundCryptoReceipt is essentially a wrapper around a HashMap of receipts.

```
package cryptodb;

import java.util.*;

public class CompoundCryptoReceipt {

  private HashMap receipts = new HashMap();
  private String aliasId = null;
```

The `addReceipt` method adds a new receipt to the `CompoundCryptoReceipt` after first ensuring that all the receipts share the same alias ID.

```
public void addReceipt( String cryptoColumn,
  CryptoReceipt receipt )
throws MultipleAliasIdException {
  if (aliasId != null) {
    if ( ! aliasId.equals(receipt.getAliasId())) {
      MultipleAliasIdException e =
        new MultipleAliasIdException(this.aliasId,
          receipt.getAliasId() );
      throw e;
    }
  }
  else {
    this.aliasId = receipt.getAliasId();
  }
  receipts.put( cryptoColumn, receipt );

}
```

The next two methods, `getCiphertext` and `getIv`, provide access to the ciphertexts and IVs of the contained `CryptoReceipts` without actually exposing the receipts themselves.

```
public String getCiphertext( String cryptoColumn ) {
  CryptoReceipt receipt =
    (CryptoReceipt)receipts.get( cryptoColumn );
  return receipt.getCiphertext();
}

public String getIv( String cryptoColumn ) {
  CryptoReceipt receipt =
    (CryptoReceipt)receipts.get( cryptoColumn );
  return receipt.getIv();
}
```

To determine the alias ID of all the receipts in the `CompoundCryptoReceipt`, call `getAliasId`. Finally, `getAllReceipts` returns the internal `HashMap` to the caller.

```
public String getAliasId() {
  return aliasId;
}

public HashMap getAllReceipts() {
  return receipts;
}
}
```

18.3 The Provider

If the EngineWrapper is a bridge from our cryptosystem to the engine, the Provider is a bridge between the consumer and the EngineWrapper. These layers of indirection and the access modifiers applied to the classes and methods ensure that the business logic of the consumer need not (and cannot) directly access the engine.

Technically, the methods in the EngineWrapper could be placed as private methods in the Provider. These examples separate them to keep the responsibilities of both clear.

```
package cryptodb.core;

import cryptodb.*;
import java.util.*;
import java.security.SecureRandom;
import java.security.NoSuchAlgorithmException;

public class Provider {
```

18.3.1 Encrypting Business Data

When the consumer calls the Provider to encrypt data, it passes an EncryptionRequest object and the name of the key family it wants the provider to use. The encrypt method then generates an IV, retrieves the currently Live key alias, and then iterates over all the items in the EncryptionRequest. In each iteration, the EngineWrapper is called to encrypt the data in the request, and the result is stored in a CryptoReceipt. All the receipts are then bundled in a CompoundCryptoReceipt, which is returned to the consumer.

The encrypt method throws a host of exceptions that could be consolidated depending on the exception handling strategy in a particular environment. They are all shown here for completeness.

```
public CompoundCryptoReceipt encrypt(
    EncryptionRequest request, String keyFamily )
  throws LiveKeyNotFoundException, KeyNotFoundException,
    MultipleAliasIdException, NoSuchAlgorithmException {

  byte[] iv = new byte[16];
  SecureRandom ivGenerator =
    SecureRandom.getInstance( "SHA1PRNG" );

  CompoundCryptoReceipt receipts =
    new CompoundCryptoReceipt();
```

```
String cryptoColumn = null;
String plaintext = null;
byte[] ciphertext = null;
CryptoReceipt receipt = null;

EngineWrapper engine = new EngineWrapper();
KeyAlias alias =
  KeyAlias.getLiveKeyAlias(keyFamily);
String keyId = alias.getKeyId();
String aliasId = alias.getAliasId();

HashMap plaintexts = request.getPlaintexts();
Set cryptoColumns = plaintexts.keySet();
Iterator i = cryptoColumns.iterator();
while ( i.hasNext() ) {
  cryptoColumn = (String)i.next();
  plaintext =
    (String)plaintexts.get( cryptoColumn );
  ivGenerator.nextBytes( iv );

  ciphertext = engine.encrypt(
    plaintext.getBytes(),
    iv,
    keyId );

  receipt = new CryptoReceipt(
    Utils.bytes2HexString( ciphertext ),
    Utils.bytes2HexString( iv ),
    aliasId );
  receipts.addReceipt( cryptoColumn, receipt );
}
return receipts;
}
```

18.3.2 Decrypting Business Data

Decryption is not terribly different. Instead of retrieving the Live key for a specified family, the code pulls the alias ID from the CompoundCryptoReceipt and uses it to create the appropriate key alias. Then, after ensuring that the key is in a state that allows decryption, the decrypt method iterates through all the ciphertexts and decrypts each in turn. Finally, the plaintexts are placed in a DecryptionResults object and are returned to the caller.

```
public DecryptionResults decrypt(
  CompoundCryptoReceipt receiptWrapper )
throws InvalidKeyStateException, KeyNotFoundException {
```

```
DecryptionResults plaintexts =
  new DecryptionResults();

byte[] plaintext = null;
String cryptoColumn = null;
CryptoReceipt receipt = null;

String aliasId =
  receiptWrapper.getAliasId();
KeyAlias alias = new KeyAlias( aliasId );

if ( ! alias.isValidForDecryption() ) {
  throw (new InvalidKeyStateException( aliasId ));
}
EngineWrapper engine = new EngineWrapper();

HashMap receipts = receiptWrapper.getAllReceipts();
Set cryptoColumns =  receipts.keySet();
Iterator i = cryptoColumns.iterator();
while ( i.hasNext() ) {
  cryptoColumn = (String)i.next();
  receipt =
    (CryptoReceipt)receipts.get(cryptoColumn);

  plaintext = engine.decrypt(
    Utils.hexString2Bytes(receipt.getCiphertext()),
    Utils.hexString2Bytes(receipt.getIv()),
    alias.getKeyId());

  plaintexts.addPlaintext( cryptoColumn,
    new String( plaintext ) );
}
return plaintexts;
}
```

18.3.3 Replacing Keys

The final method in the Provider allows a consumer to easily replace the key used to encrypt an item. The replaceKey method takes a CompoundCryptoReceipt and key family as parameters. It decrypts the receipts and then immediately re-encrypts with the current Live key. This process is made easier because, as we saw earlier, a DecryptionResults object is also an EncryptionRequest. The class ensures that the state of the key used to encrypt the ciphertexts in the CompoundCryptoReceipt is Expired (so as not to decrypt and then reencrypt with the same Live key).

```
public CompoundCryptoReceipt replaceKey(
  CompoundCryptoReceipt receiptWrapper, String keyFamily )
throws LiveKeyNotFoundException, KeyNotFoundException,
  MultipleAliasIdException, NoSuchAlgorithmException,
  InvalidKeyStateException {

  CompoundCryptoReceipt receipts = null;
  KeyAlias alias =
    new KeyAlias(receiptWrapper.getAliasId());
  String keyState = alias.getKeyState();

  if (keyState.equals( KeyAlias.EXPIRED)) {
    DecryptionResults plaintexts =
      decrypt( receiptWrapper );
    receipts = encrypt( plaintexts, keyFamily );
  }
  else {
    throw (new InvalidKeyStateException(
      alias.getAliasId()));
  }
  return receipts;
}
```

18.4 Summary

The provider is the consumer's entry point into the cryptosystem, and this chapter presented the classes that allow the consumer to easily make use of the provider's services. Communication between the consumer and provider is accomplished by passing encryption requests and decryption results back and forth. While the encryption requests consist of plaintexts, the decryption results return cryptographic receipts containing the ciphertext, alias ID, and IV.

The provider acts as a hub and takes information from the consumer and the manifest and calls into the engine to either encrypt or decrypt. The provider also offers a convenient method for consumers to replace the keys used to encrypt data.

Chapter 19

The Consumer

The consumer represents the reason the cryptosystem exists. The consumer might be a Web application, a backend financial system, a customer relationship management suite, or any other application that handles information that needs strong protection.

The consumer needs to understand the information it handles. It needs to know which information is sensitive and, for each sensitive item, it must know the appropriate security requirements. These security requirements include the level of protection necessary and how keys are to be scoped and possibly striped.

We'll base our examples on an application that handles customers' personally identifiable information and credit card numbers. Our system will handle the following customer information:

- First name
- Last name
- E-mail address
- Zip code
- Credit card number
- Expiration date

Of these, the first and last name, e-mail address, credit card number, and expiration date have all been identified as requiring encryption. The key for the first and last name and e-mail address requires a key change every six months, while the key for the credit card number and expiration date must be replaced every three months.[1] To help with verification, the last four digits of the credit card number may remain unencrypted.

Two key families are identified to provide the necessary protection. The pii family will have keys changed every six months and is linked to an engine that uses 128-bit keys and AES in CBC mode. The cci key provides the same level of protection but is changed every three months. Wide scoping is to be used for both families.

To facilitate searching for customers, we store the first and last initial for each name unencrypted. These initials, along with the unencrypted zip code, will limit the number of customer records to decrypted and searched.

The database table that results from these specifications includes a column for each initial and columns for each encrypted data item along with their respective IVs. Two additional columns will be allocated to hold the key alias IDs.

```
CREATE TABLE customer_info
(
    customer_id          INTEGER          NOT NULL PRIMARY KEY
                                           AUTO_INCREMENT,
    first_name           VARCHAR(64)      NOT NULL,
    first_name_iv        VARCHAR(32),
    first_initial        VARCHAR(1),
    last_name            VARCHAR(64)      NOT NULL,
    last_name_iv         VARCHAR(32),
    last_initial         VARCHAR(1),
    email_address        VARCHAR(64),
    email_addr_iv        VARCHAR(32),
    zip_code             VARCHAR(64),
    credit_card_num      VARCHAR(64)      NOT NULL,
    credit_card_num_iv   VARCHAR(32),
    last_four_ccn        VARCHAR(4),
    expiration_date      VARCHAR(32)      NOT NULL,
    expiration_date_iv   VARCHAR(32),
    pii_scope_alias_id   VARCHAR(30),
    cci_scope_alias_id   VARCHAR(30)
);
```

The rest of this chapter assumes that the keys have been set up for the pii and cci families.

---

1. *These are just expirations for use in the example and aren't meant to reflect security requirements of a real organization.*

19.1 Customer Information

The `CustomerInfo` class represents a customer's personal information. The class is also an `EncryptionRequest`, meaning that it can be passed directly to the provider for encryption. As per our search criteria mentioned earlier, the customer's initials remain unencrypted, and this class supports that functionality. In addition, `CustomerInfo` contains a `CreditCardInfo` containing the customer's credit card information. The `CustomerInfo` class is an inner class of `CustomerManager`.

```
class CustomerInfo implements EncryptionRequest {

  private String custId;
  private String first; // Missing first letter
  private String firstInitial;
  private String last; // Missing first letter
  private String lastInitial;
  private String email;
  private String zip;
  private CreditCardInfo cci;

  public void setcustomerId(String custId) {
    this.custId = custId;
  }

  public String getCustomerId() {
    return custId;
  }

  public void setFirstName(String fullFirst) {
    first = fullFirst.substring(1);
    firstInitial = fullFirst.substring(0, 1);
  }

  public String getFullFirst() {
    return firstInitial + first;
  }

  public String getFirstInitial() {
    return firstInitial;
  }

  public String getFirst() {
    return first;
  }
```

```
public void setLastName(String fullLast) {
  last = fullLast.substring(1);
  lastInitial = fullLast.substring(0, 1);
}

public String getFullLast() {
  return lastInitial + last;
}

public String getLastInitial() {
  return lastInitial;
}

public String getLast() {
  return last;
}

public void setEmail(String email) {
  this.email = email;
}

public String getEmail() {
  return email;
}

public void setZip(String zip) {
  this.zip = zip;
}

public String getZip() {
  return zip;
}

public void setCreditCardInfo(CreditCardInfo cci) {
  this.cci = cci;
}

public CreditCardInfo getCreditCardInfo() {
  return cci;
}
```

Because the class implements `EncryptionRequest`, the `getPlaintexts` method assembles and returns the plaintexts. The `HashMap` it returns contains pairs of data consisting of the column label, as discussed earlier, and the plaintext to be encrypted.

```
public HashMap getPlaintexts() {
  HashMap plaintexts = new HashMap();
  plaintexts.put(CustomerManager.FIRST_NAME, first);
```

```
    plaintexts.put(CustomerManager.LAST_NAME,  last);
    plaintexts.put(CustomerManager.EMAIL_ADDR, email);

    return plaintexts;
  }
}
```

19.2 Credit Card Information

The `CreditCardInfo` class contains the credit card number and the expiration date. Like `CustomerInfo`, it is an `EncryptionRequest`. The class implements logic to handle the requirement of keeping the last four digits unencrypted. This is also an inner class of `CustomerManager`.

```
class CreditCardInfo implements EncryptionRequest {

  private String creditCard;
  private String lastFour;
  private String expDate;

  void setCreditCard(String fullCreditCard) {
    int length = fullCreditCard.length();
    lastFour = fullCreditCard.substring(length-4);
    creditCard = fullCreditCard.substring(0, length-4);
  }
  String getFullCreditCard() {
    return creditCard + lastFour;
  }
  String getLastFour() {
    return lastFour;
  }
  String getCreditCard() {
    return creditCard;
  }
  void setExpDate(String expDate) {
    this.expDate = expDate;
  }
  String getExpDate() {
    return expDate;
  }
```

The `getPlaintexts` method returns the expiration date and the credit card number without the last four digits for encryption. While AES is not vulnerable to known ciphertext attacks, that's no reason not to be conservative with the design. By removing the last four digits from the plaintexts, we improve the chances of keeping the algorithm from running into another block that would consist mostly of encrypted padding. While not a security requirement, this does help reduce the amount of encrypted data that needs to be stored. The same line of reasoning lies behind the missing first letters in the first and last names returned by getPlaintexts in CustomerInfo.

```
public HashMap getPlaintexts() {
  HashMap plaintexts = new HashMap();
  plaintexts.put(CustomerManager.CREDIT_CARD,
    creditCard);
  plaintexts.put(CustomerManager.EXP_DATE,
    expDate);

  return plaintexts;
  }
}
```

19.3 The Customer Manager

The CustomerManager class represents our consumer. Like the KeyTool, it is a command-line utility designed as an example showcase. It resides in the cryptodb.test package, where it can access only public methods in the rest of the system.

The set of static final variables at the top of the class are the labels used to identify the database source columns when working with EncryptionRequests and DecryptionResults. For instance, the FIRST_NAME variable in CustomerManager represents the first_name column in the customer_info table.

```
package cryptodb.test;

import cryptodb.*;
import cryptodb.core.*;
import java.sql.*;
import java.util.HashMap;
import java.security.SecureRandom;
import java.security.NoSuchAlgorithmException;

public class CustomerManager {

  static final String FIRST_NAME  = "first_name";
  static final String LAST_NAME   = "last_name";
  static final String EMAIL_ADDR   = "email";
  static final String CREDIT_CARD = "credit_card";
  static final String EXP_DATE    = "exp_date";
```

We won't bother showing it here, but `CustomerManager` includes its own database connection factory. The same code used in the `DbManager` class covered in Chapter 13, "About the Examples," is also in `CustomerManager`.

19.3.1 Using the Customer Manager

Issuing commands to the `CustomerManager` follows the same format as `KeyTool` commands.

```
CustomerManager <command> <arguments>...
```

The `main` method simply reads the arguments and calls the appropriate private method to handle the command. The available commands are

```
CustomerManager {add, print, find, replacePiiKey}
```

We'll cover each of these in the following sections.

```java
public static void main(String[] args) {
  String usage =
    "Usage: CustomerManager {add, print, find," +
    " replacePiiKey}";

  if (args.length == 0) {
    System.out.println(usage);
    System.exit(2);
  }

  CustomerManager mgr = new CustomerManager();
  if (args[0].equals("add")) {
    if (args.length == 7) {
      CustomerInfo cust = new CustomerInfo();
      cust.setFirstName(args[1]);
      cust.setLastName(args[2]);
      cust.setEmail(args[3]);
      cust.setZip(args[4]);

      CreditCardInfo cci = new CreditCardInfo();
      cci.setCreditCard(args[5]);
      cci.setExpDate(args[6]);

      cust.setCreditCardInfo(cci);
      mgr.addCustomer(cust);
    }
```

```
    else {
      System.out.println(
        "Usage: CustomerManager add <first> <last> <email>" +
        " <zip> <cc> <exp>");
    }
  }
  else if (args[0].equals("print")) {
    if (args.length == 2) {
      String custId = args[1];
      mgr.printAll(custId);
    }
    else {
      System.out.println(
        "Usage: CustomerManager print cust_id");
    }
  }
  else if (args[0].equals("find")) {
    if (args.length == 4) {
      try {
        CustomerInfo cust = mgr.findCustomer(
          args[1], args[2], args[3]);
        mgr.printCustomer(cust);
        mgr.printCreditCardInfo(
          cust.getCreditCardInfo());
      }
      catch (CustomerNotFoundException e) {
        System.out.println("Customer '" +
          e.getCustId() + "' not found.");
      }
      catch (InvalidKeyStateException e) {
        System.out.println("Key '" +
          e.getAliasId() +
          "' wrong state for decryption.");
      }
    }
    else {
      System.out.println(
        "Usage: CustomerManager find " +
        "<first_name> <last_name> <zip_code>");
    }
  }
  else if (args[0].equals("replacePiiKey")) {
    if (args.length == 2) {
      mgr.replacePiiKey(args[1]);
    }
    else {
      System.out.println(
        "Usage: CustomerManager replace " +
        "<alias_id>");
```

```
    }
  }
  else {
    System.out.println(usage);
  }
}
```

19.3.2 Adding a Customer

We begin with adding a customer to the customer table. Usage of the command is straightforward:

```
$ java -cp out cryptodb.test.CustomerManager add
Usage: CustomerManager add <first> <last> <email> <zip>
<cc> <exp>
$ java -cp out cryptodb.test.CustomerManager add \
Kevin Kenan kkenan@... 12345 1111222233334444 11/23
```

The `addCustomer` method takes a fully populated `CustomerInfo` object, extracts the `CreditCardInfo`, and then encrypts each with the appropriate key family (`pii` and `cci`, respectively). The encrypted data, along with the information that does not need encryption, is then saved to the database.

```
void addCustomer(CustomerInfo cust) {
  CreditCardInfo cci = cust.getCreditCardInfo();

  PreparedStatement pstmt = null;
  ResultSet rs = null;

  try {
    Provider provider = new Provider();
    CompoundCryptoReceipt piiReceipts =
      provider.encrypt(cust, "pii");
    CompoundCryptoReceipt cciReceipts =
      provider.encrypt(cci, "cci");

    String query =  "INSERT INTO customer_info " +
      "values (" +
        "NULL, " +
        "?,?,?,?,?," +
        "?,?,?,?,?," +
        "?,?,?,?,?," +
        "?" +
      ")";

    Connection conn = getDbConnection();
    pstmt = conn.prepareStatement(query);
```

```
    pstmt.setString( 1, piiReceipts.getCiphertext(
                         FIRST_NAME));
    pstmt.setString( 2, piiReceipts.getIv(
                         FIRST_NAME));
    pstmt.setString( 3, cust.getFirstInitial());

    pstmt.setString( 4, piiReceipts.getCiphertext(
                         LAST_NAME) );
    pstmt.setString( 5, piiReceipts.getIv(
                         LAST_NAME));
    pstmt.setString( 6, cust.getLastInitial());

    pstmt.setString( 7, piiReceipts.getCiphertext(
                         EMAIL_ADDR));
    pstmt.setString( 8, piiReceipts.getIv(
                         EMAIL_ADDR));
    pstmt.setString( 9, cust.getZip());

    pstmt.setString(10, cciReceipts.getCiphertext(
                         CREDIT_CARD));
    pstmt.setString(11, cciReceipts.getIv(
                         CREDIT_CARD));
    pstmt.setString(12, cci.getLastFour());

    pstmt.setString(13, cciReceipts.getCiphertext(
                         EXP_DATE));
    pstmt.setString(14, cciReceipts.getIv(
                         EXP_DATE));

    pstmt.setString(15, piiReceipts.getAliasId());
    pstmt.setString(16, cciReceipts.getAliasId());

    int rows = pstmt.executeUpdate();
}
catch (NoSuchAlgorithmException e) {
  System.out.println(e.toString());
}
catch(MultipleAliasIdException e) {
  System.out.println(
    "Attempted to put multiple alias Ids in a" +
    " compound receipt.");
}
catch (LiveKeyNotFoundException e) {
  System.out.println(
    "Key family does not have a live key.");
}
catch (KeyNotFoundException e) {
  System.out.println("Key " + e.getKeyId() +
    " not found by engine " + e.getEngine());
```

```
    }
    catch (SQLException e) {
      // handle any errors
      System.out.println(e);
    }
    finally {
      if (pstmt != null) {
        try {
          pstmt.close();
        }
        catch (SQLException e) {
          // ignore
        }
        pstmt = null;
      }
    }
  }
}
```

The CustomerManager, like much code that handles user input, treats its input as Strings. While this is convenient, it is not so good for security, as we've discussed previously. In Java, the creation of a String places it in the string pool. Because Strings are immutable, once in the string pool, a String is there until the Java virtual machine decides to remove it. This is not behavior we want in a system handling sensitive information.

If possible, sensitive data should enter the system as an array of bytes. If the data ever becomes a String, we've lost control of it. In a real system, though, it is very difficult to avoid Strings for business data. As a compromise, we grudgingly accept Strings for everything except unencrypted key data.

19.3.3 Viewing a Customer Record

Customer information is displayed through the printAll method, which first calls getCustomer and then passes the returned CustomerInfo object and the embedded CreditCardInfo to specific printing methods.

```
private void printAll(String custId) {
  try {
    CustomerInfo cust = getCustomer(custId);
    printCustomer(cust);
    printCreditCardInfo(cust.getCreditCardInfo());
  }
  catch (CustomerNotFoundException e) {
    System.out.println("Customer not found.");
  }
```

```
  catch (InvalidKeyStateException e) {
    System.out.println(
      "Key in wrong state for decryption.");
  }
}

private void printCreditCardInfo( CreditCardInfo card ) {
  System.out.println( "Credit card: " + card.getFullCreditCard() );
  System.out.println( "Expiration:  " + card.getExpDate() );
}

private void printCustomer( CustomerInfo cust ) {
  System.out.println( "First name:  " + cust.getFullFirst() );
  System.out.println( "Last name:  " + cust.getFullLast() );
  System.out.println( "Eamil:      " + cust.getEmail() );
  System.out.println( "Zip code:   " + cust.getZip() );
}
```

The getCustomer method reads from the database, reassembles the receipts, calls on the Provider to decrypt, and returns a populated CustomerInfo.

```
CustomerInfo getCustomer(String custId)
throws CustomerNotFoundException,
InvalidKeyStateException {

  CustomerInfo cust = new CustomerInfo();
  CreditCardInfo card = new CreditCardInfo();

  PreparedStatement pstmt = null;
  ResultSet rs = null;

  try {
    String query =
      "SELECT * " +
      "FROM   customer_info " +
      "WHERE  customer_id = ?";

    Connection conn = getDbConnection();
    pstmt = conn.prepareStatement(query);
    pstmt.setString(1, custId);
    rs = pstmt.executeQuery();
```

We use a pair of CompoundCryptoReceipts to hold all the receipts for the columns in scope of the pii and cci keys for a given customer. The piiReceipts object holds the columns identified by the labels FIRST_NAME, LAST_NAME, and EMAIL_ADDR, while cciReceipts holds the columns for CREDIT_CARD and EXP_DATE.

```
CompoundCryptoReceipt piiReceipts =
  new CompoundCryptoReceipt();

CompoundCryptoReceipt cciReceipts =
  new CompoundCryptoReceipt();

if (rs.next()) {
  piiReceipts.addReceipt(
    FIRST_NAME,
    new CryptoReceipt(
      rs.getString("first_name"),
      rs.getString("first_name_iv"),
      rs.getString("pii_scope_key_id")));

  piiReceipts.addReceipt(
    LAST_NAME,
    new CryptoReceipt(
      rs.getString("last_name"),
      rs.getString("last_name_iv"),
      rs.getString("pii_scope_key_id")));

  piiReceipts.addReceipt(
    EMAIL_ADDR,
    new CryptoReceipt(
      rs.getString("email_address"),
      rs.getString("email_addr_iv"),
      rs.getString("pii_scope_key_id")));

  cciReceipts.addReceipt(
    CREDIT_CARD,
    new CryptoReceipt(
      rs.getString( "credit_card_num" ),
      rs.getString( "credit_card_num_iv" ),
      rs.getString( "cci_scope_key_id") ) );

  cciReceipts.addReceipt(
    EXP_DATE,
    new CryptoReceipt(
      rs.getString( "expiration_date" ),
      rs.getString( "expiration_date_iv" ),
      rs.getString( "cci_scope_key_id") ) );
```

Once the receipts are added to the `CompoundCryptoReceipts`, we pass them to the `decrypt` method of `Provider`. The `piiPlaintexts` are added to the new `CustomerInfo` object, and the `cciPlaintexts` are added to a new `CreditCardInfo` object that is then added to the `CustomerInfo`. This `CustomerInfo` is then returned to the caller.

```
      Provider provider = new Provider();
      DecryptionResults piiPlaintexts =
        provider.decrypt(piiReceipts);
      DecryptionResults cciPlaintexts =
        provider.decrypt( cciReceipts );

      String firstName =
        rs.getString("first_initial") +
          piiPlaintexts.getPlaintext(FIRST_NAME);
      String lastName =
        rs.getString("last_initial") +
          piiPlaintexts.getPlaintext(LAST_NAME);

      cust.setFirstName(firstName);
      cust.setLastName(lastName);
      cust.setEmail(
        piiPlaintexts.getPlaintext(EMAIL_ADDR));
      cust.setZip(rs.getString("zip_code"));

      String creditCardNum =
        cciPlaintexts.getPlaintext(CREDIT_CARD) +
        rs.getString("last_four_ccn");
      card.setCreditCard(creditCardNum);
      card.setExpDate(
        cciPlaintexts.getPlaintext(EXP_DATE));

      cust.setCreditCardInfo(card);
    }
    else {
      CustomerNotFoundException e =
        new CustomerNotFoundException(custId);
      throw e;
    }
  }
  catch(MultipleAliasIdException e) {
    System.out.println(
      "Attempted to put multiple alias Ids in a" +
      " compound receipt.");
  }
  catch (KeyNotFoundException e) {
    System.out.println("Key not found.");
  }
  catch (SQLException e) {
    System.out.println(e);
  }
  finally {
    if (pstmt != null) {
      try {
        pstmt.close();
```

```
        }
        catch (SQLException e) {
          // ignore
        }
        pstmt = null;
      }
    }
  }
  return cust;
}
```

19.3.4 Searching for Customers

To search for a customer, we use the first and last initials and the zip code to narrow down the range of rows in the table that might contain the customer information we're after. Once we have that set of possibilities, we decrypt each until we find the customer we're interested in.

```
private CustomerInfo findCustomer( String firstName,
String lastName, String zipCode )
throws CustomerNotFoundException,
InvalidKeyStateException {

  String firstInitial = firstName.substring(0,1);
  String lastInitial  = lastName.substring(0,1);

  PreparedStatement pstmt = null;
  ResultSet rs = null;
  CustomerInfo cust = null;

  try {
    String query =
      "SELECT * " +
      "FROM  customer_info " +
      "WHERE  first_initial = ? " +
      "AND    last_initial = ? " +
      "AND    zip_code = ?";

    Connection conn = getDbConnection();
    pstmt = conn.prepareStatement(query);
    pstmt.setString( 1, firstInitial );
    pstmt.setString( 2, lastInitial );
    pstmt.setString( 3, zipCode );
    rs = pstmt.executeQuery();

    boolean custNotFound = true;
    while ( custNotFound && rs.next()) {
      cust =
        getCustomer( rs.getString( "customer_id" ) );
```

```
        if ((cust.getFullFirst()).equals(firstName) &&
            (cust.getFullLast()).equals(lastName)) {
          custNotFound = false;
        }
      }
    }
    catch (SQLException e) {
      // handle any errors
      System.out.println(e);
    }
    finally {
      if (pstmt != null) {
        try {
          pstmt.close();
        }
        catch (SQLException e) {
          // ignore
        }
        pstmt = null;
      }
    }
    return cust;
  }
```

This approach to searching an encrypted database assumes that no significant degree of confidentiality is lost by revealing the first and last initials. The strategy could be extended to include the first two letters of either or even both names if the resulting loss of confidentiality is acceptable. This will be true in most cases, but the less common a person's initials are, the more damage that arises from exposing those initials. "Jim Smith" is probably safe, but "Xander Zeffren" may very well be at risk.

Fast searching is problematic in an encrypted database because it is rather difficult to create information that the database can use to optimize the search and that cannot also be used by an attacker to extract information about the encrypted data. This is a fundamental conflict between encryption and searching. Any claims of fast searches on encrypted data need to be examined carefully.

19.3.5 Key Replacement

A key should be replaced soon after it is Expired, or immediately after its compromise is suspected. At first blush, key replacement seems like it ought to be functionality of the key manager. However, on closer examination, most of what needs to be done to replace a key involves the protected data. The data needs to be decrypted and then re-encrypted. Whatever class does this needs to understand the key families and scopes for the data encrypted with the Expired key. Generally, the consumer contains all this knowledge.

Key replacement is done on a family basis, and the replacement code should run periodically and check each family for Expired keys. In some environments, key replacement might be triggered manually. This keeps the cryptography operators in touch with the keys and their life cycle and keeps them in practice for when a key compromise occurs.

Other environments will probably want key replacement to be automated. It might constantly search the manifest for Expired keys and replace any it finds. This is where keeping keys limited to only one table becomes a practical benefit. As soon as the automation does not find an alias in the appropriate table, it knows the key is no longer in use and can be Retired.

The replacePiiKey takes, as a parameter, the alias ID of the key to be replaced. It then cycles through all the rows in the customer information table and extracts customer information encrypted with the Expired key. This information is bundled into a CompoundCryptoReceipt and is passed to the replaceKey method in the Provider class. The EncryptionResult returned from the replaceKey is then given to updatePii.

```java
private void replacePiiKey( String aliasId ) {

  PreparedStatement pstmt = null;
  ResultSet rs = null;
  CustomerInfo cust = null;

  try {
    // get data encrypted with that alias id.
    String query =
      "SELECT * " +
      "FROM    customer_info " +
      "WHERE   pii_scope_key_id = ?";

    Connection conn = getDbConnection();
    pstmt = conn.prepareStatement(query);
    pstmt.setString( 1, aliasId );
    rs = pstmt.executeQuery();

    Provider provider = new Provider();
    CompoundCryptoReceipt piiReceipts;
    String custId = null;
    while ( rs.next() ) {
      piiReceipts = new CompoundCryptoReceipt();
      custId = rs.getString( "customer_id" );
```

```
      piiReceipts.addReceipt(
        FIRST_NAME,
        new CryptoReceipt(
          rs.getString( "first_name" ),
          rs.getString( "first_name_iv" ),
          rs.getString( "pii_scope_key_id") ) );

      piiReceipts.addReceipt(
        LAST_NAME,
        new CryptoReceipt(
          rs.getString( "last_name" ),
          rs.getString( "last_name_iv" ),
          rs.getString( "pii_scope_key_id") ) );

      piiReceipts.addReceipt(
        EMAIL_ADDR,
        new CryptoReceipt(
          rs.getString( "email_address" ),
          rs.getString( "email_addr_iv" ),
          rs.getString( "pii_scope_key_id") ) );

      CompoundCryptoReceipt cryptoReceipts =
        provider.replaceKey( piiReceipts, "pii" );

      updatePii( cryptoReceipts, custId );
    }
  }
  catch (SQLException e) {
    System.out.println( e );
  }
  catch (LiveKeyNotFoundException e) {
    System.out.println( e );
  }
  catch (KeyNotFoundException e) {
    System.out.println( e );
  }
  catch (MultipleAliasIdException e) {
    System.out.println( e );
  }
  catch (NoSuchAlgorithmException e) {
    System.out.println( e );
  }
  catch (InvalidKeyStateException e) {
    System.out.println( e );
  }
  finally {
    if (rs != null) {
      try {
        rs.close();
```

```
      }
      catch (SQLException sqlEx) {
        // ignore
      }
      rs = null;
    }
    if (pstmt != null) {
      try {
        pstmt.close();
      }
      catch (SQLException e) {
        // ignore
      }
      pstmt = null;
    }
  }
}
```

The updatePii method simply takes a compound receipt containing encrypted PII data and updates the row in the customer information table identified by the customer ID parameter.

```
private void updatePii(CompoundCryptoReceipt receipts,
String custId ) {
  PreparedStatement pstmt = null;
  ResultSet rs = null;
  try {
    String query =
      "UPDATE customer_info " +
      "SET    first_name    = ?," +
             "first_name_iv = ?," +
             "last_name     = ?," +
             "last_name_iv  = ?," +
             "email_address = ?," +
             "email_addr_iv = ?," +
             "pii_scope_key_id = ?" +
      "WHERE  customer_id = ?";

    Connection conn = getDbConnection();
    pstmt = conn.prepareStatement(query);
    pstmt.setString( 1,
      receipts.getCiphertext( FIRST_NAME ));
    pstmt.setString( 2,
      receipts.getIv(FIRST_NAME));
    pstmt.setString( 3,
      receipts.getCiphertext(LAST_NAME));
    pstmt.setString( 4,
      receipts.getIv(LAST_NAME));
```

```
    pstmt.setString( 5,
      receipts.getCiphertext(EMAIL_ADDR));
    pstmt.setString( 6,
      receipts.getIv(EMAIL_ADDR));
    pstmt.setString( 7,
      receipts.getAliasId());
    pstmt.setString( 8, custId );
    pstmt.executeUpdate();
  }
  catch (SQLException e) {
    System.out.println( e );
  }
  finally {
    if (pstmt != null) {
      try {
        pstmt.close();
      }
      catch (SQLException e) {
        // ignore
      }
      pstmt = null;
    }
  }
}
```

19.4 Summary

The consumer is where the business logic touches the cryptosystem. In our examples the business logic handles personally identifiable information and credit card numbers, and both have been deemed sensitive enough to warrant encryption. Two classes, CustomerInfo and CreditCardInfo, where the latter is nested within the former, are both EncryptionRequests and are used to encrypt data.

The CustomerManager adds new customers and their credit card numbers to the database, searches for existing customers, and displays customer and credit card information. Finally, the CustomerManager can replace keys so that data encrypted with an Expired key is decrypted and then re-encrypted with the current Live key.

Chapter 20

Exceptions

This chapter lists all the exceptions used in the previous chapters.

20.1 Alias Exception

This is a generic exception thrown when a more specific exception is unnecessary.

```
package cryptodb;

public class AliasException extends Exception {
  public AliasException( String desc ) {
    super( desc );
  }
}
```

20.2 Invalid Key State Exception

When an operation attempt discovers that the key is not in the correct state for that operation, an InvalidKeyStateException is thrown.

```
package cryptodb;

public class InvalidKeyStateException extends Exception {

  private String keyAliasId = null;

  public InvalidKeyStateException( String keyAlias ) {
    this.keyAliasId = keyAlias;
  }
```

```
  public String getAliasId() {
    return keyAliasId;
  }
}
```

20.3 Key Not Found Exception

When the core attempts to access a key that doesn't exist, the
KeyNotFoundException is thrown.

```
package cryptodb.core;

public class KeyNotFoundException extends Exception {

  // This is the ID of the missing key.
  private String keyId;
  // This is the name of the engine which
  // couldn't find the key;
  private String engine;

  public KeyNotFoundException( String keyId, String engine ) {
    this.keyId = keyId;
    this.engine = engine;
  }

  public String getKeyId() {
    return keyId;
  }

  public String getEngine() {
    return engine;
  }
}
```

20.4 Live Key Not Found Exception

When an encryption attempt cannot find a Live key in the specified family, this
exception is thrown. Because this exception means that the data is not being
encrypted, it represents a serious problem and should generate high-
priority alerts.

```
package cryptodb;

public class LiveKeyNotFoundException extends Exception {

  private String keyFamily;
```

```
  public LiveKeyNotFoundException( String keyFamily ) {
    this.keyFamily = keyFamily;
  }

  public String getKeyFamily() {
    return keyFamily;
  }
}
```

20.5 Multiple Alias ID Exception

When building a compound receipt, all the alias IDs must be identical.
If a receipt is added that has an alias ID different from the others, a
MultipleAliasIdException is thrown. Assuming that the code is correct,
this exception means that the manifest has been corrupted.

```
package cryptodb;

public class MultipleAliasIdException
extends Exception {

  private String correctAliasId;
  private String rogueAliasId;

  public MultipleAliasIdException(
    String correctAliasId, String rogueAliasId ) {
    this.correctAliasId = correctAliasId;
    this.rogueAliasId = rogueAliasId;
  }

  public String getCorrectAliasId() {
    return correctAliasId;
  }

  public String getRogueAliasId() {
    return rogueAliasId;
  }
}
```

20.6 Customer Not Found Exception

If the consumer cannot find a customer based on the customer's ID number, it
throws this exception.

```
package cryptodb.test;

public class CustomerNotFoundException
extends Exception {

  private String custId;

  public CustomerNotFoundException(String custId) {
    this.custId = custId;
  }

  public String getCustId() {
    return custId;
  }
}
```

20.7 Summary

Exception handling is an art, and this chapter presented just a sketch of exceptions appropriate to a database cryptosystem. Depending on an organization's policies, these exceptions should generate log entries and, in some cases (such as LiveKeyNotFoundException), immediate alerts.

Chapter 21

The System at Work

This chapter presents examples of the system in use. We'll start with key management, and then, once the keys are installed, show how the system handles customer data. After detailing the typical use of the system, we'll show the key replacement feature in action.

The examples primarily feature the KeyTool and CustomerManager, but SQL queries are included to show how commands affect the database. We start with completely empty databases. No customer or key information is present anywhere.

21.1 Setting Up Keys

Key management begins with creating the key-encrypting key and ends with placing a new alias in the manifest.

21.1.1 Generating the Key-Encrypting Key

We make a quick check to ensure that the table is empty.

```
mysql> select * from key_encrypting_keys;
Empty set (0.00 sec)
```

The KeyTool is used to generate the key-encrypting key.

```
$ java -cp out cryptodb.KeyTool genKek
KEK ID: 1
```

We confirm that a key-encrypting key was created:

```
mysql> select kek_id, activation_date
    -> from key_encrypting_keys;
+--------+---------------------+
| kek_id | activation_date     |
+--------+---------------------+
|      1 | 2005-05-07 11:23:58 |
+--------+---------------------+
1 row in set (0.00 sec)
```

21.1.2 Creating a New Key

The local key store and the manifest are empty[1] when we begin.

```
mysql> select * from local_key_store;
Empty set (0.00 sec)
mysql> select * from key_manifest;
Empty set (0.00 sec)
```

We create the key and its manifest entry with a single KeyTool command.

```
$ java -cp out cryptodb.KeyTool load sample local pii 0
```

We check the key store (the result is reformatted to fit on the page):

```
mysql> select * from local_key_store;
+--------+----------------------------------+--------+
| key_id | key_data                         | kek_id |
+--------+----------------------------------+--------+
|      1 | EFCC4E283005D85C0BD9E86D8EDA80E2 |      1 |
+--------+----------------------------------+--------+
1 row in set (0.00 sec)
```

and the manifest.

```
mysql> select * from key_manifest;
+----------+-----------+------------+--------+--------
| alias_id | key_alias | key_family | engine | key_id
+----------+-----------+------------+--------+--------
|        1 | sample    | pii        | local  | 1
+----------+-----------+------------+--------+--------

   +---------------------+--------+
   | key_activation_date | status |
   +---------------------+--------+
   | 2005-05-07 11:25:32 | ACTIVE |
   +---------------------+--------+
1 row in set (0.00 sec)
```

---

1. *While these two tables are presented here as if they are in a single database, in a production system, the key store would be locked up in a separate database.*

The key exists and is ready to use. We confirm with the `KeyTool`.

```
$ java -cp out cryptodb.KeyTool print 1
Alias Id:        1
Alias:           sample
Family:          pii
Engine:          local
Key Id:          1
Activation date: 2005-05-07 11:25:32.0
Status:          ACTIVE
State:           LIVE
```

We'll also create a pending key that will become live in 10 days:

```
$ java -cp out cryptodb.KeyTool load sample local pii 10
```

and then update it to go live in about half an hour.

```
$ java -cp out cryptodb.KeyTool update date 2 \
> '2005-05-07 12:00:00'
$ java -cp out cryptodb.KeyTool print 2
Alias Id:        2
Alias:           sample
Family:          pii
Engine:          local
Key Id:          2
Activation date: 2005-05-07 12:00:00.0
Status:          ACTIVE
State:           PENDING
```

We've created a `pii` key, but we still need a `cci` key.

```
$ java -cp out cryptodb.KeyTool load sample local cci 0
$ java -cp out cryptodb.KeyTool print 3
Alias Id:        3
Alias:           sample
Family:          cci
Engine:          local
Key Id:          3
Activation date: 2005-05-07 11:27:04.0
Status:          ACTIVE
State:           LIVE
```

Just to be sure, we check for live keys for both families.

```
$ java -cp out cryptodb.KeyTool printLive pii
Alias Id:        1
Alias:           sample
Family:          pii
Engine:          local
Key Id:          1
```

```
Activation date: 2005-05-07 11:25:32.0
Status:         ACTIVE
State:          LIVE
$ java -cp out cryptodb.KeyTool printLive cci
Alias Id:       3
Alias:          sample
Family:         cci
Engine:         local
Key Id:         3
Activation date: 2005-05-07 11:27:04.0
Status:         ACTIVE
State:          LIVE
```

21.2 Working with Customer Information

Now that the keys have been created, we can begin loading customer information into the system. The customer information table starts empty.

```
mysql> select * from customer_info;
Empty set (0.00 sec)
```

We use the `CustomerManager` to insert customers.

```
$ java -cp out cryptodb.test.CustomerManager add \
> Don Smith dsmith@... 12345 1111222233334444 11/06
```

A quick look at the customer table shows the entries (this example has been reformatted for the page).

```
mysql> select * from customer_info;
customer_id:          1
first_name:           84F678F6FBE49197047BCD6FC0FB9A83
first_name_iv:        555EA440921382533FF53FBDA06E4611
first_initial:        D
last_name:            A236713D71F3F4F6EA91F5ADBF3BE4BB
last_name_iv:         A5B0E1AA3170AC20DA1D10A72142BA9D
last_initial:         S
email_address:        BBCDA3B08BE2FA4EEB2570D2CEE4FB5E
email_addr_iv:        67F9CA3877DB7812C4F1A0021AA629AE
zip_code:             12345
credit_card_num:      004DFD264588D71F0651CB90FA3C5488
credit_card_num_iv:   EFAE37B060CEB1FC3CBC67A745CE8170
last_four_ccn:        4444
expiration_date:      D1EEC23D610BE8EF16C969385FEB2FA7
expiration_date_iv:   2B4EE769BD9968B2A16144D013414EA4
pii_scope_alias_id:   1
cci_scope_alias_id:   3
```

We can see that it is encrypted; now we check that it is retrievable.

```
$ java -cp out cryptodb.test.CustomerManager print 1
First name:  Don
Last name:   Smith
Eamil:       dsmith@...
Zip code:    12345
Credit card: 1111222233334444
Expiration:  11/06
```

We add some more customers:

```
$ java -cp out cryptodb.test.CustomerManager add \
> Donna Simpson dsimpson@... 12345 1234123412341234 08/06
$ java -cp out cryptodb.test.CustomerManager add \
> David Sanders dsanders@... 12345 1123581321345589 05/06
.
.
.
```

and then do a search for one of them.

```
$ java -cp out cryptodb.test.CustomerManager find \
> david sanders 12345
First name:  David
Last name:   Sanders
Eamil:       dsanders@...
Zip code:    12345
Credit card: 1123581321345589
Expiration:  05/06
```

21.3 Replacing a Key

During the work just shown, our first key expired.

```
$ java -cp out cryptodb.KeyTool print 1
Alias Id:       1
Alias:          sample
Family:         pii
Engine:         local
Key Id:         1
Activation date: 2005-05-07 11:25:32.0
Status:         ACTIVE
State:          EXPIRED
```

Since that key has expired, we need to replace it. We'll check to see how much data is encrypted with that key.

```
mysql> select customer_id, pii_scope_alias_id
    -> from customer_info
    -> where pii_scope_alias_id = 1;
+-------------+--------------------+
| customer_id | pii_scope_alias_id |
+-------------+--------------------+
|           1 | 1                  |
|           2 | 1                  |
+-------------+--------------------+
2 rows in set (0.00 sec)
```

Apparently the key expired after Donna was entered but before David.

```
$ java -cp out cryptodb.test.CustomerManager print 2
First name:  Donna
Last name:   Simpson
Eamil:       dsimpson@...
Zip code:    12345
Credit card: 1234123412341234
Expiration:  08/06
$ java -cp out cryptodb.test.CustomerManager print 3
First name:  David
Last name:   Sanders
Eamil:       dsanders@...
Zip code:    12345
Credit card: 1123581321345589
Expiration:  05/06
```

We can verify that David's PII was encrypted with a different key.

```
mysql> select customer_id, pii_scope_alias_id
    -> from customer_info
    -> where customer_id = 3;
+-------------+--------------------+
| customer_id | pii_scope_alias_id |
+-------------+--------------------+
|           3 | 2                  |
+-------------+--------------------+
1 row in set (0.00 sec)
```

The CustomerManager class provides the key replacement functionality. We tell it to replace key 1

```
$ java -cp out cryptodb.test.CustomerManager \
> replacePiiKey 1
```

and confirm that the change occurred:

```
mysql> select customer_id, pii_scope_alias_id
    -> from customer_info
    -> where pii_scope_alias_id = 1;
Empty set (0.00 sec)
mysql> select customer_id, pii_scope_alias_id
    -> from customer_info
    -> where customer_id in (1,2);
+-------------+--------------------+
| customer_id | pii_scope_alias_id |
+-------------+--------------------+
|           1 | 2                  |
|           2 | 2                  |
+-------------+--------------------+
2 rows in set (0.00 sec)
```

We also can check that the values in the customer information table changed (the output has been reformatted to fit on the page).

```
mysql> select *
    -> from customer_info
    -> where customer_id = 1;
customer_id:          1
first_name:           767257EA7A3C67E87113446B308170E2
first_name_iv:        994B22CD7EB7094129384E44C3509E9B
first_initial:        D
last_name:            EBFB69CC00BC6878F72D324B1F57CDC2
last_name_iv:         BA4A02537E3D0F9BE7CD22792EBC376E
last_initial:         S
email_address:        7DF0326F958B76F9FE28538312B9279A
email_addr_iv:        000292502FF30714DD153AC1292F9336
zip_code:             12345
credit_card_num:      004DFD264588D71F0651CB90FA3C5488
credit_card_num_iv:   EFAE37B060CEB1FC3CBC67A745CE8170
last_four_ccn:        4444
expiration_date:      D1EEC23D610BE8EF16C969385FEB2FA7
expiration_date_iv:   2B4EE769BD9968B2A16144D013414EA4
pii_scope_alias_id:   2
cci_scope_alias_id:   3
```

Note that this confirms that a change took place, but even though the encrypted values are different, we can't conclude that the key is what caused the change. It's possible that the key remained the same and that the new encrypted values are due to the new IVs.

However, the `pii_scope_alias_id` does say that the alias ID is 2. We can check the manifest and confirm that the different aliases do point to different keys in the key store.

```
mysql> select alias_id, key_id
    -> from key_manifest
    -> where alias_id in (1,2);
+----------+--------+
| alias_id | key_id |
+----------+--------+
|        1 | 1      |
|        2 | 2      |
+----------+--------+
2 rows in set (0.29 sec)
```

So we can informally conclude that the key has been replaced. This validation would not satisfy a quality assurance test, but it is sufficient for our casual purposes.

The next step in the replacement strategy is to retire the replaced key. We turn to the `KeyTool` for this.

```
$ java -cp out cryptodb.KeyTool retire 1
$ java -cp out cryptodb.KeyTool print 1
Alias Id:        1
Alias:           sample
Family:          pii
Engine:          local
Key Id:          1
Activation date: 2005-05-07 11:25:32.0
Status:          RETIRED
State:           RETIRED
```

This key can no longer be used, and its retired state indicates that no data is encrypted with the key.

Sometime after the key has been retired, it should be terminated. Terminating a key involves removing it from the key store. The `KeyTool` provides the necessary functionality.

```
$ java -cp out cryptodb.KeyTool terminate 1
$ java -cp out cryptodb.KeyTool print 1
Alias Id:        1
Alias:           sample
Family:          pii
Engine:          local
Key Id:          1
Activation date: 2005-05-07 11:25:32.0
Status:          TERMINATED
State:           TERMINATED
```

We can check the `local_key_store` to ensure that the key has been deleted.

```
mysql> select * from local_key_store;
+--------+----------------------------------+--------+
| key_id | key_data                         | kek_id |
+--------+----------------------------------+--------+
|      2 | 9AA04F178C4A2B4F19BB2A8F5298AE26 |      1 |
|      3 | D75E51BCF4FA6D8388AA178E04A52229 |      1 |
+--------+----------------------------------+--------+
2 row in set (0.00 sec)
```

21.4 Replacing the Key-Encrypting Key

Replacing the key-encrypting key is exactly the same as creating the initial key.

```
$ java -cp out cryptodb.KeyTool genKek
KEK ID: 2
```

Not only does the `genKek` command create a new key-encrypting key, it also re-encrypts the keys. We can confirm this by looking at the affected tables. First we can see that there are now two rows in the `key_encrypting_keys` table.

```
mysql> select count(*) from key_encrypting_keys;
+----------+
| count(*) |
+----------+
|        2 |
+----------+
1 row in set (0.00 sec)
```

In addition, the `local_key_store` shows that a different key-encrypting key is in use.

```
mysql> select * from local_key_store;
+--------+----------------------------------+--------+
| key_id | key_data                         | kek_id |
+--------+----------------------------------+--------+
|      2 | 9AA04F178C4A2B4F19BB2A8F5298AE26 |      2 |
|      3 | D75E51BCF4FA6D8388AA178E04A52229 |      2 |
+--------+----------------------------------+--------+
2 row in set (0.00 sec)
```

We can verify that changing the key-encrypting key did not break access to customer data.

```
$ java -cp out cryptodb.test.CustomerManager print 1
First name:  Don
Last name:   Smith
```

```
Email:       dsmith@...
Zip code:    12345
Credit card: 1111222233334444
Expiration:  11/06
```

21.5 Summary

This chapter presented a tour of the cryptosystem in action. Keys were created, encrypted with key-encrypting keys, and then used to encrypt and decrypt data. Keys were replaced, and business data encrypted with an expired key was re-encrypted with the current live key. A key-encrypting key was also replaced. Nearly all the functionality presented in the previous chapters was exercised directly or indirectly. In many examples, database queries were used to illustrate exactly what the command did to the information in the underlying tables.

These examples should be enough to help a team field, at the very least, a prototype of a database encryption system. With confidence and experience gained from the prototype, the team should be in a good position to identify exactly what their environment needs from a database cryptosystem and be clear on how to rework the prototype into a production-quality infrastructure to meet those needs.

Bibliography

[1] MySQL AB. *MySQL Connector/J Documentation*, 2005. Available at
`http://dev.mysql.com/doc/connector/j/en/index.html`.

[2] Bob Blakley, Craig Heath, and members of The Open Group Security Forum. *Technical Guide: Security Design Patterns*. The Open Group, 2004. ISBN 1-931624-27-5. Available at `http://www.opengroup.org/publications/catalog/g031.htm`.

[3] Frank Buschmann, Regine Meunier, Hans Rohnert, Peter Sommerlad, and Michael Stal. *Pattern-Oriented Software Architecture, Volume 1: A System of Patterns*. John Wiley & Sons, 1996. ISBN 0-471-95869-7.

[4] National Computer Security Center. *A Guide to Understanding Data Remanence in Automated Information Systems*. September 1991. Available at `http://www.radium.ncsc.mil/tpep/library/rainbow/ncsc-tg-025.2.pdf`.

[5] International Business Machines Corporation. *IBM Java JCE FIPS 140-2 Cryptographic Module*, December 2004. Available at `http://www-128.ibm.com/developerworks/java/jdk/security/142/secguides/JCEFIPSDocs/JCESecurityPolicy.html`.

[6] Darrell M. Kienzle, Ph.D., Matthew C. Elder, Ph.D., David Tyree, and James Edwards-Hewitt. *Security Patterns Repository, Version 1.0*, 2002. Available at `http://www.scrypt.net/~celer/securitypatterns/`.

[7] Morris Dworkin. *Recommendation for Block Cipher Modes of Operation*. NIST Special Publication 800-38A. National Institute of Standards and Technology, 2001. Available at `http://csrc.nist.gov/publications/nistpubs/index.html`.

[8] Niels Ferguson and Bruce Schneier. *Practical Cryptography*. Wiley Publishing, Inc., 2003. ISBN 0-471-22357-3.

[9] Erich Gamma, Richard Helm, Ralph Johnson, and John Vlissides. *Design Patterns: Elements of Reusable Object-Oriented Software*. Addison-Wesley, 1994. ISBN 0-201-63361-2.

[10] Mark G. Graff and Kenneth R. van Wyk. *Secure Coding: Principles and Practices*. O'Reilly & Associates, Inc., 2003. ISBN 0-596-00242-4.

[11] Greg Hoglund and Gary McGraw. *Exploiting Software: How to Break Code*. Addison-Wesley, 2004. ISBN 0-201-78695-8.

[12] Michael Howard and David LeBlanc. *Writing Secure Code*. Microsoft Press, 2nd edition, 2003. ISBN 0-7356-1722-8.

[13] RSA Laboratories. *PKCS #5 v2.0: Password-Based Cryptography Standard*, March 1995. Available at `http://www.rsasecurity.com/rsalabs/`.

[14] RSA Laboratories. *PKCS #11 v2.20: Cryptographic Token Interface Standard*, June 2004. Available at `http://www.rsasecurity.com/rsalabs/`.

[15] Scott Oaks. *Java Security*. O'Reilly & Associates, Inc., 2nd edition, 2001. ISBN 0-596-00157-6.

[16] United States Department of Health and Office of Civil Rights Human Services. *Summary of the HIPAA Privacy Rule*. May 2003. Available at `http://www.hhs.gov/ocr/privacysummary.pdf`.

[17] National Institute of Standards and Technology. *Advanced Encryption Standard (AES)*. FIPS PUB 197. November 2001. Available at `http://csrc.nist.gov/publications/fips/index.html`.

[18] National Institute of Standards and Technology. *Security Requirements for Cryptographic Modules*. FIPS PUB 140-2. May 2001. Available at `http://csrc.nist.gov/publications/fips/index.html`.

[19] George Reese. *Database Programming with JDBC and Java*. O'Reilly & Associates, Inc., 2nd edition, August 2000. ISBN 1-56592-616-1.

[20] Frank Swiderski and Window Snyder. *Threat Modeling*. Microsoft Press, 2004. ISBN 0-7356-1991-3.

[21] John Viega and Gary McGraw. *Building Secure Software*. Addison-Wesley, 2002. ISBN 0-201-72152-X.

[22] Xiaoyun Wang, Dengguo Feng, Xuejia Lai, and Hongbo Yu. Collisions for hash functions MD4, MD5, HAVAL-128 and RIPEMD. Cryptology ePrint Archive, Report 2004/199, 2004. Available at `http://eprint.iacr.org/`.

Glossary

cipher block chaining mode A method of using a symmetric cryptographic algorithm to protect the confidentiality of data by mixing the previous block of ciphertext into the next plaintext block prior to encryption.

consumer A component that manages sensitive business data and consumes the cryptographic services offered by the cryptosystem.

counter mode A method of using a symmetric algorithm to protect the confidentiality of data by encrypting a sequence of counters to produce a key stream.

electronic codebook mode A method of using a symmetric algorithm to protect the confidentiality of data by relying entirely on the algorithm itself.

engine The component that performs cryptographic operations on data.

hardware security module (HSM) A dedicated, secure device that includes the functionality of an engine and a key vault.

initialization vector (IV) In cipher block chaining mode, the string of bits mixed with the first plaintext block.

key alias A unique reference used by the cryptosystem to identify keys.

key family A set of keys used to protect the same information. While multiple families may be assigned to a single table, a family is generally assigned to only a single table and often to just a column in that table.

key fatigue A condition that limits the amount of data a single key should encrypt due to "leaked" information.

key ID   A reference to a key in a particular key vault; several keys may have the same key ID if they all reside in different vaults.

key migration   The automatic decryption of data encrypted with an Expired key and re-encryption with the current Live key due to changed data.

key scope   Describes how keys are mapped across a row in the database. Narrow scopes indicate that keys can vary for each encrypted field, and wide scopes mean that multiple fields share the same key.

key state   Indicates where the key is in terms of the key life cycle and determines how the key can be used.

key vault   The component that stores the cryptographic key for operational use.

manifest   The component that stores the key alias and tracks the key state.

provider   The component that provides cryptographic services to the consumer by taking the consumer's requests and passing them as needed to the rest of the cryptosystem.

receipt   Data returned by the provider to the consumer containing the encrypted data, the alias of the key used, and the initialization vector.

striping   A strategy of assigning key families to a table based not on columns but on some row criteria such as a modulus of the row ID.

Index

P

packet sniffing, 3

padding schemes, 85, 87

passing statements to databases, 18

PCI (Payment Card Industry)
PCI Data Security Standard, 15
PCI connections in HSM
communications, 57

pending keys
defined, 47
timeline indicating relationship between
states and activation dates, 78

penetration testing
main discussion, 146–149
defining roles in security-enhanced
cryptographic projects, 100–101
requirements review, 110–112

periodic key replacement, example code,
176–179

permissions. *See* credentials and
permissions

personally identifiable information.
See privacy and confidentiality

plaintext attacks, 28

platform security guides, 139–140

policies. *See* standards and policies

practical implementations of design and
methodology, 157–254

presentation tier, defined, 38

primary keys, 17

privacy and confidentiality
applying cryptography, 23–25
Children's Online Privacy Protection
Act, 14–15
common threats, 109

credit card numbers, 131
definition of confidentiality, 4
e-mail addresses, 131
example code, personally identifiable
information, 221–240
legislation related to privacy, 11–14
names, 131
phone numbers, 131
reasons for database security, 5–6
requirements, documenting, 109–110
SHA-1-based profiles, 131
social security numbers, 131
testing, 145

privileges
design phase, 121
development phase, 135–136
digital signatures, 21–22
See also credentials and permissions

profiles
defined, 131
designing security, searching and
profiles, 130–132

program memory, testing, 148

programmers
in development phase. *See* development
phase of security-enhanced projects
reasons for database security, 10
separation of duties, 122–123

project managers
managing security-enhanced
cryptographic projects, defining
roles, 100–101
requirements review, 110–112

project methodology for building database
cryptosystems, 93–156

protected data, defined, 40

The Executive Guide to
Information Security
Mark Egan with Tim Mather
ISBN 0-321-30451-9

Mapping Security
Tom Patterson with
Scott Gleeson Blue
ISBN 0-321-30452-7

(SCTS) Symantec Certified
Technical Specialist
Nik Alston, Mike Chapple, and
Kalani Kirk Hausman
ISBN 0-321-34994-6

The Art of Computer Virus
Research and Defense
Peter Szor
ISBN 0-321-30454-3

The Symantec Guide to Home
Internet Security
Andrew Conry-Murray and
Vincent Weafer
ISBN 0-321-35641-1